COLLEGE CURRICULUM AT THE CROSSROADS

College Curriculum at the Crossroads explores the ways in which college curriculum is complicated, informed, understood, resisted, and enriched by women of color. This text challenges the canon of curriculum development which foregrounds the experiences of white people, men and other dominant subject positions. By drawing on Black, Latina, Queer, and Transnational feminism, the text disrupts hegemonic curricular practices in post-secondary education. This collection is relevant to current conversation within higher education, which looks to curriculum to aid in the development of a more tolerant and just citizenry. Women of color have long theorized the failures of injustice and the promise of inclusion; as such, this text rightly positions women of color as true "experts in the field."

Across a variety of approaches, from reflections on personal experience to application of critical scholarship, the authors in this collection explore the potency of women of color's presence with/in college curriculum and emphasize a dire need for women of color's voices at the center of the academic process.

Kirsten T. Edwards is Assistant Professor of Adult and Higher Education and Women's and Gender Studies affiliate faculty at the University of Oklahoma. She earned a Ph.D. in Higher Education Administration with cognates in both Curriculum Theory and Women's and Gender Studies at Louisiana State University. Her research merges philosophies of higher education, college curriculum, and pedagogy. More specifically, Dr. Edwards is interested in the ways that socio-cultural identity and context influence faculty, teaching, and learning in post-secondary education. She is co-editor (with Denise Taliaferro Baszile and Nichole A. Guillory) of *Race, Gender, and Curriculum Theorizing: Working in Womanish Ways*.

Maria del Guadalupe Davidson is Associate Professor and Director of the Women's and Gender Studies Program, and Co-Director for the Women's and Gender Studies Center for Social Justice at the University of Oklahoma. She earned her Ph.D. in Rhetoric from Duquesne University. She researches in the areas of rhetorical theory and criticism, Black feminism, and Africana philosophical thought. Her most recent publication is *Black Women, Agency, and the New Black Feminism* (2017). She has co-edited several volumes including: *Our Black Sons Matter: Mothers Talk about Fears, Sorrows, and Hopes* (2016); *Exploring Race in Predominantly White Classrooms* (2014); and *Critical Perspectives on bell hooks* (2009). She is currently working on a book about the artist Kara Walker.

THE CRITICAL SOCIAL THOUGHT SERIES

Edited by Michael W. Apple, University of Wisconsin—Madison

COLLEGE CURRICULUM AT THE CROSSROADS

Women of Color Reflect and Resist

Edited by Kirsten T. Edwards and Maria del Guadalupe Davidson

Routledge
Taylor & Francis Group

NEW YORK AND LONDON

First published 2018
by Routledge
711 Third Avenue, New York, NY 10017

and by Routledge
2 Park Square, Milton Park, Abingdon, Oxon, OX14 4RN

Routledge is an imprint of the Taylor & Francis Group, an informa business

Library of Congress Cataloging-in-Publication Data
A catalog record for this book has been requested

ISBN: 978-1-138-72099-2 (hbk)
ISBN: 978-1-138-72100-5 (pbk)
ISBN: 978-1-315-19475-2 (ebk)

Typeset in Bembo
by Deanta Global Publishing Services, Chennai, India

For Bruce Edwards Sr., my daddy
September 10, 1951–March 07, 2015
Kirsten T. Edwards

For Clarke Stroud
Maria del Guadalupe (Lupe) Davidson

CONTENTS

SERIES EDITOR'S INTRODUCTION

Michael W. Apple

One of the most significant advances that has been made in education is the transformation of the question of "What knowledge is of most worth?" into "Whose knowledge is of most worth?" This rewording is not simply a linguistic issue. In changing the focus, it asks that we engage in a radical transformation of our ways of thinking about the connections between what counts as important knowledge in educational institutions and in the larger society, and existing relations of domination and subordination and struggles against these relations. This has crucial implications for what we choose to teach, how we teach it, and what values and identities underpin such choices (Apple 2014).

Just as importantly, the question also demands that one word in the final sentence be problematized—the word *we*. Who is the "we"? What group arrogates the center to themselves, thereby seeing another group as The Other? That word—"we"—often symbolizes the manner in which ideological forces and assumptions work inside and outside of education. "We" functions as a mechanism not only of inclusion, but powerfully of exclusion as well. It is a verb that masquerades as a noun, in a manner similar to the word "minority" or "slave." No one is a "minority." Someone must *make* another a minority; someone or some group must *minoritize* another person and group, in the same way that no one can be fully known as a slave. Someone or some group must *enslave* someone else. Ignoring this understanding cuts us off from seeing the often ugly realities of a society and its history. Perhaps even more crucially, it also cuts us off from the immensely valuable historical and current struggles against the gendered/sexed, classed, and raced processes of othering. By severing the connections between nouns and verbs, it makes invisible the actions and actors that make dominance seem normal. It creates a vacant space that is all too often filled with dominant meanings and identities.

This vacant space is legitimated by many things, but one of the most powerful forces of legitimation is the way we even think about rationality and objectivity. The stories of real people's lives, the realities of our real connections to the ways in which racial dominance is built and maintained—all of these are hidden by the fiction of neutrality and of keeping ourselves above any substantive commitment to challenge such dominance. This is perhaps best seen in Charles Mills's (1997) exceptional analysis of the way in which the development of our belief in the rational individual that lies at the heart of our usual conceptions of the public sphere is deeply connected to the construction of an "other" who is irrational, not fully worthy—Black, Indigenous, Woman, and the list goes on. Accepted conceptions of rationality require the creation of the irrational. It is no accident that the relational aspect of this guiding principle of "being a rational person" has its roots in empire and the history of racial judgments.

These points may seem too abstract. But behind them is something that lies at the heart of the book you are about to read. The book articulates both a vision and a reality of the fully engaged critical scholar and educator, someone who refuses to accept an education that doesn't simultaneously challenge the unreflective "we" and also illuminates the path to a new politics of voice and recognition in education. It gives embodied examples of critical pedagogies and of a more robust sense of socially informed educational action as it is lived out by women of color at institutions of higher education.

Teachers and scholars in multiple disciplines have spent years challenging the boundaries of that usually unexamined space of the "we" and resisting the knowledge, perspectives, epistemological assumptions, and accepted voices that underpin them. This is not new, of course. There was no time when resistance was not present. This is especially the case in education, a field where the issues surrounding what and whose knowledge should be taught and how it should be taught are taken very seriously, especially by those people who are not included in the ways in which dominant groups define that oh-so-dangerous word of "we" (Apple 2013; Apple and Au 2014; Au, Brown and Calderon 2016; Warmington 2014).

While this continuing history of counter-hegemonic educational work is always there, it needs to be made even more visible. One of the most significant ways of making it visible is through the actual experiences of women of color as they tell their stories of doing critically reflexive pedagogic work at universities. All of this makes *College Curriculum at the Crossroads: Women of Color Reflect and Resist* such a valuable book. Kirsten T. Edwards and Maria del Guadalupe Davidson have brought together a set of authors who detail the personal and institutional processes, contradictions, tensions, and victories involved in creating an educational environment that interrupts dominant understandings, and at the same time builds more critical and affirmative possibilities. The women of color included here document why it is so important to affirm a broader "we." They draw upon some of the very best theoretical and historical resources built by the long tradition of critical reflections of women of color, of various strands of critical race theory, and of the multiple counter-hegemonic critical traditions both within and outside of education (see, e.g., hooks 1994). The implications for curriculum development, for critical pedagogy, for teacher education, and for building supportive classroom environments are clearly articulated.

Equally significant is the fact that the authors do not minimize the risks or deny the difficulties. To do so would be to deny that the challenges that critical educators, and especially critical educators of color, face are real and substantial. But difficult does not mean impossible. After reading these accounts, I am even more convinced that their analyses and pedagogic/political actions provide us with ways to live out a more powerful politics of recognition (Fraser 1997) in our daily educational lives, something that is so very necessary today.

Michael W. Apple

John Bascom Professor of Curriculum and
Instruction and Educational Policy Studies,
University of Wisconsin, Madison.

References

Apple, M. W. (2013) *Can Education Change Society?* New York, NY: Routledge.

Apple, M. W. (2014) *Official Knowledge* (3rd ed.). New York, NY: Routledge.

Apple, M. W. and Au, W. (2014) *Critical Education, Volumes I–IV*. New York, NY: Routledge Major Works.

Au, W., Brown, A., and Calderon, D. (2016) *Reclaiming the Multicultural Roots of U.S. Curriculum: Communities of Color and Official Knowledge in Education*. New York, NY: Teachers College Press.

Fraser, N. (1997) *Justice Interruptus*. New York, NY: Routledge.

hooks, b. (1994) *Teaching to Transgress: Education as the Practice of Freedom*. New York, NY: Routledge.

Mills, C. (1997) *The Racial Contract*. Ithaca, NY: Cornell University Press.

Warmington, P. (2014) *Black British Intellectuals and Education: Multiculturalism's Hidden History*. New York, NY: Routledge.

ACKNOWLEDGMENTS

To my sweet, kind, resilient, and supportive sister-girl-friend, Dr. Maria del Guadalupe (Lupe) Davidson, thank you! Thank you for agreeing to labor with me on this project. I would also like to thank all of the chapter contributors. Your words are balm and light for so many. To my academic-brother, Dr. T. Elon Dancy II, thank you for your unwavering commitment to the most vulnerable, the dispossessed and displaced, the marginalized, the beloved community of color. Lastly, to the next generation of women of color scholars who inspired this collection, you are fierce beyond words. The academy is not ready for you, but you are more than ready for it!

Kirsten T. Edwards

I would like to thank my friend and colleague Dr. Kirsten T. Edwards for inviting me to work with her on this incredibly important project. I would like to thank the contributors for offering their brilliant work to this collection. May your words and thoughts provide strength, clarity, validation, and insight to all who read them. Special thanks to my friend Dr. T. Elon Dancy II for doing a remarkable job supporting students and faculty of color on our campus. And finally, to Scott, it's been twenty years; I'm looking forward to many, many more. *Te amo.*

Maria del Guadalupe Davidson

INTRODUCTION

Why Curriculum?

Kirsten T. Edwards and Maria del Guadalupe Davidson

For years, educationalists have theorized the implications of effective curriculum development on successful college student matriculation (Barman & Konwar, 2011; Nygaard, Højlt, & Hermansen, 2008; Wolf, 2007). Typically, higher education institutions assess curriculum effectiveness not simply by material retention, but by its ability to promote student engagement in multiple contexts. Educators and theorists have long regarded curriculum as a primary vehicle for encouraging ethical and democratic ideals (Dewey, 1990; Miller, 2005; Pinar et al., 2008). In recent history, the push for student development through curriculum has taken on an imperative for social justice (Park & Denson, 2009). Moreover, there has been evidence of increased interest in issues of diversity, equity, and access in United States (U.S.) higher education (Chang, 2001; Dancy, 2010; Hurtado, 2001; Johnson & Harvey, 2002; Leslie, McClure, & Oaxaca, 1998; Palmer & Gasman, 2008). With this relatively modern emphasis on critical examinations of difference, there remains a dearth of scholarship focused on the complexities of women of color's experiences in U.S. higher education (Alston, 2012; Patton, 2009; Watt, 2006). Limited existing scholarship is often narrowly focused on difficulties this population faces and strategies employed to survive in academe (Berkel & Constantine, 2005; Harley, 2008; Henry, 2008; Johnson-Bailey, 2004; Winkle-Wagner, 2009). Even less scholarship exists on the benefits and insights women of color bring to college campuses (Edwards, 2017; Edwards, Clark, & Bryant, 2012; Patton, 2009). While women of color's erasure from multiple facets of the intellectual project is a perennial phenomenon, we suggest in this book that the implications for erasure has particular and manifold import in regards to curriculum work.

As academicians seek to promote equity and access in higher education, they look to curriculum to support these intentions. However, as Lorde (2008) suggests, because "survival is not an academic skill," only those individuals who exist at the intersections of oppression, and therefore "outside the structures" of power, are equipped to define a socially just agenda supportive of all people (p. 50). Heeding Lorde's call, *College Curriculum at the Crossroads: Women of Color Reflect and Resist* explores the ways in which college curriculum is complicated, informed, understood, resisted, and enriched by women of color. All students benefit when curriculum attends to the lived experiences and speaks to the needs of women of color. Likewise, women of color are often most vulnerable to its effects when curriculum creates an educational space where the most marginalized are harmed. Consider, for example, curricular models that normalize whiteness, patriarchy, heterosexuality, and middle-class interpretations of *being-in-the world*. These practices silence, exclude, diminish, write out, and at their most destructive erase the humanity of women of color. These troubling realities also produce a context in which women of color become most cognizant of the potential of inclusive curricular design.

This project explores the influence women of color's intersectional perspectives have on the development of college curriculum for resistance, equity, and justice. It highlights the ways in which a specific aspect of the educational process—curriculum development—is complicated, informed, and enriched by those most susceptible to its effects. Rending the veil of silence and erasure that shrouds the lived experiences of women of color reveals potent tools for transformation. Living at the intersections of multiple systems of injustice, an intricate and multifaceted relationship with oppression produces both injury and insight. This book project is situated on the premise that women of color academicians can offer new tools to dismantle the Master's (educational) House as curriculum workers for the benefit of the whole academic community (Lorde, 2008).

Purpose: What We're Up To

College Curriculum at the Crossroads disrupts and challenges in four critical ways. First, because by using women of color feminism, women of color discourse analysis, and framing a women of color pedagogy (Edwards, 2013), this text critiques the canon of curriculum development which foregrounds the experiences of white people, men, and other dominant subject positions. Second, by drawing on Black, Latina, Queer, Transnational and so on, feminism, the text uses grassroots and collective models of resistance to disrupt hegemonic curricular practices in post-secondary education. Third, this text critically analyzes the political aspect of curriculum development. Women of color designing curriculum *about us from our* embodied position is a political act. It reminds (perhaps even teaches) those in the field about the importance of first person authorship, and the problems associated with objectification or writing/teaching about a group that one does not belong to. Finally, *College Curriculum at the Crossroads* is relevant to the current conversation within higher education, which looks to curriculum to aid in the development of a more tolerant and just citizenry. As women of color have long theorized the failures of injustice and the promise of inclusion, this text positions women of color as "experts in the field."

College Curriculum at the Crossroads engages in a rich interdisciplinary, intersectional, intergenerational conversation about the life and breath of curriculum, arguably the cornerstone of the collegiate experience; interrogating the ways curriculum frames, values, politicizes, dismisses, and delivers knowledge. Contributors to this text reflect on the multilayered ways in which all of these curricular realities are influenced by identity at the intersection of race and gender. Questions contributors ponder include:

- How is curriculum designed and deployed by the raced and gendered body in college settings?
- How is curriculum read through the woman of color's body, and how does the body become text with/in the curriculum? (Baszile, 2008). How do women's diasporic and indigenous epistemes inform college curriculum design?
- How do the writings and offerings of women of color become part of the curriculum, and what is the impact?

The individual authors featured in this book take up these questions in a variety of ways. Camara (Chapter 1) opens the collection with an account of her twenty-year evolution as a Black woman pedagogue and curriculum designer in a multiracial classroom. Reflecting primarily on her experience teaching a Hip Hop course, she reveals the ways that identity necessarily complicates course design and the development of student consciousness. Similarly, Marrun (Chapter 2) draws on personal experience to assess what she describes as ambivalence regarding the Latina academic transition. She introduces the terms *gente estudiada* and *convivencia* to illustrate the ways she resists hegemonic approaches to curriculum.

In Chapter 3, Caldera offers the reader in-depth analysis on twenty-five years of Black feminist and womanist theorizing. Presenting the transformational potential of these approaches, she cogently argues for the centering of Black women's scholarship in college curriculum. In Chapter 4, Edwards also considers the role of Black women's scholarship in college curriculum. Engaging the issue from an alternate perspective, she questions the impact dominant approaches to teaching Black feminist writings have on Black women graduate students' personal and communal development. Furthering the voices of women of color graduate students, Poon in collaboration with her students Sihite, Turman, Griffin, and Bishundat contribute the fifth chapter in this text. Seemingly a response to Edwards (Chapter 4), Poon and associates (Chapter 5) describe the pedagogical strategies necessary when incorporating critical perspectives into course curriculum. Their chapter describes the transformative possibilities for women of color students and teachers when critical consciousness is central to the pedagogical project. Using the concept of disidentifiction, Davidson (Chapter 6) evaluates the benefits and liberatory possibilities of a Black feminist curriculum that addresses taboo subjects related to Black women's bodies, desire, and commodification. Building on hooks' (1994) notion of "teaching to transgress," Guillory (Chapter 7) challenges conventional assumptions about school-community partnerships in teacher education programs. Exposing the dominant narrative latent in common-place practices, she complicates how scholars and practitioners negotiate tensions across institutional boundaries. In Chapter 8, Kelly also draws on "teaching to transgress" to challenge conventional wisdom about the university. Recounting fifteen years of experience as a Black woman teaching in higher education, she notes the ways reflection on and development of her multiple identities have strengthened her ability to design curriculum for "community-building, libera-tion, resistance and empowerment."

Through personal *testimonios*, Velazquez (Chapter 9) describes her life as a Puerto Rican teacher and scholar. She notes the ways in which women of color serve as bridges for survival within hostile academic contexts, not only for themselves but their communities. In a similar vein, Alavi (Chapter 10) testifies to her experiences as an immigrant Iranian woman teaching through damaging and stereotypical frames placed upon her within the university setting. Her chapter offers academicians' suggestions for inclusive practices that respond to the systemic injustices emerging within college classrooms. Mirroring the opening, this collection closes with a Black woman's reflection on course development. Wallace (Chapter 11) guides the reader through her curricular design informed by Africana Studies and intersectionality, devel-oped as a response to race-based police violence and socio–political activism. Through curricular content that connects historical social movements to con-temporary realities, she equips her students to develop their own activism on and off campus.

Across a variety of approaches, from reflections on personal experience to application of critical scholarship, the authors in this collection explore the potency of women of color's presence with/in college curriculum. As scholars, researchers, teachers, and theorizers, our relationship to curriculum is compli-cated and complex. What this text makes clear is the dire need for women of color's voices at the center of the academic process. The insights and perspectives these women provide not only support the intellectual development of women of color, but also the entire academic community's pursuit of justice and equity. To be sure, academe will accomplish its highest ideals with us not on the periphery, but at the fore.

References

Alston, J. (2012) Standing on the promises: A new generation of Black women scholars in educational leadership and beyond, *International Journal of Qualitative Studies in Education* 25(1), 127–129.

Barman, A. & Konwar, J. (2011) Competency based curriculum in higher education: A necessity grounded by globalization, *Revista Romaneasca Pentru Educatie Multidimensionala*, 3(6), 7–15.

Baszile, D. T. (2008) Beyond all reason indeed: The pedagogical promise of critical race testimony, *Race Ethnicity and Education*, 11(3), 251–265.

Berkel, L. A. & Constantine, M. G. (2005) Relational variables and life satisfaction in African American and Asian American college women, *Journal of College Counseling*, 8, 5–13.

Chang, M. J. (2001) The positive educational effects of racial diversity on campus, in G. Orfield (Ed.), *Diversity Challenged: Evidence on the Impact of Affirmative Action*. Cambridge, MA: Harvard Education Publishing Group.

Dancy, T. E. (2010) *Managing Diversity: (Re)Visioning Equity on College Campuses*. New York, NY: Peter Lang.

Dewey, J. (1990) *The School and Society/ The Child and the Curriculum*. Chicago, IL: The University of Chicago Press.

Edwards, K. T. (2013) Fluidity and possibility: Imagining woman of colour pedagogies. In N. Wane, J. Jagire, & Z. Murad (Eds.) *Ruptures: Anti-colonial and Anti-racist Feminist Theorizing*, pp. 139–156. the Netherlands: Sense Publishers.

Edwards, K. T. (2017) College teaching on sacred ground: Judeo-Christian influences on Black women faculty pedagogy, *Race Ethnicity and Education*, 20(1), 117–131.

Edwards, J. B., Clark, T. T. & Bryant, S. (2012) African American female faculty in predominantly White graduate schools of social work, *Journal of Teaching in Social Work*, 32(1), 90–107.

Harley, D. A. (2008) Maids of academe: African American women faculty at predominately White institutions, *Journal of African American Studies*, 12(1), 19–36.

Henry, W. J. (2008) Black female millennial college students: Dating dilemmas and identity development, *Multicultural Education*, 16(2), 17–21.

hooks, b. (1994) Teaching to transgress: Education as the practice of freedom. New York, NY: Routledge.

Hurtado, S. (2001) Linking diversity and educational purpose: How diversity affects the classroom environment and student development, in G. Orfield (Ed.), *Diversity Challenged: Evidence on the Impact of Affirmative Action*, pp. 187–203. Cambridge, MA: Harvard Education Publishing Group.

Johnson-Bailey, J. (2004) Hitting and climbing the proverbial wall: Participation and retention issues for Black graduate women, *Race Ethnicity and Education*, 7(4), 331–349.

Johnson, B. J. & Harvey, W. B. (2002) The socialization of Black college faculty: Implications for policy and practice, *The Review of Higher Education*, 25(3), 297–314.

Leslie, L. L., McClure, G. T. & Oaxaca, R. L. (1998) Women and minorities in science and engineering: A life sequence analysis, *Journal of Higher Education*, 69(3), 239–276.

Lorde, A. (2008) The master's tools will never dismantle the master's house, in A. Bailey & C. Cuomo (Eds.), *The Feminist Philosophy Reader*, pp. 49–51. New York, NY: McGraw Hill.

Miller, J. L. (2005) *Sounds of Silence Breaking: Women, Autobiography, Curriculum*. New York, NY: Peter Lang.

Nygaard, C., Højlt, T., & Hermansen, M. (2008) Learning-based curriculum development, *The Journal of Higher Education*, 55(1), 33–50.

Palmer, R. & Gasman, M. (2008) It takes a village to raise a child: The role of social capital in promoting academic success for African American men at a Black college, *Journal of College Student Development*, 49(1), 52–70.

Park, J. J. & Denson, N. (2009) Attitudes and advocacy: Understanding faculty views on racial/ethnic diversity, *The Journal of Higher Education, 80*(4), 415–438.

Patton, L. D. (2009) My sister's keeper: A qualitative examination of mentoring experiences among African American women in graduate and professional schools, *The Journal of Higher Education, 80*(5), 510–537.

Pinar, W. F., Reynolds, W. M., Slattery, P., & Taubman, P. M. (2008) *Understanding Curriculum.* New York, NY: Peter Lang.

Watt, S. K. (2006) Racial identity attitudes, womanist identity attitudes, and self-esteem in African American college women attending historically Black single-sex and coeducational institutions, *Journal of College Student Development, 47*(3), 319–334.

Winkle-Wagner, R. (2009) The perceptual homelessness of college experiences: Tensions between home and campus for African American women, *The Review of Higher Education, 33*(1), 1–36.

Wolf, P. (2007) A model for facilitating curriculum development in higher education: A faculty-driven, data-informed, and educational developer–supported approach, in P. Wolf and J. C. Hughes (Eds.), *New Directions for Teaching and Learning, 112*, 15–20. San Fransisco, CA: Jossey-Bass.

1

PEDAGOGICAL POETICS AND CURRICULAR DESIGN IN THE INTERRACIAL CLASSROOM

A Black Female Perspective

Catherine John Camara

This chapter will address some of the strategies that shaped the design and implementation of my college curricula, developed over the course of nearly twenty years of teaching at the University of Oklahoma. I will discuss how my pedagogy evolved as I learned from the environment I found myself in. I will treat as a case study the rationale behind the development of one of my most popular courses, utilizing this as a way to explain the logic behind my decisions. Finally, I will meditate on the larger significance and implications of this work. My scholarly emphasis has been on the Black Atlantic, more specifically the overlap between African–American and Afro-Caribbean literary and cultural conversations and traditions. My theoretical approach is heavily informed by both postcolonial theory and the Black radical tradition of thought emerging from African–American scholars in the late 1960s and early 1970s.

In the spring semester of 2017, I taught a graduate seminar entitled, "Introduction to African American Literature and Theory." There were six students in the course, four female, two male and all white. We covered literature and critical debates from the late nineteenth and early twentieth centuries, as well as contemporary drama, poetry, film, and theories of race and subjectivity. As final papers rolled around, student anxieties increased. One of the male students, looking for something challenging, wanted me to suggest a text not studied in the class as a possible option for his analysis. I recommended that he read Jamaica Kincaid's novel *Lucy*.

Kincaid's second novel is a text that impacts various readers in different ways. Put frankly, white American students were often annoyed by the character Lucy, whose critique of the world of her white female employer Mariah functions as an ethnography of bourgeois white subjectivity. Not used to this reciprocal function of "the gaze," Kincaid's narrative is often experienced by this demographic as uncomfortable and disconcerting. Furthermore, her text exposes the political dynamics of personal interactions between Black and white women, thus linking abstract systems of colonialism and imperialism to everyday life. On the other hand, students of color frequently identify with Lucy, seeing her as a type of anti-colonial heroine of sorts.

All too predictably the male graduate student wrote a paper that underestimated the complexity of the text, revealed by his rhetorical enactment of the kinds of reactions to the novel previously mentioned. He confessed to finding the character Lucy annoying and took to waging war against her positions without recourse to any textually based evidence. Once he received my grade, a generous low B in my opinion, he wrote me a sharp and hasty email requesting a meeting while also stating that I had assessed his paper based on my assumptions about his personal reactions to the text rather than objectively engaging his argument. He was reacting to a line in my final comments stating that by the end of his paper he had not only ceased to quote from the text but appeared to be defending the character Mariah against perceived rhetorical attacks from the character Lucy, as if the attacks were personally launched against him.

Before we met I consulted with two white male colleagues about the issue. One stated that had he received such an email from a student, the breach of decorum alone would have been enough for him to have a whole meeting exclusively addressing professional etiquette. The other suggested that were he in my place the "meeting" would simply have functioned as an opportunity for the student to state his grievances and for him to reiterate that they had a difference of opinion about the quality of his work. The actual meeting was surprisingly pleasant and functioned as an opportunity to further communicate principles I had addressed in the class itself—these being an awareness of one's worldview and social location, learning how to read the ideology of the literary text in a theoretical way, paying precise attention to detail, and also interpreting the complex way notions of race function and are situated in various texts. Yet the process of his reaction and resistance to my comments on his paper made explicit a series of implicit raced and gendered dynamics at play between white students and professors of color.

First, I felt a need to defend myself and justify my critique once I read his email despite my being the professor and he being the student. This was quite different from the reactions of my male colleagues, yet not so far afield from conversations I had had in the past with female colleagues about their own interactions with male students. Second, the tone of his initial email to me, hardly one of deference, made me wonder how the politics of the interaction would have played out if I were a Black female student and he were the white male professor and *I* sent *him* such an email. Third, in the fallout in which we had to meet and talk the episode through, I was aware that despite being the professor, I was at a sort of disadvantage in that while the paper had certain universal weaknesses, only readers who were either familiar with the novel or more importantly, racially and culturally literate in a postcolonial theoretical sense would understand that element of my critique of his paper. The world around us implicitly validated his perspective with regards to race and the onus was on me to prove to him why my reading of the text was more correct than his own. It is with this as a preamble that I turn to the task of addressing my pedagogical practices and experiences while teaching at the university level for the last two decades.

Emerging Pedagogical Strategies in the Early Years

Opening her text *Teaching to Transgress* with a quote from Paulo Friere (1968), bell hooks (1994) states:

> To educate as the practice of freedom is a way of teaching that anyone can learn. That learning process comes easiest to those of us … who believe that there is an aspect of our vocation that is sacred … that our work is not merely to share information but to share in the intellectual and spiritual growth of our students.
>
> *(13)*

hooks (1994) goes on to state that it was, "Friere's insistence that education could be the practice of freedom that encouraged [her] to create strategies for what he called "conscientization" in the classroom" (14). She goes on to speak about developing the conviction that the classroom is a space for the "active participant" rather than the "passive consumer." The "objectification of the teacher within bourgeois educational structures" denigrates a holistic approach to learning and social change in favor of an abstract, alienated notion of the academic as "smart" even if "emotionally unstable" (16).

bell hooks's (1994) utilization of Friere's (1968) ideas to situate her approach to teaching is a fitting way to describe my own pedagogical investments. I began teaching at the University of Oklahoma in the spring of 1998. At that time, in a department of twenty-eight faculty members, I was one of four faculty of color and the only Black faculty member. In my first semester I was assigned two lower division survey courses: one in American literature that covered material from 1865 to the present. This course fulfilled both general education and major departmental requirements. The other was an African–American literature survey, a course that was then part of the African–American Studies Program's core curriculum. The American literature survey had forty-one students, thirty-six Euro–Americans, three African–Americans, and two Native Americans. In the African–American literature course, of the twenty-seven students enrolled, seventeen were African–American, eight were Euro–American, one was Asian–American, and one was Native American. I soon realized that the atmosphere in both classes reflected racial and cultural tensions in Oklahoma as evidenced by the social segregation both on campus as well as in the world outside.[1]

The shock that I encountered in this first semester of teaching was twofold. First, the atmosphere in the predominantly white classroom on almost any given day was one of stony silence with severely masked white faces staring back at me. The students were by and large unresponsive and hard to read. This was different from the predominantly white classrooms I had encountered in graduate school in California. On the other hand, the predominantly Black class was loud and raucous to an uncontrollable extreme forcing me into an anxious disciplinarian stance from time to time. In the white classroom, I felt as if I was perceived by the dominant majority as an "alien" presence—someone introducing unorthodox anti-imperialist approaches. In the Black classroom, I appeared to be an unpredictable entity, one who used too many abstract academic phrases and not enough culturally and recognizably familiar Black patterns of speech. Further, I was teaching a Black studies course in a university context in which such courses historically had a reputation for being intellectually lightweight and more or less occasions for Black students to socialize and chill.

The second shock I experienced was the sharp discrepancy between the responses to the African–American literary material in both classes. While there were nuances to the reactions on both sides of the racial divide, I realized that I had been effectively trained to teach Black literature to white students rather than to Black students or other students of color. In other words, I rapidly discovered that both racial groups of students asked very different kinds of questions of the material. This became abundantly apparent when I prepared the same lecture for both classes on days when the material overlapped. For the white students in the American literature survey, by and large African–American literature and culture functioned as an exotic fish bowl; a world so different from theirs that even the most basic cultural references had to be explained. Once these things were established they were most interested in analyses that emphasized the aesthetics of form, structure, trope, and allusion. For the Black students and to an extent other students of color within the predominantly Black African–American literature survey course, there was a clear desire for more active rather than static theories of knowledge. They wanted me to elucidate the connection between the material and the reality of their lives in the world outside the university.

At the end of the semester in the African–American literature survey, the material had had the most substantial impact on the white students enrolled in this class while not appearing to have seriously influenced the Black students. The white students in the African–American literature survey experienced a kind of immersion in the African–American literary and cultural tradition and gained insights and knowledge they had not previously had. I realized that if I wanted to impact the worldviews of the Black students in that same class in the future, then I would have to aggressively and systematically plan a course that kept this goal specifically in mind with regards to the structure of their consciousness. On their course evaluations they stated that while the material had been interesting, the course was not organized enough. I suspected, however, that the material, in the form that I presented it, simply had not reached them. On the other hand, at the end of the American literature survey, I was taken by surprise by the racist nature of the commentary made by the majority of the class on the student evaluations. They stated repeatedly that the course focused on "too many blacks, too many women and not enough American literature." Probably due to the power relationship and their fear of my difference, their feelings about the literature that fell outside the Euro–American literary canon was not made apparent before the semester's end. This was my first lesson in race, pedagogy, and classroom dynamics.

In the early years, experiences in the predominantly white class made certain power relations clear. As the only Black faculty member in a department, and one who was interested in anti-imperialist pedagogical paradigms of teaching, the degree to which I could successfully "unsettle the coloniality of power" in the mainstream predominantly white classroom was directly proportionate to the racism and hostility that white students at any educational level had the power to unleash. Anything other than total hostility from white students in this regard was a result of tremendous luck and strategic skill. I put myself to the task of developing pedagogical strategies that could reach the students I would continue to encounter.

The Theory and the Practice: A Curriculum Case Study

In 2006, I designed and taught a course entitled, "Hip Hop as Poetry, Literature and Cultural Expression." My family migrated from Jamaica to Boston and specifically to urban Dorchester in the 1980s when Rap music was just becoming a culturally commercial phenomenon and hitting the airwaves. I came of age in an era when this music was considered violent, misogynist noise while simultaneously "snatching" a large cross section of youth across racial lines with the hypnotic rhymes and beats. I decided to teach a whole class on Hip Hop since it addressed a nexus of contested social and political issues, contained both sacred and profane poetry, as well as wildly secular and deeply philosophical worldviews expressed through unconventional and frequently complex artistry. Put plainly, issues of gender, race, violence, oppression, sexuality, and more all found voice in the wide-ranging world of oral and visual Hip Hop culture. No other pop culture medium was more divisive, and yet as the controversy increased the popularity exploded with Hip Hop rapidly influencing advertising, music production and sales, sports, television shows, movie themes and soundtracks as well as how young people viewed themselves and their lives.

By this time, now tenured and eight years into the teaching career, I was no novice when it came to the controversial course curriculum. As a matter of fact, I thrived on it. I had been nominated for and received one of the more elite teaching awards and six years later I received another one. I had successfully designed and repeatedly taught at least four African diaspora courses. My classroom was notorious for the unconventional discussions in which students with radically different social and cultural backgrounds could have heated discussions and emerge alive and energized. Some students hated my classes, more loved them and it was a mystery to some of my colleagues how I could teach such radical Black material in a place like Oklahoma and get positive student evaluations. My secret was fairly simple. I knew how to generate a good discussion and I had found out that controversial subjects could make for great discussion if one knew how to structure the organizing questions. Another part of my success can be attributed to my talent for thinking quickly on my feet in the midst of tension and animosity and figuring out how to maintain dialogue under these conditions. This was not pedagogy for the faint of heart. This involved instinctively knowing how to utilize the awkward silence, seeing the connection between various threads of a conversation, keenly reading participant facial expressions and learning when to draw into the dialogue silent bystanders.

The Logic Behind the Syllabus

In the first year of the Hip Hop class, I organized the syllabus into three sections. In the first part of the semester we read and discussed essays, books, and documentaries, with both an ancient to contemporary historical reach, the goal being to give students an historical understanding of the social conditions that shaped the emergence of the music and poetry. In the second part of the semester we addressed the form and content of the music. In this segment, we analyzed the lyrics, rhyme scheme, message and philosophical worldview of the albums of various artists. We treated the albums as texts that had been strategically organized with the same coherence as a novel or a collection of short stories. The last part of the semester was and always has been devoted to live performances. Students have to participate in three performances organized around inspiration, technique, and improvisation, respectively. For the inspiration segment, they have to write, memorize, and perform an original spoken word poem. For the technique segment, they have to memorize and perform a minute of lyrics from a list of songs that I either choose or approve.[2] For the freestyle segment, they have to engage in a freestyle battle for 30–45 seconds with a classmate on one of the selected topics. The first two-thirds of the course is heavy on writing, analysis, and interactive small and big group discussions. The last third emphasizes an appreciation for the aesthetics of the art form. The structure of this course has stayed consistent over the years.

Eleven years later, the Hip Hop course (also part of the university's general education core curriculum) has become so popular that I offer it twice a year, once in the summer. My goal is to use the material to tell them a story. Part of this story involves quick immersion and basic comprehension of key concepts that will lay a foundation for the comprehension of the stories in the music. These key concepts are: (1) **Colonialism** and the relationship between racial and economic oppression, (2) **Mis-education** and among other things the internalization of the oppressive society's worldview, and (3) **Resistance/Resilience** as consistent strategies of survival emanating most often from the folks at the bottom rung of Black cultures and societies.

To educate them about colonialism, I often use selections from Walter Rodney's *How Europe Underdeveloped Africa* coupled with excerpts from relevant documentaries and contemporary texts. I pair these texts with Hip Hop albums such as Common's *Be* and Notorious B.I.G.'s *Ready to Die*. To address mis-education, I always return to Carter G. Woodson's *The Mis-Education of the Negro* juxtaposed with the Eyes on the Prize documentary segment addressing the Ocean Hill-Brownsville school district in Brooklyn and the failed attempt at community-run schools in the 1960s. Woodson also works nicely with Dead Prez's song "They Schools" from their album *Let's Get Free*. To address Resistance/Resilience, I juxtapose Langston Hughes's 1928 Harlem Renaissance manifesto "The Negro Artist and the Racial Mountain" with Barbadian poet Kamau Brathwaite's essay, "The History of the Voice: Nation Language in Anglophone Caribbean Poetry." We also watch at this juncture David LaChappelle's documentary *RIZE* about the rise of Krumping as an art form in south central Los Angeles among urban youth following the 1992 Los Angeles riots.

There are a variety of texts that can do this work and based on student suggestions I often incorporate new music. But while I periodically add or make substitutions, I treat these texts like good math books: why reinvent the wheel if something is a success? My goal is less the transmission of information for information's sake and more a kind of decolonization of the mind, one that will go hand in hand with receptivity to the complexity of concepts and principles that arise from the music the students will study next.

Pedagogical Tools

The organization of the syllabus and the ordering of the course material is part of my pedagogical strategy. Understanding the historical conditions and analyzing the music comes before the performances, which require students to not only delve into self-expression but also self-assessment and awareness. The texts studied in the course are organized in a way akin to a crescendo. I believe that there are concepts that need to be understood before other concepts can be introduced. If one doesn't understand basic math, calculus will be a foreign language. For example, the fundamental nature of racial and economic oppression as part of the lived reality and psyche of those who were the descendants of formerly enslaved Africans was something that I believed could not really be grasped without having an understanding of capitalism as a system of economic and hierarchical power. This was why teaching Walter Rodney's text from the 1970s alongside occasional selections from John Perkins's 2004 James Bond-like exposé *Confessions of an Economic Hit Man* helped to shed light on Hip Hop songs such as Common's "The Corner" and Notorious B.I.G.'s "Things Done Changed" or "Gimme the

Loot." Without Rodney and Perkins, Common and especially Biggie just seemed like gangsters without a cause. After Rodney and Perkins, their albums began to be seen by many of the students, often without my prodding, as descriptions of both individual and communal reactions to economic oppression; Perkins and Rodney explained the wasteland of economic exploitation on a world scale, Biggie and Common localized it.[3]

In addition to the actual material on the syllabus, a crucial aspect of my strategic success involved assessing where the students were in terms of both their literacy in Hip Hop as well as their familiarity with African–American culture. This involved the two-fold strategy of a quiz on the first day as well as strategic use of classroom discussion and writing assignments in a variety of ways throughout the semester. The quiz asked them to specify the five original elements of Hip Hop culture[4] and also identify some old school Hip Hop tracks by song and artist that I played live in the classroom.[5]

In terms of writing assignments, the Hip Hop class is in many ways writing intensive for the first two thirds of the semester. There is a 10–12 page take home midterm, three or four single-spaced 1–2 page music analyses, two or three film analyses and "Paragraph Assignments."[6] In my second semester of teaching, I came up with the idea of the "Paragraph Assignment." The syllabus contains a paragraph question that isolates a central issue raised by some aspect of the material. Students have to write a response to the question and upload their answers before class begins. Despite the additional grading, this was a key aspect of my success in the early years. It ensured that grade hungry students would not only study the course material in advance but have thought about it in depth. It also gave me intimate insight into their thought process, and this was useful as I constructed lectures.

There were two reasons why I decided that the last third of the class should be reserved for actual student performances. The first was to disenchant them of the notion that Rap and Spoken Word were simplistic art forms that were "catchy and fun maybe" but not at all as complex as the literature they were used to reading and studying. There was no better way to understand the complexity of an artist's rhythm, rhyme, and cadence than to have to recite a few bars from memory. The second reason was that performance functioned as a pedagogical tool that connected them to the last and most frequently forgotten element of foundational Hip Hop culture, that being Knowledge of Self. I discovered that the process of creation and self-revelation was a psychologically liberating thing for all students across racial and cultural lines; it was something that made them feel empowered when they were studying material that was psychologically disempowering. They were also being exposed to a cultural secret without realizing it; the "how" of turning pain into joy. Having to write a Spoken Word poem about any topic of their choice reversed the position they occupied as consumers of the material and instead they became cultural agents.

In 2016, I added something called a "Journal of Consciousness" to my pedagogical writing tools in the Hip Hop class. The Journal of Consciousness was meant to create a context for students to chart and see their own reactions to the material at each stage while also giving me a form of concrete validation for my theories about what they were going through. They were also assigned a journal buddy. After they had submitted their journal they had a week to exchange journals with their buddy and have a conversation. They then had to write and submit a brief response to whatever the takeaway was from their conversation with their buddy.

This was an improvisational strategy meant to address a challenge that presented itself in previous courses. I felt as if the students went through a process of transformation throughout the semester that ebbed and flowed. I had also become painfully familiar, as noted earlier, with white mainstream students' bitter resentment of material that addressed issues of white privilege and racism. I knew from previous experiences with classroom discussion that the first part of the material that addressed economic and social oppression often functioned as a period of invigorating awakening for the students of color while for many of the white students this was a period characterized by shock, resentment, and feelings of betrayal.[7]

During the second segment of the course when we addressed the lyrics, form, and content of the music, some of the African–American students who were either familiar with the music or the world the music depicted suddenly became star pupils whose ability to decode and comprehend the poetry in the songs was often superior to my own. For many of the white students, even those who were self-proclaimed "Hip Hop heads," there was often surprise, confusion, and shame even, at their lack of mastery of the material. This was particularly true for students who were used to studying alone producing textual mastery as opposed to being in a situation where the cultural knowledge of other students gave them an added advantage.

In the final portion of the course, almost everything would equalize itself on the first day of Spoken Word performances. Students sat in rapt attention listening to each other's very personal stories, while each semester also came with two or three students who broke down in tears in front of the class, not from fear of performance, but rather from the sheer shock of publicly sharing private, sometimes painful, parts of themselves that they had not realized they had repressed. This was all the more astonishing since I never, ever assigned topics for the Spoken Word so every experience that a student shared in this segment was a choice. The Technique segment was often humbling since most students who were not professional rappers underestimated the skill set it takes to imitate the rhythm and rhyme of even the most rudimentary MC. Finally, the freestyle was so terrifying for almost everyone that the hysteria and anxiety evolved into sheer hilarity and abandon, thus functioning as the ultimate release from the semester's challenges. By the end of the performances many students across racial lines were openly declaring that the class had been one of their most rewarding. The pathway to this point of consciousness was often different for Black and white students, but there was unity in the end result. After the first few years, I created a writing assignment in which they addressed what their experiences of the performances had been while I also gave them the opportunity to have open discussion in a large group at the end of each performance. The performances never took place in our regular classroom with desks and chairs and a chalkboard. Instead, I always reserved the department lounge or a room on campus with couches, comfortable chairs, and the space for everyone to sit in a full circle with the student performers taking center stage in the middle.

The Evolution of Pedagogy and the Take Away

In Vèvè Clark's (2009) article "Developing Diaspora Literacy and Marasa Consciousness," Clark observes that due to the Western master/slave dichotomy we frequently think of our experience in binary terms. Searching for a strategy to help us develop not just literacy but a consciousness capable of assisting us with the difficult work of transforming our societies, Clark (2009) turns to two sets of theories, one from the intelligentsia and one from the folk context for answers. An improvisational praxis was isolated by Clark when she applied both Houston Baker's theories and the notion of Marasa consciousness emanating from Vodoun principles, to John Coltrane's rendition of "My Favorite Things." She states that it was through improvisation that Coltrane reformed the conflicting registers. My own pedagogical strategy within the context of the classroom has required constant improvisation and innovation to bridge the conflicting tensions created by the diverging histories and cultural experiences of Black and white students as well as other students of color in my classroom.

Over the course of my twenty years of teaching, my goals evolved. At their best, my courses aimed to give students a basic understanding of the literature and culture of African people, focusing on both their experiences of oppression and the resilience of their cultural matrix. I wanted my students to understand that the strength and the psycho-spiritual complexity of these cultures have been underestimated. Ultimately, I aimed to expose them to the transformation-oriented aesthetic that is the most vibrant aspect of these cultures in the hopes that they would develop an interest in both personal and societal transformation. What follows are brief selections from the final journals of four students from the fall 2016 sections of the Hip Hop class.[8]

Ben (white male)

In some sense, I identify with those who feel personally attacked by the ideas of white privilege and cultural appropriation. Towards the beginning of the semester, I was more likely to feel that my input would be disregarded due to a lack of personal experience. I now feel like I was missing the mark. While my lack of experience as a target of racism means that I can't speak from first-hand experience about this, I still have a lot to say about my own experiences. I've talked a lot this semester about ways in which I feel that whiteness differs from other racial identifiers. Most of all, due to its status as a perceived "default," it tends to mean far less than other identifiers, except as a tool to establish power. Outside of white racist groups, it is generally frowned upon to identify with one's whiteness. This class has prompted me to think about what a theoretical racially accepting white pride might be or if it is possible. In parallel, I've started to think about other parts of myself that I should have some more appreciation for, [such as] my upbringing, or my culture. Most of all, I've decided that, as long as I approach these questions in earnest and acknowledge the value of all people, I can allow these questions to take me to their logical conclusions.[9]

Edgar (Latino male)

Class has been getting down to business the last couple days. I cannot believe the amount of time I have spent thinking about the topics we talk about in class. Every day I am seeing the world from a whole new perspective and I cannot believe how different I feel compared to the start of the semester. I can see that my fear of public speaking has not really changed, but I can at least say this class has provided me with the insight to better myself. When I mentioned to my girlfriend about the poem I performed in front of class, she could not believe I did that and told me how amazed she was [by] me, because she knows about how nervous I get in front of crowds; her saying that made me feel a whole lot better about this class and about myself. Time and time again, I am glad I took this class *this* semester. It has been an eye-opening experience all throughout the days. One thing that has stuck with me all semester long is that in order to keep a level head, I must keep an open mind. Failure to do so [would mean that] I would not [have been] able to get through [this] class. This is a good way to live my life because this can be applied in the real world setting and not just to class. People out there are willing to stand up for their opinion, and I need to do the same. If I am to make myself known, I need to make my thoughts known. This class has taught me the importance of speaking my mind, while allowing other people's thoughts to enter and shape my own opinions.[10]

Lauren (white female)

In relation to this class, I feel peace and I feel charged. I am not sure if those are contradictory, but I do know that I feel both. I want to take what this class has given me and do more, do better. I do not intend to stop exploring the topics that we discussed, and I am not afraid of dialogue anymore (or at least not as much as I used to be). As I continue to work on my first feature film/performance post-graduation, this class will be on my mind. I am starting to think that it will be on my mind for the rest of my life.[11]

Savanna (Asian–American female)

All of the readings in THIS class were actually the ones that I really did read compared to all my other classes. I won't lie … even though I missed like about 2–3 writing assignments, I did do all of the readings. These readings intrigued me like no other, and that says a lot. This class was one that I really, really enjoyed, and that says a lot! I wish I can just continue taking classes like this throughout college, but I probably can't.[12]

Final Thoughts

While these student responses are rewarding and the Hip Hop class has broken the mold in an exceptional way, teaching a wide variety of courses has also brought me to more somber conclusions about the limits of my pedagogy. In classrooms in which there are critical masses of talkative Black students and other students of color, white students are usually pushed beyond their comfort zone by the nature of the questions raised. Typically what Black students and other students of color find empowering, many white students appeared to find dis-empowering. Many white students viewed material and perspectives that had a critique of capitalism or a discussion of reparations as direct attacks on their personal identities and frequently reacted with anger or paralyzed silence when students of color raised questions about the legacy of white privilege and complicity. They were hard pressed to acknowledge the existence of race privilege or anti-Black racism in the present, since this disrupted their assumptions about a post-racial reality, not realizing that the future existence of such a society depended on direct confrontation with these denied and repressed truths. This type of deep-rooted ideology is the kind of "racial mountain" that the white student will have to climb to get to the dream of the post-racial society, to quote Langston Hughes (1997) in reverse.

Because of these observations, after the first six years of teaching, I came to the conclusion that what was good for the goose *was not* good for the gander. I believed that white students and professors who were equally invested in what songwriter Bob Marley would refer to as the task of "emancipation from mental slavery" would have to develop strategies that are specifically relevant to the structures of their consciousness. While strategies created for and by people of color could raise the awareness and consciousness of white students, I believed that there were limits in terms of what was possible at the level of real ideological transformation. This is because the problems facing both groups are quite different. One racial group has to come to terms with what it would mean, on the deepest level, to no longer be the universal standard by which everything else is judged. Other groups of color are still trying to maintain basic survival, and beyond that are looking towards a liberated future in which their cultural realities realistically set the terms for institutions and policies that shape the lives of their own people.

After twenty years of teaching, my view is somewhat different. In certain ways the Hip Hop class proved that to some extent students from white racial contexts are impacted and transformed when exposed to Black politically radical material as well as to the resilience of the culture of what Zora Neale Hurston calls, "the God-making man in the gutter who is the creator of everything that lasts."[13] As we see from Lauren and Ben's journals above, the takeaway for them was significant and they were not alone among their demographic over the years. Yet most classes are not structured like the Hip Hop class and it is an uphill battle in the traditional classroom to make the kind of "sacred consciousness" inroads that bell hooks (1994), borrowing from Paulo Friere (1968), identifies, and that most Black female educators have explicit or implicit investments in.

The investments of Black professors and Black female faculty in particular have historically run deeper than the mere transmission of information. For those of us who are the descendants of formerly enslaved Africans, the task of the preservation and restoration of the psyches of our children and families often fell to us, the proverbial "Big Mamas," "Aunties," and "Nanas." Extending this generosity beyond the family has been our historical social tendency. What I have learned over the years is that African diaspora culture has a lot to teach members of the dominant society. However, it is not a free pass. The white students who have gained the most from my classes are those who were not afraid to have painful conversations. The rewards were then substantial because African diaspora cultures have developed internal mechanisms of collective compassion as by-products of the Afro-indigenizing impulse that transforms pain into power and sometimes joy.[14] The students who had the courage to confront their pain and complicity were then able to reap some of the benefits of this magnificent diasporic cultural resonance.

Institutions, however, do not have access to this knowledge and most Black female teachers are simply seen as having nothing significant to offer that is out of the ordinary. The knowledge that we have has not been quantified and by and large has been more a product of our ability to interpret the history of our experiences, personal and cultural, than information gathered from graduate programs and study alone. What I am trying to say is that twenty years later, I have come to the conclusion that the type of knowledge that I am able to deploy pedagogically in the classroom is a product of my upbringing, cultural socialization, institutional training, and ancestral ways of understanding things that have been handed down to me from my lineage. It has been fairly easy to transmit some of what I know to students who share my cultural and racial background and worldview but harder to reach others whose worldview I understand less. Still, I have had some successes. Were Black women given the freedom to create and structure institutions in the image of the knowledge that they have gained implicitly, we could transform the world.

Notes

1 The most substantial example of this was the fact that at the time of my arrival there were full-fledged scholarship pageants devoted to each ethnicity. These included a Miss OU, a Miss Black OU, as well as a Miss Hispanic, Native American, and Asian OU.
2 I control the list in order to maintain consistency with regards to the level of difficulty of the songs. This way there is no danger of similar grades being assigned for a song with exceptionally difficult flow as well as another that is simple in its structure.
3 "If I wasn't in the rap game I'd probably have a key knee deep in the crack game/ Because the streets is a short stop Either you're slingin' crack rock or you got a wicked jumpshot/Shit, it's hard being young from the slums/Eatin' five cent gums not knowin' where your meals comin' from"—"Things Done Changed" by Notorious B.I.G.
4 The five elements of Hip Hop are the DJ or disc jockey, the MC or Master of Ceremonies; aka the Rapper, the B-Boy or break dancer, the Graffiti artist, and the last most elusive, often excluded element is Knowledge of Self.
5 The quiz usually functions as the first sign to students that although the class deals with popular culture it is not only rigorous but there is an actual knowledge base associated with Hip Hop beyond familiarity with commercially popular rappers and current music.
6 The midterm has two parts. In Part 1, students had to analyze the literary form of a particular song (including rhythm and rhyme, tone, structure, message, philosophical worldview), while in Part 2, they have to compare and contrast male and female relations and the depiction of women in four specifically assigned songs by various artists.
7 For many of the students of color, historically in this class, this portion of the material was invigorating because it appeared to validate much of their lived understanding of reality. For white mainstream students, on the other hand, the sense of betrayal was proportionate to their belief in a color-blind American dream that was accessible to all Americans. This was often followed by a sense of resentment towards me, or the material, for being the messenger of such bad news.
8 Each of these students gave their consent for the selection from their journals to be used for this article.
9 Ben Russell was an Economics major.
10 Edgar Akuna was a Psychology major with a minor in Sociology.
11 Lauren Bumgarner was a Film and Video Studies major.
12 Savanna Thao was a Human Relations major.
13 This quote was found in Valerie Boyd's 2003 biography, *Wrapped in Rainbows: The Life of Zora Neale Hurston*, p. 182.
14 The concept of Afro-Indigenization as an African diasporic cultural way of making meaning within the context of oppressive situations is the subject of my current manuscript entitled, *Afro-Indigenization: Internal Power as Cultural Practice*.

References

Boyd, Valerie. *Wrapped in Rainbows: The Life of Zora Neale Hurston*. New York, NY: Scribner Press, 2003.
Clark, VèVè. "Developing diaspora literacy and *Marasa* consciousness." *Theatre Survey 50*, pp. 9–18, 2009.
Friere, Paulo. *Pedagogy of the Oppressed*. New York, NY: Seabury Press, 1968.

hooks, bell. *Teaching to Transgress: Education as the Practice of Freedom.* New York, NY: Routledge Press, 1994.

Hughes, Langston. "The negro artist and the racial mountain." In *Norton Anthology of African American Literature,* edited by Henry Louis Gates, Jr., 1266–69. New York, NY: Norton, 1997.

2

SOMOS GENTE ESTUDIADA

Creating Change Within and Outside the Walls of Academia

Norma A. Marrun

Nuestra gente [our people] can tell by the way we dress and speak that we are *gente estudiada.*[1]*¿Porque te quejas* [Why do you complain]? You do not have to clean other people's homes or work at a factory for minimum wage. You get paid to sit on a comfy chair to read books and write. For many of us who are the first in our family to pursue an academic position it is difficult to explain the intellectual and emotional labor involved in our work without sounding self-absorbed or apathetic to the everyday struggles of our families and communities. Although in their eyes "we have made it," it is difficult to explain that because of our racial, ethnic, class, gender, physicality (i.e., short, brown), sexual identities, or "non-traditional" scholarship, we are often perceived as second-class academics (Garcia, 2005; Turner, 2002).

Should I return to my community and help out *mi gente* or can I create change within academia? *Gente estudiada* are always crossing *fronteras*—moving between intersectional identities—while confronting our relatively privileged status as college educated and academics. *Las mujeres* [the women] are told by their *gente* to get *una buena educación*[2] *para valerse por si mismas* [to be self-reliant] (Villenas & Moreno, 2001). However, when some of us challenge our mothers' way of treating *los hombres* [the men] in our *familias*, we are told to relax with those *femenista* ideas (Latina Feminist Group, 2001). Similar sentiments are reflected in Aida Hurtado's (2003) study about the contradictions that Chicana students experience between their mothers' *consejos* [advice giving narratives] centered on feminism and their mothers' actions. One of Hurtado's (2003) Chicana participants spoke to this contradiction:

> My mom is probably the closest thing to a feminist, even though she didn't
> want to stand up to my dad, she told us, "Don't get married when you're

young. Live your life; do what you want to do; don't be dependent on a man"—even though she never took her own advice.

(p. 210)

The inconsistency between what we learn at home and newfound knowledge and ways of thinking creates dissonance between our families, communities, and academic worlds. Dissonance is not only heighted by our participation in higher education, but by colleagues who perceive our status as second-class academics. We are *gente estudiada* living and moving across physical, social, emotional, spiritual, and intellectual borderlands. The dissonance created by these intense contradictions has helped me develop a tolerance for ambiguity and a recognition of the funds of knowledge that my students and I bring into higher education (González, Moll, & Amanti, 2005).

In this chapter, I draw from my own personal struggles as a first-generation college student and the first *mujer* in my *familia* to be in academia. Women of color have documented similar experiences about feeling torn between their commitment to their families, communities, and careers (González, Jovel, & Stoner, 2004; Rendón, 1992; Turner & Myers, 2000). Although my family has never fully understood my journey, they have been a strong source of emotional support in my academic journey; their stories of resilience have inspired my research, and my family's pedagogies of the home including *convivencia* [communalism] have guided my pedagogy (Delgado Bernal, 2001). Additionally, I share how my experiences and reflections about my research, positionality, and work in the community are mutually informed and shaped in my curriculum. I foreground *gente estudiada* as a term for (re)defining intersectional identities and (re)asserting connections with family and communities of color within and without the academy. I draw from women of color feminist frameworks as resistance to the hegemony of Eurocentric thoughts, values, norms, and knowledge production in academia.

Defining *Gente Estudiada*

My work evolves from women of color feminism; it comes from engaging in my own process of gaining *conocimiento* [reflective consciousness] as a result of (un) learning about my racialized, gendered, classed, and (un)documented[3] intersectional identities. My work introduces *gente estudiada*, a term used in the Latina/o community to refer to people who are college educated.[4] *Gente estudiada* is cohesive and gender neutral and is about following a path to *conocimieno,* a strong sense of community commitment and responsibility to take action. So far, *gente estudiada* has not been used in educational or Chicana/Latina feminist scholarship; hence, my work draws from the assets found in Latino communities, while carrying out a critical analysis of these communities. To honour and respect where I come from, I show the stories, wealth, and knowledge found within Latino communities and using a term like *gente estudiada,* even if it is not yet an academic term. A useful

analytical concept, *gente estudiada* carries discursive meanings of both empowerment as well as otherness and helps to keep the tension around education clearly
in view. Because it comes from how communities name students, it also recognizes both the community origins of learning and the sometimes-present, com-
munity-based suspicions about those who are educated. That is, *gente estudiada*
marks one's status as educated and thus admired by family and community for
his/her accomplishments. It often marks the person as an exception, especially if
he/she/they are the first in the family to attend college. This process of reflecting from within and without one's home and community is part of belonging
to a group of *gente estudiada,* an ongoing process of crossing-over into multiple
knowledges, paradigms, ideologies, and conflicting sets of values (i.e., collectivism
versus individualism).

In my research with first-generation Latina/o students, I realized that we
shared a similar experience of feeling partially understood and constantly having
to negotiate uncomfortable tensions. As one Latino male participant shared:

> As soon as you get a college education and you don't go back home, you're
> seen as a traitor to your family. They start saying things to your face like,
> "*Te crees muy chignón*" [you think you're a bad ass] just because I'm col-
> lege educated.

In her writing, Gloria Anzaldúa (1999) also described the dissonance she experienced as the first in her family in six generations to leave her home in Texas
to pursue higher education. Anzaldúa (1999) wrote about her desire to "leave
home so I could find myself" by "way of education and career and becoming
self-autonomous" (pp. 38, 39). She was also afraid of being "abandoned by the
mother culture" for critiquing its patriarchal constraints placed on women and its
homophobia (p. 42). Choosing to leave her home to find herself came with the
cost of being marked as a traitor and *creida* [arrogant or stuck-up] to her family.
She wrote, "If you don't behave like everyone else, *la gente* will say that you think
you're better than others, *que te crees grande*" (p. 40).

Similar to my participants' and Anzaldúa's (1999) experiences, I noticed that my
family treated me differently when I returned to visit. Sometimes I felt embraced
by them, but, more often, I felt a growing distance. I did not always have the words
to describe how I felt because I was made to feel the pride of the family. However,
there were instances when I overheard comments about how I was changing.
Internally I wondered if in fact I had changed and had turned my back on them.
I started to make sense of my unease when I read Margaret E. Montoya's (1994)
"Mascaras, trenza's y greñas: Un/masking the self while un/braiding Latina stories
and legal discourse." It was the first academic article that I read that used personal
narrative to reflect on one's resilience in navigating higher education. Montoya
(1994) also interwove legal scholarship to "unmask" academia's additive approach
to diversity, which tends to focus on cosmetic representations and tokenism. She

retold stories about the isolation and alienation she experienced as a first-year law student at Harvard, and her work revealed the ambivalence and contradictions that Latinas/os confront in moving between worlds. Montoya (1994), too, reflected on the pain and "internal doubts about what one has given up in order to achieve academic success. Concerns about ethnic identity and personal authenticity are embedded with the question, 'Who am I really?' We have been told, 'You don't seem Latina', or have been asked, 'How Latina are you?'" (p. 11). Thus, we often are marked as the exception.

Creating a Classroom Space of *Convivencia* (communalism)

When I started teaching I was unsure of how to arrange classroom space. I thought about the professors who created classroom spaces where I felt I belonged, where I felt safe to be vulnerable, and where I experienced intellectual growth. Their approaches resembled what Chicana/Latina education feminists have described as teaching and learning centered on *convivencia*[5] to create compassionate pedagogical spaces (Villenas, 2005). At the end of each semester, a few students always admit how at first they were uncomfortable about my pedagogy because they were unaccustomed to it; many expected me to deliver information by lecture and were nervous about my approaches to teaching that included problem-posing dialogue, gallery walks, listening to music while students worked in small groups, and other approaches that got students to move and to engage their affective and emotional sensibilities (Clark, 2002; Freire, 1970). These students' admissions caused me to reflect on how my family instilled *convivencia* at home and within our community. *Convivencia* is grounded on community-building, respect, active listening, caring, trust, critical dialogue, and empathy. My mother welcomed anyone who entered our home with a warm greeting, offered them *un cafesito*, and engaged in long conversations embedded with compassion, humor, and affirmation. My mother dropped whatever it was she was doing and always gave her full attention to whomever walked through our door, even if it was people with whom she disagreed; like individuals who tried to push a different religion. She always welcomed them into our home and listened with an open heart. My mother's pedagogies of home, specifically *convivencia*, have inspired and guided how I organize the classroom space.

Following my mother's ways of teaching and learning, I always arrange classroom space to maximize interaction. I often reposition the physical space of the classroom into a circle because I find that it creates a more intimate space of learning. For the first few weeks I have students place name tents on their desks to help their peers and me learn each other's names. I organize each course as a series of *pláticas* [talking circles/open conversations] that encourage active participation; problem-posing dialogue, compassion, reflection, and listening with respect are embraced (Delgado Bernal & Elenes, 2011; Fierros & Delgado Bernal, 2016). The purpose of *pláticas* is to create a collaborative learning space for students to get to know their peers and eventually to develop friendships. I open each *plática* by asking the class how they are feeling or how their week has been going. If I am aware of a student's accomplishment, I announce it in class and then open it up for others to share. I ask students to be mindful of their participation and to pay close attention to how much they are or are not contributing to the *plática*. Active participation also requires listening to each other sympathetically, respecting the contributions of others, and reframing disagreement in constructive ways. The goal of *pláticas* is to learn from each other and for my students and me to expand our understanding of issues from a perspective different from our own.

I usually teach evening courses that meet around dinnertime. Many of my students come straight from a full day at work or from another class, so I bring food to the first week of class. I then have groups of students take turns bringing food. Breaking bread together helps build a classroom community; sharing food encourages them to walk around the classroom and create opportunities to get to know their peers. I realize that some students might not have the funds to purchase food so I encourage them to talk with me if they cannot contribute. Like my mother's offering of *un cafesito*, I break bread with my students as a form of developing *convivencia*.

Centering the Knowledge of Scholars of Color and Marginalized Communities

In developing the curriculum, I employ scholarship that highlights the perspectives of and analyses by women of color and scholars from other marginalized identities. I privilege texts, counter narratives, and *testimonios* by scholars of color reflecting on their schooling experiences and documenting their family and community wealth; throughout my teaching years, students have expressed grasping the course content from reading *testimonios* centered on the schooling experiences of marginalized students. A year after enrolling in one of my courses, I was surprised when a student took the time to write:

> Being a white female, I grew up with the impression that racism was when someone said, "I don't like Black people" or "I am not giving you this job because you are Chinese." It wasn't until your class that I was introduced to the systemic racism and underlying issues of racism in society. The class really impacted my views of the world and me. The readings that stood out to me the most were the two readings about the experiences of "hiding their Latino-ness" in school. Because of my privilege, it was only through these readings that I could begin to understand what minorities go through … The main point of me writing is that your class sparked my interests in these issues … Just thought you deserved to know that.

I also develop assignments that allow students to engage in self-reflection, and to develop a better understanding of the sociopolitical, historical, and structural inequalities that continue to disproportionally impact marginalized families and communities. In particular, I draw on González, Moll, and Amanti's (2005) funds of knowledge, Delgado Bernal's (2001) pedagogies of the home, and Yosso's (2005) community cultural wealth models. I use these pedagogical approaches to place my students, their family, community assets, and cultural wealth at the center of the knowledge construction, curriculum, and pedagogy of the classroom. Most importantly these approaches lead students to believe that their lived experiences and knowledge are valued in the classroom space.

Every assignment is developed with the intention of reflecting on students' backgrounds, allowing them to draw from the course materials and their personal and professional experiences. One assignment in particular allows students to develop the knowledge and skills to engage in everyday self-reflection. The first part is a critical narrative assignment, which allows students to examine the interconnectedness of their multiple identities and to reflect on how they might consciously or subconsciously emphasize or disregard certain aspects of their identity (Crenshaw, 1991). Sample questions and reflective statements from the assignment include:

1 Identify an aspect of privilege that you take for granted every day or that makes you uncomfortable. Explain why you are uncomfortable thinking about this privilege. Examples of privileged identity can be whiteness, religion (e.g., Christian), heterosexual, middle class, able-bodied, or U.S. citizen.
2 What messages did you receive (e.g., from your community, school, media) growing up about what it means to be a member of your group? How did these messages influence, inform, and/or challenge how you interact with others, either in or out of your group?

This assignment is a powerful tool that helps students to understand classroom power dynamics and to disrupt social categories of oppression and privilege.

The second assignment involves students interviewing a family to understand their experiences in navigating their child's schooling. Many students are surprised by the family's generosity, as some of them open their homes and invite them for dinner. By interviewing a family, students find that although they might not participate in school events, families are involved in their child's education by making sure their child arrives on time to school, completes homework, and talking to the child about the importance of education. Although not all the students are changed or convinced because of their own deeply held biases, many become more aware of the socioeconomic pressures and constraints placed on families living in poverty. Embedded in this assignment are tools and lenses that help students move away from deficit models and move towards recognizing the assets of families and communities, and to identifying systematic inequities, and to finding solutions.

Through readings and course assignments students explore the connections between their schooling experiences, family histories, and communities. The feedback from some of my students has indicated that many of the readings and assignments enabled them to relate their lived experiences to the theories, ideas, and analyses of the issues discussed in class. Whereas some students from more privileged identities appreciate feeling challenged to see beyond their experiences and to understand the position of others, others tend to respond defensively by denying their white privilege or remarking, "I didn't have any privileges because I had to work hard to get into college." I do not claim to have figured out a balanced and critically engaging curriculum, but my pedagogical goal is to expand the possibilities for both students of color and white students to stand up against systemic oppression and to use their knowledge and positions to reseed notions of equity and social justice.

Validation: Affirming Student Capabilities to Succeed

Although I did well throughout my undergraduate education, few professors took the time to praise my work. When professors did acknowledge my work my confidence improved, and I thought I was capable of graduating and pursuing graduate school. Although my writing could always use improvements, many of my professors complimented me on my ideas and encouraged me to keep working on my writing. As faculty, I always provide both constructive feedback on student papers and highlight their strengths. Semester after semester, at least one student comments on how I am their first Latina professor or how they thought their experiences and personal and academic identities were validated. One particular undergraduate Latina student was quiet in class, but her writing was critical and creative. She left as soon as class ended, but one day as I was returning papers, I made sure to return hers last. Before handing back her paper, I complimented her on her writing and expressed how much I enjoyed reading her work. I hoped she would respond, but she stood still without saying a word. I did not know what to think so I returned her paper. Later in the day, I received the following message from that student:

> I wanted to reach out to you and thank you once again for the compliment that you gave me in class regarding my writing assignments. To some a compliment like that may not be a big deal but to me it meant something special. In case you didn't notice I had to fight back a tear because your words really touched me. The reason for that being is because for the first time in my five years of college someone noticed my work. Attending this university as a female who is a minority has always made me feel as if I have to compete to show others that my work could be just as good or even better, but unfortunately it always went unnoticed, until now. To hear that someone thinks my work is good and that they enjoy reading what I have to say makes me feel that I am doing something right, despite others opinions, because for the first time I feel as if someone understands me.

> As silly as this may sound, you made my last month at the [university] a
> memorable one because I leave this university knowing that my hard work
> did not go unnoticed.

I was filled with conflicting emotions of warmth, hope, anger, and sadness; I was
sad because for five years her writing and presence made her feel invisible in the
classroom. For Latina/o students, these experiences do not happen in isolation.[6] I
received a similar message from a Latino male student:

> First, I wanted to tell you that I appreciate the comments you left for me on
> my paper. They really hit me with positive feelings and I ended up tearing
> up in my car because I felt validated.

For these two Latino students, this was the first time that a professor had expressed
caring and the first time that they believed that their writing, knowledge, and
presence in the classroom were valuable. While these praises from students are
comforting and invigorate my spirit, I am reminded that I cannot afford to sit
back and wait for change, nor can I wait for more of us to be hired; I must continue to do my part. I am saddened and frustrated that, like my students, many
of our marginalized students' assets go unnoticed because they do not uphold
white, Eurocentric values in their thinking and writing. I am also reminded of the
countless faculty from marginalized backgrounds who have supported me and
saw in me what I could not see in myself. Thus, it is my turn to pay it forward.

Passion: Detaching the Body from Teaching

> Displaying a passion for one's culture is a radical risk for people of differ-
> ence within the academy: passion—or anger, fear, pleasure, commitment—
> becomes synonymous with "primitive," and that primitive voice is then
> okay to discount, deride, or even turn against itself.
>
> *(Miranda, 2002, p. 195)*

As a woman of color in the classroom, I am expected to detach my body from
my teaching. My students read that showing any kind emotion or feeling in my
teaching is biased, opinionated, and unintelligent. The academy expects us to be
'objective' and 'neutral' in our teaching. Many students, especially white students,
believe that schools and universities are apolitical spaces and that the knowledge
taught to them is 'neutral' and 'objective.' However, I remind students to look
around the classroom and to imagine a space with only white men. Changes in
attendance, curriculum, and faculty diversity have resulted from civil rights struggles and decades of activism, including physical violence against students of color.
Additionally, admissions policies have changed, ethnic studies programs have been
established, and more faculty of color and women have been hired. University

leaders began to recruit more women and people of color into institutions of higher education not because they believe it is the right thing to do, but because students at colleges across the country pressured campus leaders into hiring more diverse faculty. So, when I hear the words "neutral" and "objective," it feels like a thousand stabs to my body because universities are not now, nor have they ever been, politically neutral spaces of learning.

My desire to prepare culturally responsive teachers propelled my decision to pursue academia, especially because 84 percent of our country's teachers are white (U.S. Department of Education, 2016). Although I grew up in the Bay Area, a racially and ethnically diverse community, most of my teachers were white, with the exception of a few Latina/o teachers in elementary school; this was mainly because the school offered a Spanish and English bilingual program. I never thought I could be a teacher because I never saw teachers who reflected my racial, ethnic, and cultural identity. It was not until I was accepted into the Ronald E. McNair Postbaccalaureate Achievement Program[7] that I was encouraged to pursue graduate school and academia. My desire to be in the classroom and to connect with all students fueled my determination to pursue academia, but, more importantly, I wanted to connect with students with whom I shared similar backgrounds.

Teaching about multicultural education has been rewarding, but it has also been emotionally taxing and caused me to constantly question my presence in academia. Throughout my years of teaching, students generally have been generous on my teaching evaluations. Occasionally, I am called out for being 'biased' in my teaching and too 'passionate' about my research. One student commented about my teaching:

> It was awesome to have a teacher with such passion about the material. Just be careful on some of the political topics to not let your emotions teach, it's one thing to be passionate, but don't let your own experiences get in the way especially over controversial topics.

The student thought that my passion for teaching about 'controversial topics' like working with undocumented students and their families was an inappropriate teaching topic. The student also warned me to not let my lived experiences obscure my ability to teach.

I have taught at historically white universities but currently teach at a minority serving institution. My students have been pre-service and in-service teachers, many of whom are white and often perceive me as 'biased' or find me 'too passionate' about my research and teaching. I am marked as an outsider by my education, gender, and Latinidad because my identity does not fit neatly in people's imaginations. In the classroom, I am marked as an outsider by the way I look and speak. Physically, my students read me as a feminine heterosexual woman of color. Students cannot always point out my ethnicity and I am usually racially profiled as

Persian; when I share that I identify as Latina of Mexican descent, always one student says, "Ah, I see it now, because of your accent." I have never asked students to explain what they mean by my accent, possibly because it is challenging to engage students on the first day of class about how the history of having a Spanish 'accent' has been used in schools to justify the legal segregation of Mexican–American students. As a Latina faculty, my teaching brings an approach that has historically been absent, silenced, and devalued in academia. Institutions of higher education need to look at who is sitting in their classrooms because the faculty in many universities and colleges does not reflect the diversity of our students.

Faculty Orientation: Am I the Only Latina?

I walked into the College of Education's building, excited to meet my new colleagues and to learn about their research projects. Two weeks before the college's orientation, I attended the campus wide orientation: two long days of information overload, but one message that was repeated over and over was how much pride the university had in being the second most diverse campus in the nation (Summers, 2015). Almost every speaker at the orientation made a connection to the statement and after the second day, I found myself calling my friends and family and telling them how lucky I was to work at the second most diverse campus in the nation. I was inspired by the idea of being surrounded by so much diversity, especially because I had previously been at three historically white institutions. I sipped the diversity Kool-Aid and I must admit, it tasted damn good. After taking that first sip, I felt like diversity was an issue of the past because I was part of an institution that had fulfilled its mission.

Two weeks later, I walked into the College of Education's faculty orientation and that sweet taste turned sour as the new faculty introduced themselves and discussed their research. After the introductions, I asked myself, "Am I the only Latina who was hired?" And then it hit me. The student population is diverse, but neither the faculty nor staff is diverse. The institution has capitalized on the diversity of the student population to access more resources for the university. For example, the University of Nevada, Las Vegas, (UNLV) has achieved federal designation as both Minority Serving Institution (MSI) and Asian American and Native American Pacific Islander Serving Institution (AANAPISI), opening up additional avenues to fund academic programs under the Higher Education Act of 1965 (Gasman, Baez, & Turner, 2008). UNLV hit the jackpot with its diverse student population without having to do heavy recruitment. Another layer to the university's diverse student population is that Las Vegas is among the world's top tourist destinations and depends on marginalized bodies to provide labor for the tourist industry. In 2015, Las Vegas attracted more than 42.3 million visitors (Velotta, 2016), an average of 3.5 million visitors per month who need to have their rooms cleaned, meals cooked, drinks served, gambling machines working, and sexual fantasies met.

After leaving the orientation, I realized that I could not wait for the university to hire more faculty of color. I must take a more intersectional approach to deepen collaboration between and across social change. Lorde (2007) and Anzaldúa (1999), and other feminist scholars of color, remind us that the feminist project is about imagining a better world where we can all flourish. Lorde (2007) echoed the sentiment that we cannot afford to wait for others to create change. She explained:

> Change is the immediate responsibility of each of us, wherever and however we are standing, in whatever arena we choose … And if we wait to put our future into the hands of some new messiah, what will happen when those leaders are shot, or discredited, or tried for murder, or called homosexual, or otherwise disempowered? Do we put our future on hold?
>
> *(p. 141)*

I am a faculty member in the second most diverse university where many of our students are graduates of the Clark County School District (CCSD), the fifth largest and most diverse district in the nation. As of 2016, students of color in CCSD make up 73.8 percent of the student population, while only 27.1 percent of teachers are of color (Clark County School District Fast Facts 2015–2016). While we at UNLV have a diverse student population, many of our undergraduate students do not major in education. My colleagues, our graduate students, staff and I in the Department of Teaching and Learning are working to transform the leaky pipeline for teachers of color (Putman et al., 2016). We received funding through the Nevada Department of Education's Great Teaching and Leading Fund to study why there are so few teachers of color within the district, and so few students of color pursuing teaching as a career. Through the *Abriendo Caminos/ Opening Pathways for Students of Color into the Teaching Profession: Giving Back to the Community through Teaching* grant project, we are focusing on Nevada's persistent teacher shortage and growing student-teacher diversity gap so that durable local and national solutions may be developed and put into action. Each of us on the team comes from a diverse background and experiences, but we are working together to diversify the teaching workforce as we continue to fight for the humanity of our *gente*.

Notes

1 I coin the phrase *gente estudiada;* the term's literal translation is a studied person. However, I am defining it as a concept to illuminate the dissonance that many Latina/o students experience as they enter higher education and their strong commitment to remain committed to family and community. The use of Spanish and code-switching is a critical component of Chicana/Latina feminist discourse. Using different forms of Spanish affirms one's commitment to community, and demonstrates a form of resistance against assimilation.

2   Although *educación* is a direct translation of the English word education, its meaning is much broader than just succeeding academically; the Spanish term embodies moral and ethical values and social behavior.

3   When I immigrated to the U.S. I was undocumented; I became documented through my adoption, and thus obtained permanent residence status.

4   Within the Latino community there are people who are *mal educadas/os* and there are people who are *bien educadas/os. Una persona mal educada/o* is formally educated and can hold advanced degrees, but may still be disrespectful, ignorant, dishonest, and insensitive. *Una persona bien educada/o* might not be formally educated, but is acknowledged by the Latino community as being generous, kind, well mannered, and honest. *Una persona educada* can also mean a person who is perceived as being *preparada* (or more highly prepared/formally educated); in essence, a college education is seen as the gateway to better opportunities that then validates our families' risks, hard work, and sacrifice.

5   The literal translation of *convivenica* is living together.

6   In 2016, BuzzFeed News covered a story about a Latina college student and McNair Scholar who was accused of plagiarism by one of her professors; the professor circled the word "Hence," in disbelief that the student could write in a scholarly way. Her blog post generated 3,733 comments, the majority of which shared similar experiences. https://www.buzzfeed.com/tamerragriffin/a-professor-circled-hence-on-a-latina-students-paper-and-wro?utm_term=.qiQaX3QAvA#.qtY1XR8zkz

7   The McNair Program prepares eligible students from disadvantaged backgrounds for doctoral studies through involvement in research and other scholarly activities, summer internships, seminars, and other educational activities designed to prepare students for doctoral study. In addition to tutoring and academic counseling, activities are designed to assist participating students in securing admission to and financial assistance for enrollment in graduate programs (U.S. Department of Education).

References

Anzaldúa, G. (1999) *Borderlands/La Frontera: The New Mestiza*. San Francisco, CA: Aunt Lute Books.

Clark, C. (2002) Effective multicultural curriculum transformation across disciplines. *Multicultural Perspectives*, 4(3), 37–46.

Clark County School District (2015) *CCSD Fast Facts 2015–16*. Retrieved from http://static.ccsd.net/ccsd/content/media-files/fast-facts-15-16-final-5.pdf

Crenshaw, K. (1991) Mapping the margins: Intersectionality, identity, politics, and violence against women of color. *Stanford Law Review*, 43(6), 1241–1299.

Delgado Bernal, D. (2001) Learning and living pedagogies of the home: The mestiza consciousness of Chicana students. *International Journal of Qualitative Studies in Education*, 14(5), 623–639.

Delgado Bernal, D. & Elenes, C. A. (2011) Chicana feminist theorizing: Methodologies, pedagogies, and practices. In R. R.Valencia, (Ed.), *Chicano School Failure and Success: Present, Past, and Failure* (3rd ed.), pp. 99–119, New York, NY: Routledge.

Fierros, C. O. & Delgado Bernal, D. (2016) Vamos a platicar: The contours of platicas as Chicana Latina feminist methodology. *Chicana Latina Studies*, 15(2), 98–123.

Freire, P. (1970) *Pedagogy of the Oppressed*. New York, NY: The Seabury Press.

Garcia, A. (2005) Counter stories of race and gender: Situating experiences of Latinas in the academy. *Latino Studies*, 3, 261–273.

Gasman, M., Baez, B., & Turner, C. S.V. (2008) *Understanding Minority-serving Institutions*. Albany, NY: State University of New York Press.

González, K. P., Jovel, J. E., & Stoner, C. (2004). Latinas: The new majority in college. *New Directions for Student Services, 105,* 17–27.

González, N., Moll, L. C., & Amanti, C. (2005) *Funds of Knowledge: Theorizing Practices in the Households, Communities and Classroom.* Mahwah, NJ: Lawrence Erlbaum Associates.

Hurtado, A. (2003) *Voicing Chicana Feminisms: Young Women Speak out on Sexuality and Identity.* New York, NY: New York University Press.

Latina feminist group. (2001) *Telling to Live: Latina Feminist Testimonies.* Durham, NC: Duke University Press.

Lorde, A. (2007) *Sister Outsider: Essays & Speeches by Audre Lorde.* Berkeley, CA: Crossing Press.

Miranda, D. A. (2002) "What's wrong with a little fantasy?" Storytelling from the (still) ivory tower. In G. E. Anzaldúa & A. Keating (Eds.) *This Bridge We Call Home: Radical Visions for Transformation,* pp.192–201, New York, NY: Routledge.

Montoya, M. (1994) Mascaras, trenzas, y greñas: Un/masking the self while un/braiding Latina stories and legal discourse. *Chicano-Latino Law Review, 15,* 1–37.

Putman, H., Hansen, M., Walsh, K., & Quintero, D. (2016) High hopes and harsh realities. The real challenges to building a diverse workforce. Brown Center on Education Policy at Brookings. Retrieved from https://www.brookings.edu/research/high-hopes-and-harsh-realities-the-real-challenges-to-building-a-diverse-teacher-workforce/

Rendón, L. I. (1992) From the barrio to the academy: Revelations of a Mexican American "scholarship girl". *New Directions for Community College, 80,* 55–64.

Summers, K. (2015, September 9) UNLV ranked second most diverse campus in the nation. *Campus News.* Retrieved from https://www.unlv.edu/news/release/unlv-ranked-second-most-diverse-campus-nation

Turner, C. S. V. (2002) Women of color in academe. Living with multiple marginality. *The Journal of Higher Education, 73*(1), 74–93.

Turner, C. S. V. & Myers, S. L., Jr. (2000) *Faculty of Color in Academe: Bittersweet Success.* Boston, MA: Allyn and Bacon Press.

U.S. Department of Education. (2016, July) *The State of Racial Diversity in the Educator Workforce.* Retrieved from https://www2.ed.gov/rschstat/eval/highered/racial-diversity/state-racial-diversity-workforce.pdf

Velotta, R. N. (2016, January 10) Las Vegas hosted record 42.9M visitors in 2016. *Las Vegas Review-Journal.* Retrieved from http://www.reviewjournal.com/business/tourism/las-vegas-hosted-record-429m-visitors-2016

Villenas, S. (2005) Latina literacies in *convivencia*: Communal spaces of teaching and learning. *Anthropology and Educational Quarterly, 36*(3), 273–277.

Villenas, S., & Moreno, M. (2001) To valerse por si misma: Between race, capitalism and patriarchy-Latina mother/daughter pedagogies in North Carolina. *International Journal of Qualitative Studies in Education, 14*(5), 671–687.

Yosso, T. (2005) Whose culture has capital? A critical race theory discussion of community cultural wealth. *Race Ethnicity and Education, 8*(1), 69–91.

3

BLACK FEMINIST/WOMANIST EPISTEMOLOGIES, PEDAGOGIES, AND METHODOLOGIES

A Review of Literature

Altheria Caldera

Introduction: Finding an Ocean

This literature review began as resistance to a class project. In a graduate seminar on feminist theory, I was assigned to lead a discussion using principles of feminist pedagogy. "Why *feminist pedagogy* and not *Black feminist pedagogy?*" I wondered. As Taliaferro Baszile (2016, p. 13) wrote in *Race, Gender, and Curriculum Theorizing,* this was an effort "to think outside the white norm and outside the education literature." At this point in my graduate studies, I had been more inspired by Black feminist theory than feminist theory. This inspiration combined with curiosity led me to pursue an answer to a foundational question:

- How does Black feminist pedagogy differ from feminist pedagogy?

As I began my research, my initial findings led to more complex, more substantial ones:

- What theoretical contributions have Black feminists (and other Black women critical scholars) made to the study of teaching and learning?
- How have Black feminists helped to shape the praxis of Black women academics?

Again, quoting Taliaferro Baszile (2016, p. 13), "This [learning] was really life changing stuff." As an African–American woman embarking on a career in academia, I knew that my project had shifted from a class assignment to a monumental work that would shape my career in the professorate. This "eureka" moment is summed-up perfectly by Taliaferro Baszile, Taylor-Brandon, Guillory, and Salaam (2016, p. 148):

It was like finding an ocean after walking for years in a desert. It was not that we did not appreciate the many other readings we were doing in graduate school—Freire, Foucault, Dewey, Derrida, and many others—they were informative, thoughtful, critical, but simply could not compare to what it was like reading a language we actually understood and lived with and through daily.

The scholarship I found was indeed an ocean in the desert of graduate studies that I had found interesting at best, sterile and dry at worst. As an outsider to the academy, I found this literature affirming to my work, to my presence even.

In her appraisal of *Women's Ways of Knowing: The Development of Self, Voice, and Mind*, Banks-Wallace (2006, p. 313) wrote of the book's authors, "They challenged dominant paradigms regarding the nature of truth, reality, knowledge, and one's relationship to the larger world." This statement encapsulates the scholars whose work is featured in this review of literature. These Black feminist and womanist scholars[1] raised "critical questions about the complex and simultaneous systems of oppression" (Henry, 2005, p. 91). Such questions have given birth to conceptions of epistemological, pedagogical, and methodological theoretical orientations that greatly impact knowledge creation and acquisition in higher education. Their theoretical work is reflected in a wide range of Black feminist and womanist scholarship.

My purpose, then, is to synthesize their work—over two decades of salient literature that evidence ways Black feminist and womanist thinkers resist hegemonic structures in academia—in order to necessarily advance the legitimacy of their theories and to inform diverse scholars of possibilities outside of dominant paradigms to enrich their scholarship and teaching. This review follows the tradition of Taliaferro Baszile, Edwards, and Guillory (2016), Bay, Griffin, Jones, and Savage (2015), and Waters and Conaway (2007), and those who have strived to legitimate the intellectual contributions of African–American women. My work is distinctive in its exclusive emphasis on Black women's theorizing about epistemologies, pedagogies, and methodologies that are characterized by resistance to oppressive practices in academic settings. Their theorizing is most apropos to Black women and other women of color in the academy. Literature included in this review had to be

- written by a Black feminist/womanist, or by a Black woman with a critical lens, or by a woman of color with implications for Black women;
- focused on epistemologies, pedagogies, and methodologies; and
- published in the last 25 years.

The first section is a discussion of Black feminist/womanist epistemologies, followed by an analysis of Black feminist/womanist pedagogies. In the last section, Black feminist research methodologies are explored.

Black Feminist/Womanist Epistemologies

Since scholars' classroom pedagogies and research methodologies are usually undergirded by her epistemological views, this literature review begins with Black feminist/womanist epistemologies. (See Table 3.1.) Six "culturally consistent epistemological frameworks," espoused by women of color, are analyzed here (Banks-Wallace, 2006, p. 314). One such system of knowing is Black feminist epistemology, as characterized by Allen (2009, p. 75):

> Black feminist epistemology stresses the importance of Black women's social locations for how they create and validate knowledge, claiming that their shared experiences can foster group knowledge that can inform political action. It emphasizes the fact that Black women can face multiple, interlocking oppressions of gender and race as well as classism and heterosexism.

Like much of the scholarly research on African–American women over the last two decades, Allen (2009) drew upon the work of Patricia Hill Collins. In her groundbreaking work, *Black Feminist Thought,* Hill Collins (2000) posited a shift in European approaches to the study of Black women. Instead of viewing Black women simply as objects to be examined, Hill Collins (2000) argued for a centering of Black women and valuing their unique standpoint. She defined Black feminist thought as consisting of "theories or specialized thought produced by African–American women intellectuals designed to express a Black women's standpoint" (Hill Collins, 1990, p. 32). Although she argued the importance of Black women intellectuals, she did not exclude others from participating in Black feminist thought.

From Black feminist thought emerged Hill Collins' closely related Afrocentric feminist epistemology. She explained epistemology as "the study of the philosophical problems in concepts of knowledge and truth" (Hill Collins, 1990, p. 202). What constitutes truth and how knowledge is validated are key research issues that shape thought and action. Hill Collins espoused four dimensions of Afrocentric feminist epistemology: (1) concrete experience as a criterion of meaning, (2) the use of dialogue to assess knowledge claims, (3) the ethic of caring, and (4) the ethic of personal accountability. Each of these aspects of Afrocentric feminist epistemology reflects values that are devalued or completely ignored in the Eurocentric masculinist knowledge validation process. These typically positivistic approaches neglect the value of lived experiences, dialogue between researcher and subjects, care for individuals, and respect for an individual's ethics and viewpoints. Summarily, "The existence of a self-defined Black woman's standpoint using an Afrocentric feminist epistemology calls into question the content of what currently passes as truth and simultaneously challenges the process of arriving at that truth" (Hill Collins, 1990, p. 219). This interrogation of traditional epistemological paradigms and the introduction of alternative paradigms have begun to shape knowledge and truth validation in the academy.

Since the publication of Hill Collins' (2000) work, several other scholars of color have expanded her pioneering theories. In "Racialized discourses and ethnic epistemologies," Ladson-Billings (2000, p. 258) argued "The hegemony of the dominant paradigm makes it more than just another way to view the world—it claims to be the only legitimate way to view the world." To counter this hegemony, many scholars of color look to paradigms outside of dominant discourse and embrace ethnic epistemologies to give meaning to their work and to validate subjugated knowledge. According to Ladson-Billings (2000, p. 27), they use their positions as they return to their communities to do field work "uncovering the complexities of difference—race, class, and gender." Further, Ladson-Billings (2000, p. 272) offered crucial insight on the relevance of critical race theory to qualitative research. She contended that the "gift" of critical race theory is that it "challenges the scholarship that would dehumanize and depersonalize us." In addition, critical race theorists deliberately include themselves in their research and raise important questions about knowledge creation and validation, especially knowledge about people of color (Ladson-Billings, 2000, p. 272). Ladson-Billings' contributions are not labeled feminist, but are pertinent to any marginalized populations, thus are relevant to Black feminist epistemology.

Aligned with Ladson-Billing's (2000) thoughts on ethnic epistemologies and critical race theory are Delgado Bernal's (2002) critical raced-gendered epistemologies. Critical raced-gendered epistemologies (1) view the experiential knowledge of communities of color as a strength, (2) allow for the creation of new theories that understand multidimensional identities, and (3) "affirm experiences and responses to different forms of oppression and validates them as appropriate forms of data" (Delgado Bernal, 2002, p. 116). In this way, critical raced-gendered epistemologies, among which are Chicana feminism and other third world feminisms, allow researchers to bring together layered identities and experiences for examination.

Similarly, Dillard and Okpalaoka (2011) offered the following definition of endarkened feminist epistemology. "Endarkened feminist epistemology articulates how reality is known when based in the historical roots of global Black feminist thought" (Dillard & Okpalaoka, 2011, p. 148). They acknowledged a difference in cultural standpoint from White feminist epistemology in that it is located at the overlap of multiple oppressions. As with the aforementioned theories, endarkened feminist epistemology places an emphasis on reciprocity between the researcher and the researched based on the African value of community wellbeing. Dillard and Okpalaoka (2011) described research as a responsibility instead of as a recipe. Distinctly central to this epistemology are spirituality and sacredness (Dillard & Okpalaoka, 2011). Spirituality refers to having a consciousness of the spirituality in one's work, an acknowledgement that one's work is connected to a larger purpose. Sacredness denotes carrying out work with honor and respect. Another distinguishing facet of endarkened feminist epistemology is its transnational lens, recognizing that all African ascendant women have a shared oppression as a result of slavery and colonization. Deeply rooted in African cosmology, endarkened feminist epistemology insists on wholeness, the engaging of body, mind, and spirit. Summarily, endarkened feminist epistemology strongly values the experiences and perspectives of African–American women and supports the uncovering of these stories through qualitative research methods. In conjunction, these theories of Black feminist epistemology recognize the need for alternative paradigms for the traditional, European, patriarchal ways of studying people of color, namely Black women.

Central to each of these epistemologies are (1) the importance of social location, (2) recognition of ways of knowing that provide alternatives to traditional, dominant systems of knowing that are mostly positivistic, and (3) the role of experience in knowledge-validation. An epistemological framework that relies very little on social location based on identity is womanist epistemology.

Maparyan (2012) addressed fundamental epistemological questions—what is good knowledge and how do we know—in her explication of womanist epistemology. Womanists regard "knowledge that helps people and other beings, promoting balance and well-being within Creation" as good knowledge (Maparyan, 2012, p. 37). Good knowledge, then, is practical, beneficial, and facilitates problem-solving, healing, and self-development. With an emphasis on spirituality and sacredness, womanist epistemology is akin to endarkened feminist epistemology. Maparyan (2012) believes that human beings are divine, spirit connects humans to each other and other beings, and because spirit pervades everything, knowledge is everywhere. Knowledge is verified in one or more ways: internal validation ("it feels right"), social validation (community consensus through dialogue), recourse to the observation of nature/discernment, (signs, symbols, patterns, and messages), bodily intelligence (gut knowledge, instinct, or sixth sense), and deductive/inductive reasoning (scientific method) used in conjunction with one of the above knowledge validation methods. According to Maparyan (2012, p. 40), a distinguishing feature of womanist epistemology is "the ability to sustain paradox comfortably," respecting different belief systems and the people who hold them without giving in to conflict and dissension. Womanist epistemology, like the aforementioned epistemologies, places a strong emphasis on alternate ways of knowing and validating knowledge. Noticeably absent from Maparyan's womanist

TABLE 3.1 Epistemological Approaches

Epistemology	Scholar	Year
Black feminist epistemology	Allen	2009
Afrocentric feminist epistemology	Hill Collins	1990 & 2000
Ethnic epistemologies	Ladson-Billings	2000
Critical raced-gendered epistemologies	Delgado Bernal	2002
Endarkened feminist epistemology	Dillard & Okpalaoka	2011
Womanist epistemology	Maparyan	2012

epistemology, however, is any mention of the socially constructed identities that are central to Black feminists.

Black Feminist/Womanist Pedagogies

Black feminists' epistemological beliefs influence their approaches to curriculum and instruction, leading them to define Black feminist/womanist pedagogies. I use Black feminist/womanist pedagogies to describe the diverse range of teaching practices Black feminists and womanists employ to accomplish their course learning goals. Simply stated, Black feminist/womanist pedagogies are intentional *ways of being* between teachers and students enacted by Black feminists and womanists in academic settings. Despite their marginalization, Black feminist/womanist pedagogies have been well-theorized (Russell, 1982; TuSmith, 1989/1990; Omolade, 1987; Joseph, 1995; Thompson, 1998; Beaubeouf-Lafontant, 2005; Westfield, 2006; Brock, 2011; White, 2011; Patterson, Mickelson, Hester & Wyrick, 2011; Nyachae, 2016). Siddle Walker (1996; 2000; 2001) extensively studied African–American teachers in the South but did not, in these works, analyze her findings through the lens of Black feminism or womanism and does not label herself as either. I have found, however, that there is significant overlap between her findings and the tenets of Black feminist/womanist pedagogies.

Perhaps the most comprehensive theorizing of Black feminist pedagogy was undertaken by Joseph (1995) in "Black feminist pedagogy and schooling in capitalist white America." Though the essay was published in 1995, Joseph indicated in the essay that she wrote it in the 1980s, making it one of the earliest writings on Black feminist pedagogy. Joseph (in Guy-Sheftall 1995, p. 465) professed Black feminist pedagogy as

> designed to raise the political consciousness of students by introducing a worldview with an Afrocentric orientation to reality, and the inclusion of gender and patriarchy as central to an understanding of all historical phenomena.

She acknowledged the influences of Paulo Freire, who is highly regarded as the pioneer of critical pedagogy. Joseph furthered Freire's theories by articulating a Black feminist pedagogy, a pedagogy of liberation, that is useful in bringing about revolutionary change in a capitalistic society—one that is oppressive to people of color and women, a perspective that "goes beyond the Marxist sociology of education" (in Guy-Sheftall 1995, p. 464). Key themes in Joseph's Black feminist pedagogy include political consciousness for radical change, students as active change agents, liberation for humankind, and Afro-centrism.

Remarkably similar to Joseph's Black feminist pedagogical vision is bell hooks' conception of a transformative, liberatory pedagogy. Though hooks (1994) did not label her theory Black feminist or womanist, it mirrors the thoughts of Joseph and other Black feminist/womanist pedagogues. Instead, hooks branded her ped-agogical stance as feminist critical, and she, too, drew heavily upon the work of Paulo Freire, citing the notion of pleasure in teaching and learning as a major difference between the two. Like Joseph, she argued for education that is lib-eratory, active students who are critically aware, and the centering of subjugated knowledge. But hooks went much further. Other components of engaged, trans-formative pedagogy include creating a caring community of learners, validation of individual voices, and openness on behalf of the teacher. Teachers, as part of the community, should include their own voices, and students should not be the only ones asked to share and confess.

Further, two additional tenets are intriguing. First, hooks (1994) advocated for teachers to be committed to inner wellbeing—their own and their students. This commitment to self-care is an act of resistance. As Lorde (1988) recognized, "Caring for myself is not self-indulgence, it is self-preservation, and that is an act of political warfare." In this way, hooks' pedagogy extends beyond the classroom and to the Black woman's body, mind, and spirit. Further, teachers should strive to educate the whole person by recognizing the union among body, spirit, and mind. She cited this emphasis on wholeness as one way in which engaged peda-gogy differs from feminist pedagogy. (This theme of wholeness will be explored in greater depth when analyzing Brock's (2011) pedagogy of wholeness.) According to hooks, students do not want book knowledge but knowledge of how to live in the world. Second, hooks (1994) challenged the notion of the classroom being a safe, harmonious space in contrast with a classroom that might sometimes be a place of chaos and confusion because biases and truths are exposed. Since sponta-neity is an element of these learning environments, all learners, including teach-ers, must be flexible and adaptable. She advised, "We cannot despair when this is conflict. Our solidarity must be affirmed by shared belief in a spirit of intellec-tual openness that celebrates diversity, welcomes dissent, and rejoices in collective dedication to truth" (hooks, 1994, p. 33). This, according to hooks, is transgres-sive teaching.

Beaubeouf-Lafontant (2005) also explored the idea of transgressive teaching in "Womanist ideas for reinventing teaching." She claimed, "Teaching was never meant to be a transgressive or subversive activity for female educators or their students" (p. 436). According to Beaubeouf-Lafontant (2005), if education is to be liberatory instead of oppressive, then teaching must be reinvented. One of her three ideas for reinventing teaching is embracing care as the basis for social activism, also found in hooks' philosophy. This idea of womanist care is preva-lent in other studies of Black female teachers of Black children (Siddle Walker 1996; 2000; 2001). Womanist caring is both "affect and advocacy" (Beaubeouf-Lafontant, 2005, p. 442). Patterson, Mickelson, Hester, and Wyrick (2010, p. 268) add to this concept of caring: "African American teachers' caring was more than the provision of affection to students; it was political and took a variety of forms." In this way, womanist care provides the impetus for transgressive teaching. Because of the potential to confuse womanist care with care espoused by other pedagogies, Beaubeouf-Lafontant (2005, p. 443) clarified the parameters of womanist care in a manner worth noting:

> Unlike many White, middle-class, and mainstream depictions of women's relational qualities, the caring of womanist educators is typically neither framed nor experienced as a dyadic, largely apolitical, or selfless undertaking (e.g., Casey, 1993; Gilligan, 1993). It is also not universalized to the point of being disingenuous about being specific to a social order and location within that order. Instead, womanist caring is deeply contextual, responsive to particular instances of injustice, and tied to concrete action.

Caring, then, in this manner will likely manifest itself differently in learning environments in which the student population is comprised of homogenous minoritized students versus a slightly heterogeneous, though majorly Caucasian student population. The idea of contextualized caring is worthy of further theorizing.

An in-depth handling of womanist caring and other mothering is found in "Remembering teachers in a segregated school: Narratives of womanist pedagogy" (Patterson, Mickelson, Hester, & Wyrick, 2010). The findings of this study indicate that womanist caring, the key component of womanist pedagogy, is not color-blind, acknowledges the experiences of African–American teachers, extends to the community, and equips African–American children to survive in hostile environments.

Two other scholars (Westfield, 2006 and TuSmith, 1989/1990) theorized about womanist pedagogy. Westfield (2006) emphasized the notion of "Black female patriarchy" far more than she analyzed her womanist pedagogy, but her contribution is significant because it highlights a challenge that may be common to Black female academics—being validated. In Westfield's narrative, she encountered a Black female student who legitimated Westfield's faculty position in the academy only after the student learned that Westfield had been published alongside male scholars in her field. The student's comment, "Had I known you were somebody, I would have done better in your class," exemplified what Westfield described as Black female patriarchy, defined as African–American women taking ownership of male domination and participating in the maintenance of male power and privilege. Westfield suggested that one practice of womanist pedagogy is for male and female scholars to co-teach and co-think, implying, problematically, that the presence of a respected male academic adds validity to Black female academics' work as teachers and researchers. She concluded her brief narrative with a call for further research on how womanist pedagogy might address Black female patriarchy.

TuSmith (1989/1990) treated the notion of womanist pedagogy much more extensively than Westfield (2006) in her article, "The cultural translator: Toward an ethnic womanist pedagogy." Many themes in TuSmith's (1989/1990) theory echo previously stated Black feminist/feminist critical/womanist ideas: shared author-ity, encouraging student voice, and tolerance for ambiguity. While an argument can be made that these features characterize feminist pedagogy as well, TuSmith (1989/1990, p. 20) detoured from feminist pedagogy and argues that "race, ethnic-ity, and class are additional complicating factors which the feminist process cannot adequately address." She argued that ethnic pedagogues, like womanist pedagogy, must enter the debate at this juncture. TuSmith's (1989/1990) most substantial contribution to the idea of ethnic womanist pedagogy is the proposition that teachers of color, whose learners are mostly Caucasian, take on the role of cultural translator—making the unfamiliar familiar for the Caucasian student. She stressed the importance of assisting Caucasian students in accessing cultures in meaning-ful ways by starting with an awareness of their own ethnic cultural identity. The womanist pedagogical concept of cultural translator is also explored by Patterson, Mickelson, Hester, and Wyrick (2010). They found that African–American teach-ers often had to serve as cultural translators for their Caucasian colleagues to help bridge the gap between these teachers and their African–American students. Additionally, TuSmith (1989/1990) supported a pedagogy that counters tradi-tional pedagogy whose aim is the elimination of oppression from multiple systems of oppression, as did Joseph (1995) and hooks (1994). She contended, "As feminist and ethnic theorists are realizing, isolating gender promotes racism, isolating race promotes sexism, and so on (TuSmith, 1989/1990, p. 22). In this way, womanists and Black feminists view effective pedagogy as encompassing intersectional analy-sis of systemic oppression.

Similar to TuSmith's womanist pedagogy, Sheared (2006, p. 270) proposed a womanist instructional pedagogy, created to "give voice to those whom tradi-tional and unidimensional methods of instruction have silenced." Sheared's (2006) model of instruction centers around the concept of "polyrhythmic realities," described as a belief that individuals experience intersecting realities simultane-ously, as opposed to Western linear notions of the world and reality. These inter-twining realities must be acknowledged for individuals to be fully recognized as interconnected human beings. Womanist instructional pedagogy is a communal experience in which the teacher decenters herself or himself and "allows students to seek and interpret their world and their words in a political, social, historical, and economic context" (Sheared, 2006, p. 273). It is designed to "give voice" through critical reflective dialogue.

Although Brock (2011) acknowledged the importance of "reconceptualiz[ing] all dimensions of the dialectic of oppression," she applied this importance spe-cifically to the experiences of Black women. She emphasized the need to not only raise political consciousness but to do so based on an Afrocentric worldview. Brock argued that Black women's knowledge has been subjugated, and as a result, Black feminist pedagogy should center their knowledge and experiences. This centering of previously marginalized knowledge proves to be a key component of Black feminist pedagogy. Brock's Black feminist pedagogy shows parallels to hooks' feminist critical pedagogy in its focus on transformative education as a result of students grappling with injustices by interrogating historical and existing social structures. She referenced her non-traditional transformative "pedagogy of wholeness" that stresses community over individualism and that suggests the possibility for life transformation, not just social transformation. This emphasis on educating the whole student also mirrors hooks' concern with education of body, mind, and spirit.

Omolade (1987) clarified that Black feminist pedagogy is not just about Black women, for Black women, by Black women. Instead, it "aims [sic] to develop a mindset of intellectual inclusion and expansion that stands in contradiction to the Western intellectual tradition of exclusivity and chauvinism" (Omolade, 1987, p. 31). This acknowledgement of Black feminist pedagogy being a departure from traditional pedagogy is seen throughout several of Black feminist pedagogies. Omolade (1987) illuminated the need for teachers to confess the power differential between them and students and offered a solution to this challenge—intellectual partnership and mutual sharing. The role of a Black feminist pedagogue, according to Omolade (1987), is that of clarifier or consultant. She cautioned, however, that a lack of structure leaves students without "a clear sense of where the course is going" (Omolade, 1987, p. 38). As with other theorists of Black feminist pedagogy, Omolade (1987) described a classroom environment that is liberatory, inclusive of the experiences of Black women, and that invites students to generalize their life experiences within a community of learners. This environment also has tensions and discomfort but should be one in which students feel safe to take risks and make mistakes (Omolade, 1987).

Two enacted pedagogies in which the students are African–American girls are Brown's (2009) hip-hop feminist pedagogy and Nyachae's (2016) Black feminist pedagogy in *Sisters of Promise*. Hip-hop feminist pedagogy can be categorized as a Black feminist pedagogy in that it centers the experiences and resists devaluation of African–American girls. Brown (2009) advanced hip-hop feminist pedagogy as a pedagogy that focuses on relationships (with Black girls) that respect their contexts and communities, which are shaped by hip-hop culture. Hip-hop feminist pedagogy is a "political act of resistance that values Black girls' ways of being" (Brown, 2009, p. 4). Hip-hop music is used as a tool through which identity is formed and negotiated. Like other Black feminist pedagogies, it interrogates the process of marginalization based on membership in several identity categories—race, gender, class, sexuality, and age. Hip-hop pedagogy, responsive to twenty-first century girlhood, strongly encourages the use of hip-hop language instead of, and in addition to, academic language used in classroom settings.

Nyachae (2016) also expressed a need for pedagogy that is effective with African–American girls in her article, "Complicated contradictions amid Black feminism and millennial Black women teachers creating curriculum for Black girls." She alleged

> Curriculum created by millennial Black teachers for Black girls may not recognize the nuances of how schools oppress Black girls as compared to Black boys. This shortcoming is partly due to the absence of Black feminism, by means of Black women educational scholarship in curriculum studies.
>
> *(Nyachae, 2016, p. 787)*

She further argued that pedagogical strategies that stem from black feminism can serve to resist racialized gendered status quo pedagogy that disempowers Black girls (Nyachae, 2016). Nyachae (2016) examined how her work with African–American girls exhibited key characteristics of Black feminist pedagogy. According to Nyachae (2016), her project reflected four aspects of Black feminist pedagogy:

1   Study of social constructions—In order to understand others and their perceptions of you, it is necessary to understand how perception is influenced by socially constructed notions of Blackness.
2   Education for liberation—The very notion that a Black girl could live with a clear understanding of who she is … is in itself an act of empowerment and liberation.
3   Political commitment via activism and social change—Black girls should not only care about their personal situations, but also work towards social change through activism.
4   Connecting Black women to each other—Black feminist pedagogy emphasizes connecting Black girls to each other through sisterhood.

A major contradiction to Black feminist pedagogy, as she viewed it, included the program's failure to include Black women's history, *her stories.*

White (2011) defined Black feminist pedagogy based on her experience teaching in Ethiopia. Her Black feminist pedagogy is a holistic, intersectional approach to teaching that includes the teacher honestly interrogating her identity and risking self-disclosure. This self-disclosure is a prerequisite for establishing rapport with students. In these ways, White is not unlike other Black feminist pedagogues. Her goal was to create a classroom with "varying degrees of safety" (White, 2011, p. 203). She posed the following arguments to her class that led to an atmosphere that allowed for the unpacking of dangerous politics:

1   Culture is dynamic.
2   All cultures have harmful traditional gender practices.
3   Language is dynamic.
4   Sexuality issues are linked to gender inequalities.

By offering these propositions, White (2011) hoped to prevent students from essentializing culture and language, to admit shameful aspects of their culture without feeling singled out, and to realize connections between gender and sexuality oppressions, providing an example of how to build a classroom ethos for classes that explore what could be volatile issues.

This review of existing literature on Black feminist pedagogies reflects practices that hold the potential to enhance learning and critical consciousness for all students. For Black feminist pedagogues, grappling with challenging real world issues involving systemic inequities and injustices is pertinent. This critical stance, along with the centering of subjugated voices, is a cornerstone of Black feminist/womanist pedagogies. With a deep respect for the knowledge and experiences that students bring to the classroom, Black feminist/womanist pedagogues stand in contrast to pedagogues who practice a traditional, hierarchical dissemination of knowledge from all-knowing teacher to unknowing students. A table depicting these pedagogies is helpful in organizing the literature, please see Table 3.2 on page 47.

Research Methodologies

Three research approaches (listed in Table 3.3)—Mullings' (2000) Black feminist research methodology, Lindsay-Dennis' (2015) Black feminist/womanist (BFW) research paradigm, and Tillman's (2002) culturally sensitive research framework—closely align with Black feminist epistemologies. In "African–American women making themselves: Notes on the role of Black feminist research," Mullings (2000) characterized Black feminist research practices as informed by feminist research that aim to include women, Black studies that describe research as corrective and prescriptive, and left/progressive scholarship with the aim to not only study the world but to change it. What makes Black feminist research unique is its "grounding in the interaction of race, class, and gender from which emerges the experience of African American women" (Mullings, 2000, p. 27). Fundamentally, Black feminist research practices center the lives of African–American women in ways that refute stereotypical representations. Based on her experience as a social scientist, she suggested qualitative research methodologies such as participatory action research, oral history, ethnography, and other methodologies that value the unique standpoint of participants.

Mullings (2000) listed three central components of Black feminist research: (1) These practices must be collaborative and aim for the establishment of non-hierarchical relationships between researchers and participants. For Mullings (2000), these relationships are of utmost importance in Black feminist research. (2) The research relationship must evidence the researchers' "identification with and responsibilities towards the African–American community" (Mullings, 2000, p. 27). Ethical practices that ensure the protection of informants, disposition of data, and framing of results should be employed when conducting research with groups who have limited control over how knowledge is presented and represented. (3) The research must link itself to social action that allow for change. In this way, the research is not descriptive; it is prescriptive.

TABLE 3.2 Pedagogical Approaches

Pedagogy	Scholar	Year	Educational Setting
Black feminist pedagogy/a pedagogy of liberation	Joseph	1995	Higher education
Engaged, transformative, liberatory pedagogy	hooks	1994	Higher education
Womanist/liberatory pedagogy/transgressive	Beaubeouf-Lafontant	2005	Higher education
Womanist pedagogy	TuSmith	1989/1990	Higher education
	Westfield	2006	
Pedagogy of wholeness	Brock	2011	Higher education
Black feminist pedagogy	Omolade	1987	Higher education
Hip-hop feminist pedagogy	Brown	2009	K–12 & Higher education
Black feminist pedagogy	White	2011	Higher education
Womanist instructional methodology	Sheared	1994 (first publication)	Higher education/Adult education
Black feminist pedagogy	Nyachae	2016	K–12

Black feminist/womanist research (BFW) is a response to the increased interest in the study of African–American girls. Lindsay-Dennis (2015, p. 511) utilized a dual cultural lens (Black feminism and womanism) to outline a culturally congruent model that allows for "consideration of intersectionality and metaphysical aspects of African American girls' cultural perspectives." Similar to Mullings' (2000) Black feminist research, BFW insists on a commitment to action that leads to social change and a duty to community support. BFW demands an acknowledgment of the context within which African–American girls live and their intergenerational influences. Moreover, a BFW researcher's commitment to Black girlhood scholarship stems from a personal and professional responsibility that allows the researcher's own lived experiences to emerge. Significant to note as well is the emphasis on the researcher as bricoleur who gathers data from a wide variety of sources to reveal the intricacies of African–American girls' lives.

In addition to the principles of Black feminist research espoused by Mullings (2000) and Lindsay-Dennis' (2015), I appreciate Tillman's (2002) five-pronged framework for culturally sensitive research, particularly with African–Americans. Though not specific to African–American women, the framework, with its likeness to feminist research methodologies, can be extended to research with African–American women. Tillman (2002) argued for culturally sensitive research as resistance to mainstream research that tends to present communities of color as deficient and that fail to consider cultural and historical contexts. She contended that culturally sensitive research "must be viewed as legitimate, appropriate, and critical to understanding the experiences of African Americans" (Tillman, 2002, p. 4). Without culturally sensitive research approaches, voids will continue to exist in what we know and understand about the lived experiences of African–Americans. Culturally sensitive research approaches

1 use qualitative methods such as interviews (individual, group, life history), observation, and participant observation.
2 use the particular and unique self-defined (Black self-representation) experiences of African–Americans.
3 attempt to reveal, understand, and respond to unequal power relations that may minimize, marginalize, subjugate, or exclude the multiple realities and knowledge bases of African–Americans.
4 position experiential knowledge as legitimate, appropriate, and necessary for analyzing, understanding, and reporting data. Analysis and presentation that is appropriate to the research topic and the individual or group under study is co-constructed.
5 can lead to the development of theories and practices that are intended to address the culturally specific circumstances of the lives of African–Americans (Tillman, 2002, p. 6).

TABLE 3.3 Research Methodological Approaches

Methodological Approaches	Scholar	Year
Black feminist research	Mullings	2000
Black feminist/womanist research (BFW) paradigm	Lindsay-Dennis	2015
Framework for culturally sensitive research	Tillman	2002

Dantley (2010, p. 151) applauded Tillman's framework for its "cultural resistance to theoretical dominance." He further argued that Tillman's framework for culturally relevant research is useful in revealing the ways traditional qualitative research paradigms silences and minimizes the voices of communities of color.

Mullings' (2000) Black feminist research, Lindsay-Dennis' (2015) Black feminist/womanist research paradigm, and Tillman's (2002) culturally sensitive research framework fit within the critical paradigm in qualitative inquiry, in which the impetus for research is the study of oppressive social structures on disenfranchised individuals. The goal of critical scholars like the Black feminists and womanists included in this review, then, is for critique to lead to transformation and emancipation.

Conclusion

This literature review is an analysis of epistemologies, pedagogies, and methodologies as shaped by Black feminist theory and womanist theory. All three aspects of scholarly work are included because "none of the three—epistemology, methodology, and pedagogy—can be isolated from one another, as they are closely interdependent" (Delgado Bernal, 2002, p. 115). Though still devalued, Black feminist and womanist scholars continue to make robust contributions to the academy in a wide range of disciplines. My aim was to bring together these voices of resistance as evidence of the multitude of ways that scholars are responding and reacting to European, masculinist research and teaching. African–American women and other women of color in the academy continue to be sustained from this ever-expanding ocean.

Note

1   In short, Black feminists and womanists are (primarily) Black women activists devoted to eradicating racism, sexism, classism, and, in most cases, heterosexism. Both Black feminists and womanists contend that Black women's historical sociocultural contexts are distinct from white women's and Black men's contexts. The decision about which label to claim rests with the individual Black woman.

References

Allen, B. J. (2009) Black feminist epistemology. In S. W. Littlejohn & K. A. Foss (Eds.), *Encyclopedia of Communication Theory*, pp. 75–76, Thousand Oaks, CA: Sage Publications.

Banks-Wallace, J. (2006) Womanist ways of knowing: Theoretical considerations for research with African American women. In L. Maparyan (Ed.), *The Womanist Reader*, pp. 313–326, New York, NY: Routledge.

Bay, M. E., Griffin, F. J., Jones, M. S. & Savage, B. D. (2015) *Toward an Intellectual History of Black Women*. Chapel Hill, NC: University of North Carolina Press.

Beaubeouf-Lafontant, T. (2005) Womanist lessons for reinventing teaching. *Journal of Teacher Education*, 56(5), 436–455.

Brock, R. (2011) Recovering from 'yo mama is so stupid': (En)gendering a critical paradigm on Black feminist theory and pedagogy. *International Journal of Qualitative Studies in Education*, 24(3), 379–396.

Brown, R. N. (2009) *Black Girl Celebration: Toward a Hip-Hop Feminist Pedagogy*. New York, NY: Lang Publishing, Inc.

Casey, K. (1993) Teacher as mother: Curriculum theorizing in the life histories of contemporary women teachers. *Cambridge Journal of Education*, 20, 301–320.

Dantley, M. E. (2010) Leadership and a critical spirit of resistance: New ways to conceptualize qualitative research on leadership and spirituality. In R. H. Milner IV (Ed.), *Culture, Curriculum, and Identity in Education*, pp. 143–160, New York, NY: Palgrave Macmillan.

Delgado Bernal, D. (2002) Critical race theory, Latino critical theory, and critical raced gendered epistemologies: Recognizing students of colors as holders and creators of knowledge. *Qualitative Inquiry*, 8(1), 105–126.

Dillard, C. B. (2000) The substance of things hoped for, the evidence of things not seen: Examining an endarkened feminist epistemology in educational research and leadership. *International Journal of Qualitative Studies in Education*, 13(6), 661–681.

Dillard, C. B. & Okpalaoka, C. (2011) The sacred and spiritual nature of endarkened transnational feminist praxis in qualitative research. In N. Denzin & Y. Lincoln (Eds.), *The Sage Handbook of Qualitative Research* (4th ed.), pp. 147–162, Thousand Oaks, CA: Sage Publications.

Gilligan, C. (1993) *In a Different Voice: Psychological Theory and Women's Development* (Reissue ed.). Cambridge, MA: Harvard University Press.

Henry, A. (2005) Black feminist pedagogy: Critiques and contributions. *Counterpoints, 237*, 89–105.

Hill Collins, P. (1990) *Black Feminist Thought: Knowledge, Consciousness, and the Politics of Empowerment*. New York, NY: Routledge.

Hill Collins, P. (2000) *Black Feminist Thought: Knowledge, Consciousness, and the Politics of Empowerment* (second edition). New York: Routledge.

hooks, b. (1994) *Teaching to Transgress: Education as the Practice of Freedom* (4th ed.), New York, NY: Routledge.

Joseph, G. (1995) Black feminist pedagogy and schooling in capitalist white America. In B. Guy-Sheftall (Ed.), *Words of Fire: An Anthology of African–American Feminist Thought*, pp. 462–471, New York, NY: The New Press.

Ladson-Billings, G. (2000) Racialized discourses and ethnic epistemologies. N. Denzin & Y. Lincoln (eds). *Handbook of Qualitative Research* (Second edition). Thousand Oaks, CA: Sage.

Lindsay-Dennis, L. (2015) Black feminist-womanist research paradigm: Toward a culturally relevant research model focused on African American girls. *Journal of Black Studies, 46*(5), 506–520.

Lorde, A. (1988) *Burst of Light: Essays by Audre Lorde*. Ann Arbor, MI: Firebrand Books.

Maparyan, L. (2012) *The Womanist Idea*. New York, NY: Routledge.

Mullings, L. (2000) African-American women making themselves: Notes on the role of Black feminist research. *Souls: A Critical Journal of Black Politics, Culture, and Society, 2*(9), 18–29.

Nyachae, T. M. (2016) Complicated contradictions amid Black feminism and millennial Black women teachers creating curriculum for Black girls. *Gender and Education, 28*(6), 786–806.

Omolade, B. (1987) A Black feminist pedagogy. *Women's Studies Quarterly, 15*(3/4), 32–39.

Patterson, J. A., Mickelson, K. A., Hester, M. L., & Wyrick, J. (2010). Remembering teachers in a segregated school: Narratives of womanist pedagogy. *Urban Education, 46*(3), 267–291.

Russell, M. (1982) "Black-eyed blues connections: Teaching Black women." In G. Hull, P. Bell Scott, & B. Smith (Eds.), *All the Women Are White, All the Blacks are Men, But Some of Us are Brave*, pp. 196–207, New York, NY: The Feminist Press.

Sheared, V. (2006) Giving voice: An inclusive model of instruction—A womanist perspective. In L. Maparyan (Ed.), *The Womanist Reader*, pp. 269–279, New York, NY: Routledge.

Siddle Walker, V. (1996) *Their Highest Potential: An African American School Community in the Segregated South*. Chapel Hill, NC: University of North Carolina Press.

Siddle Walker, V. (2000) Valued segregated schools for African American children in the South, 1935–1969: A review of common themes and characteristics. *Review of Educational Research, 70*(3), 253–285.

Siddle Walker, V. (2001) African–American teaching in the south: 1940–1960. *American Education Association Research Journal, 38*(4), 751–779.

Taliaferro Baszile, D. (2016) Getting on with the business of the rest of her life: On the curriculum of her blackness. In D. Taliaferro Baszile, K.T. Edwards, & N.A. Guillory (Eds.), *Race, Gender, and Curriculum Theorizing: Working in Womanish Ways*, pp. 1–16, Lanham, MD: Lexington Books.

Taliaferro Baszile, D., Edwards, K. T. & Guillory, N. A. (2016) *Race, Gender, and Curriculum Theorizing: Working in Womanish Ways.* Lanham, MD: Lexington Books.

Taliaferro Baszile, D., Taylor Brandon, L. U., Guillory, N. A. & Salaam, T. (2016) For/four colored girls who do curriculum theory. In D. Taliaferro Baszile, K. T. Edwards, & N. A. Guillory (Eds.), *Race, Gender, and Curriculum Theorizing: Working in Womanish Ways*, pp. 147–170, Lanham, MD: Lexington Books.

Thompson, A. (1998) Not the color purple: Black feminist lessons for educational caring. *Harvard Educational Review, 68*(4), 522–555.

Tillman, L.C. (2002). Culturally sensitive research approaches: An African American perspective. *Educational Researcher, 31*(9), 3–12.

TuSmith, B. (1989/1990) The cultural translator: Towards an ethnic womanist pedagogy. *MELUS, 16*(2), 17–29.

Waters, K. & Conaway, C. B. (2007) *Black Women's Intellectual Traditions: Speaking Their Minds.* Burlington, VT: University of Vermont Press.

Westfield, L. N. (2006) Researching a womanist pedagogy to heal. *Religious Education, 101*(2), 170–174.

White, A. M. (2011) Unpacking Black feminist pedagogy in Ethiopia. *Feminist Teacher, 21*(3), 195–211.

4

ACADEMIC SAPPHIRES

College Curriculum at the Intersection of Race, Gender, and Black Women's Subversion

Kirsten T. Edwards

> [R]evolutionary and radical ideas are actualized through an engagement with scholars and scholarly traditions of the canonized past. Contemporary generations read, or more often reread older texts, resulting in "new" readings that do not fit the dominant reception of these texts.
>
> *(Dolphijn & van der Tuin, 2012, p. 13)*

Black women faculty and students live at the intersections of race, class, and gender (Berkel & Constantine, 2005; Gutierrez y Muhs et al., 2012; Jean-Marie & Lloyd-Jones, 2011; Wallace et al., 2012). Examining the multifaceted consequences of this intersectional existence has particular import for post-secondary institutions. There are many educative spaces where these intersections manifest in significant ways. One such site is the college curriculum. This study interrogates the role of the college curriculum as a lever for and potentially against institutionalized racism at the intersection of sexism. It considers the ways Black women's scholarship is assigned and deployed in college classrooms, and the influence that interplay has on pedagogy and the experiences of Black women faculty and graduate students.

Conversations

Examining the curricular and pedagogical fruits that arise within the lived experiences of Black women academicians encompasses much of my scholarly work. One essay that has been particularly helpful along my intellectual journey is Regina Austin's (1995) *Sapphire Bound!* Within her article, Austin constructs for the reader a professional activist trajectory for the Black woman academic; a trajectory that embraces a radical black female subjectivity and inter-subjectivity (hooks, 1992). She cogently examines the stereotypes present in and outside of academe that limit the work of Black women scholars, and testifies to the violence experienced as a result of these pervasive ideologies (Baszile, 2008; Spivak, 1988). However, instead of encouraging Black women academics to resist such stereotypes, Austin (1995) urges them to embrace their inner "Black Bitch" or "Sapphire" (p. 426)—the "tough, domineering, emasculating, strident, and shrill" (p. 426) character from the long-running 1940s and 1950s Black sitcom *Amos & Andy*. She compels Black women academics "[t]o testify" (p. 426) against the academy. Further, she urges Black women to use that testimony as a vehicle for subversive social, legal, and educational change.

Following my first reading of *Sapphire Bound!* during my doctoral studies, I believed I had acquired a fairly robust understanding of Austin's expectations for Black women academics. Austin is a legal scholar, and *Sapphire Bound!* is a cornerstone piece in critical race theory and critical race feminism (Crenshaw et al. 1995). As an education scholar, immediately following my reading, I began to consider parallel responses to Austin's call for college curricula, pedagogy, and Black women faculty. My initial engagement with *Sapphire Bound!* was also accompanied by recorded conversations with two Black women scholars. During these conversations, I invited the women to offer their insights on pedagogy, curriculum, and theory. The overarching inquiry for these semi-structured interviews being, "How would you define pedagogy?" I hoped to auto-ethnographically explore the notion of a 'Black feminized curriculum and pedagogy' in college classrooms. I envisioned our separate voices working with and against each other in tandem, co-constructing the idea, purposefully resisting a mono-vocal reality, while also appreciating a shared experience and standpoint (Collins, 1990). This *idea* would hopefully carry the spirit of its collective and conversational roots. This was my vision at least.

After interviewing these women from very disparate backgrounds—one an unmarried, West Indian doctoral candidate, college instructor, and former high school teacher; the other an African–American, married mother, and associate professor from the United States (U.S.) Midwest—both scholars of education occupying different subfields, I assumed I would walk away with something enlightening, powerful, and cohesive. At one level, I hoped that our (counter) narratives would illuminate the raced, gendered, and classed embodiment of curriculum and pedagogy in college classrooms (Apple, 2004; Asher, 2010; Baszile, 2008; Lawrence, 1995). Yet, most importantly I hoped our conversations would provide education scholars a new set of Black-feminized tools to draw from when theorizing the role of pedagogy and curriculum in higher education (Beauboeuf-Lafontant, 2005; Gutierrez y Muhs et al., 2012; Jean-Marie & Lloyd-Jones, 2011).

As I expected, I had vastly different experiences with each conversation. What I did not expect was to have less than positive experiences with either woman. I personally have a great amount of respect for each woman as a scholar and human being. However, while I found myself invigorated by the conversation with the associate professor, I struggled to identify with the politics, commitments, and practices of my doctoral student colleague. Her stance appeared less 'radical' than I expected from a Black woman academic. As is often the case, I failed to thoughtfully consider my limited understandings of the "Black woman experience" and how different locations (physical, metaphysical, and psychic) can profoundly influence thought and action (Edwards, 2014; Hawkesworth, 2006; McCarthy et al., 2003; Rhoades et al., 2008).

No Room Left in the Multicultural Section

As I reflected on my less than enthusiastic response to the conversation with the doctoral student, I had another realization. I began to question the ways canonical Black women's scholarship—the work by Black women writers that regularly appear on course syllabi and reference lists—has potentially been used to construct a particular image of the Black woman academic. These are radical, revolutionary scholars. However, their scholarship's singular use as tools necessary for addressing the experiences of Black women (and often by extension women of color) becomes problematic, particularly in light of the dearth of relevant scholarship on Black women faculty and students (Patton, 2009; Wallace et al., 2012). Instead of attending to Black women's multidimensionality, in the hands of a commodifying or commodified academy, their simplistic use can actually reinforce boundaries and stereotypes.

In an effort at clarifying this position, I draw on scholarship from media studies, specifically media representations. Representations of Black women in the media are direct reflections of the dominant culture's unjust perceptions of Black women (Brooks & Hebert, 2006; hooks, 1992; Hudson, 1998; Manatu, 2003). Owned, operated, and consumed by the white psyche, Black women are represented in ways that are *consumable* for a white audience. Characters align with already existing tropes that flatten and prescribe Black women's subjectivity. Even representations that attempt to reflect positive, empowered images of Black womanhood are filtered through an already oppressive lens. Tropes such as the *Strong Black Woman*—able to endure any and all forms of hardship and violence—re-inscribe a conception of Black women that is super(un)human. While valorized, the Strong Black Woman does not create space for the very human experience of vulnerability, weakness, and/or need.

Similarly, Black women's scholarship is narrowly deployed in ways that are comfortable and expected for the dominant academic culture. As opposed to offering a fulsome view of Black women's lives and navigational strategies in higher education, these texts serve, for more enfranchised instructors, as "perhaps a bit of 'cut-up [edginess]' thrown in to keep them credible" (Austin, 1995, p. 434). As Fasching-Varner (2009) writes,

> In a story, readers can be "shocked" and "awed" at what happens, but race and racism remain fictionalized, untrue, and quasi-literary in the imagination of

readers, particularly white readers. In this sense whites never take responsibility or action for racist behavior, belief, and treatments of whole groups of people.

(p. 816)

Questions

Based on the above analysis, I offer three inquiries. First, do constructions of Black women academics as presented in standard curriculum hinder different Black women with different forms of resistance from finding common ground? Plainly stated, I am now (seven years removed from graduate school) wondering if my understandings of what it meant to be a Black woman academic, informed primarily by the presentation of canonical Black women writers in graduate course syllabi, hampered my ability to recognize spaces of communion, embrace points of departure, and build communities without consensus (Miller, 2006) with Black women who are differently situated. Second, how might more holistic interpretations of these writings that embrace fuller notions of difference among Black women aid in reclaiming these powerful texts for the work of greater community-building and institutional subversion? Third, is the almost non-existence of Black women's scholarship in course syllabi beyond diversity discussions a reflection of academe's interpretation of what is the *consumable* Black woman scholar; and does that interpretation inhibit Black women's influence throughout postsecondary institutions?

These questions are complicated by the precarious situation of Black women in higher education. At the intersections of racism and sexism, many Black women find themselves struggling for any sense of protection and peace. Unfortunately, instead of serving as frames for recognizing resistance and subversion, these texts are often represented in ways that ultimately support the values of an academic institution fundamental to the continuation of a "white capitalist patriarchal hegemony" (Giardina & McCarthy, 2008). As Collins (1996) suggests,

> [W]e must be attentive to the seductive absorption of black women's voices in classrooms of higher education where black women's texts are still much more welcomed than black women ourselves. Giving the illusion of change, this strategy of symbolic inclusion masks how the everyday institutional policies and arrangements that suppress and exclude African Americans as a collectivity remain virtually untouched ... Similarly, capitalist market relations that transformed black women's writing into a hot commodity threaten to strip their works of their critical edge.
>
> *(p. 9)*

As a young Black woman doctoral student, I was simply grateful for the minimal curricular outlets I received, and by default found myself ill-equipped to imagine or recognize alternative methods of relief and resistance. These minimal outlets are those the academy has already assimilated, and subsequently, disempowered. I do not mean to suggest that the works of well-known Black women writers are not powerful and political. But if collectively they become the only blueprint for a "radical black female subjectivity" (hooks, 1992) as opposed to a frame, guideline, or jumping-off point for the next generation of Black women academics, then they are regrettably only serving the status quo. When used, if these texts do not receive thoughtful analyses that elucidate meaningful mergers and disconnects across a wide range of phenomena, they lose much of their transformational power. Towards the end of my doctoral studies, as I was creating my own unique contributions to the field, I began to seriously consider these queries. I endeavored to rethink my initial understanding of *Sapphire Bound!*, and instead employ it in a new project of empowerment and community-building. In this chapter, I revisit many of those early ruminations by drawing on Austin's (1995) essay as a theoretical frame in a manner apart from academically safe (colonized) expectations; in a way that instead of giving the illusion of progress, hopefully incites revolt. In this way, I will explore the flexibility of Austin's (1995) piece for theorizing varied Black-feminized subversive practices.

Sapphire-Colored Glasses

Paving the Way: A Theoretical Frame

Again, I begin this inquiry by revisiting Austin's (1995) *Sapphire Bound!*. I posit a more contemporary reading that acknowledges the slightly less overt but still pervasive manifestations of oppression that rest at the nexus of Black women's raced, gendered, sexualized, and classed lives will reveal elements of "testimony," revolt, and "cut-up" often undetectable in college classrooms. Applying Austin's (1995) article as a theoretical framing for the present study draws on Collins' (1986) notion of standpoint theory. The present study situates Austin's essay as a particular standpoint from which to understand Black women academics as "professional Sapphires." The common experience of navigating academe as a Black woman scholar requires particular tools for survival. Unlike the often simplistic use of Black women's writings in college classrooms, standpoint theory also recognizes that the particularities of individual Black women's lives will influence the ways those tools are deployed and reimagined for specific purposes.

Through a close reading of *Sapphire Bound!*, I have identified six commitments or tools by which Austin (1995) expects the "professional Sapphire" to be expressed in our intellectual lives:

1 Radicalism: "I think the time has come for us to get truly hysterical" (p. 426).

2 Specific Ontological Analysis: "Document the ... existences of minority women" (p. 426).
3 Explicit Research Agenda (and Pedagogical Practice): Evidenced exploration in written and pedagogical work of minority women's "problems and needs" in academia (p. 426).
4 Commonality: "[A] synthesis of values, traditions, and codes that bind women of the same minority group to one another and fuel their collective struggle" (p. 426).
5 Embodied Knowledge: Finally, the experiential is not to be abandoned ... She must be guided by her life, instincts, sensibility, and politics. The voice and vision reflected in her work should contain something of the essence of the culture she has lived and learned; imagine, if you can, writing a law review article embodying the spontaneity of jazz, the earthiness of the blues, or the vibrancy of salsa (p. 427).
6 Empowerment: "We must write with an empowered and empowering voice" (p. 427).

These six commitments serve as a roadmap or guide for navigating the racist and sexist political economy of higher education. Guides respond to semblance without expectations of duplication. Similarly, the final product of individual Black women's responses may be different, while simultaneously carrying markers of commonality and community.

Re-Doing: A Methodological Framework

As mentioned earlier, I participated in semi-structured conversations with two Black women academics, Yvetta[1] and Priscilla, during my doctoral studies as a way to *communally* document and archive my experiences. At the time, Yvetta was an African–American associate professor of education who taught at a mid-sized university in the Midwestern region of the U.S. Priscilla was a West Indian education doctoral candidate and college instructor at a large institution in the Southern region of the U.S. After transcription, the two individual conversations served as the unit of analysis.

For multiple reasons, I needed a methodological and analytical tool that would assist me in approaching the transcriptions in a fresh and more meaningful manner than traditional methodological frames offer. I sought a reading of the texts that were pedagogical and took seriously the women's experiences as gendered within the Black Diaspora. To this end, the chapter draws on the emerging methodological frame, Womanist Testimony (Edwards & Baszile, 2016; Edwards & Thompson, 2016). Womanist testimony lives at the intersection of three theoretical and methodological traditions: womanist theology; Black liberation theology, specifically Black Church testimony (Lincoln & Mamiya, 1990); and indigenous methodologies (Ng-A-Fook, 2007). The origins of womanist testimony are in Edwards and Baszile's (2016) description of "scholarly rearing" as:

> Black women['s] textual labor of writing ourselves in as acts of individual and collective resistance. [Womanist testimony] shift[s] attention from the power the writer [or speaker] experiences through testifying to the development the student [, reader, or listener] experiences through reading … Textual pedagogy refers to the ways in which Black women writers and readers evoke the art of teaching and learning. These pedagogical moments are serendipitous, invocative, faith-filled, and spiritual. Textual pedagogues render their testimonial offerings for various purposes. However, by virtue of their truth-telling in writing [and narrating], which is often an act of faith and spirit, they create the epistemic space where they can teach what is often silenced.
>
> *(Edwards & Baszile, 2016, p. 87)*

The present project positions Yvetta and Priscilla as textual pedagogues. While the chapter does not take up their published writing, it does engage their narratives, the testimonies they offered during the interview process. It also foregrounds relationship in intellectual and scholarly practice. Womanist testimony challenges researchers to place less emphasis on speaking to an academic audience during the analytical process. Instead, it is more concerned with the survival of the oppressed. Methodologically, it shifts the researcher's focus in academic work, while also highlighting traditional methodological frames' allegiance to the erasure of oppressed peoples. Similar to standpoint theory, womanist testimony resists Eurocentric conceptions of scholarly purpose and asserts Black women's and other minoritized groups' self-definition. By supporting indigenous and culturally specific narrating and theorizing, womanist testimony gives Black women researchers permission to engage data affectively and authentically, in ways that support the production of more culturally nuanced and resistant scholarship.

In the following section, I have coded the testimonies according to the six-point theoretical frame detailed previously. The primary goal of this project is to stretch the boundaries of understanding in regards to Black women academics and interrogate the ways that college curriculum at the intersections of racism and sexism potentially impedes more robust images of resistance and effect. Next, I will discuss the ways Black women's multiple forms of resistance go unrecognized, and how this lack of recognition compromises community-building and hinders more comprehensive implementations of Black women's scholarly contributions. Reading the testimonies through a renewed lens demonstrates how both women maintain characteristics of an "academic Sapphire," while disparately articulated. Austin's (1995, p. 426) call to a "synthesis of the values, traditions, and codes that bind women of the same minority group to one another and fuel their collective struggle" grounds the present study.

The Ties that Bind: Analysis and Findings

Radicalism

More than the other commitments, radical tendencies are interwoven—sometimes modestly, other times prominently embroidered—throughout the women's words. When Austin (1995) says she thinks it is time for Black women to get truly "hysterical," I envision a fundamentally different perspective on reality. However, conceptions of "different" and "reality" in relation to radicalism can have multifaceted interpretations. I have broadened the concept of radicalism as primarily a shift in imagination and understanding; the process of conceiving of ideas in distinctly different and resistant ways. These are conceptions that consciously contradict the academic status quo and its oppressive expectations for Black women.

Within Yvetta's narrative, I easily recognized a radical spirit. I repeatedly read in her testimony an investment in revolutionary change in the academy. In one remark I find particularly powerful, Yvetta said,

> So I think … the whole race thing for instance is such a painfully dishonest conversation. It's ridiculous you know! [T]he fact that I can go in and teach about it and be expected not to express any rage is ridiculous … and its dishonest … so I keep asking myself where are we getting really at the end of this if I can't honestly tell you how angry I actually am and you can't honestly hear that anger. So I just think again progressive folks have a fantasy about the classroom that I think is unrealistic at least in a way we view the classroom in the western world.

Yvetta made it clear that she wants to work towards a radical transformation in the college classroom. She wants a shift to take place in the way that she is able to exist, express, and educate. There is a passion to her words that places certain demands on the educative space. These are demands that are often not appreciated in higher education. While revolutionary ideals, they are also radical in the sense that Yvetta envisions a starkly different pedagogical engagement, one that is not tempered by, but responsive to racism. The desire for her students and colleagues to "hear that anger" runs counter to the white-niceness (Torres, 2002) or colorblind ideology (Edwards, 2014) is often expected in college classrooms.

Radicalism in Priscilla's narrative appeared less intense, while still laced with transformational insight. Her words consistently challenged taken-for-granted assumptions about the college classroom Black women occupy. They became that inconspicuous "too much" that would not let me rest and write comfortably (Baszile, 2010, p. 493). Early in our conversation I asked Priscilla how she defines pedagogy. After a pause for contemplation, she responded, "it's constantly an act of revising." Initially, this simple response seemed appropriate enough. Upon revisiting the testimony, the statement seemed particularly potent. The "act of revising" denotes a movement, an action, a response, a reflection, a verb. Conversely, common definitions of the term pedagogy describe the presence of a particular set of actions, the capsule that binds the action, a noun. When educators discuss pedagogy, we often document "Best Practices" or develop guides and manuals to better facilitate instruction. We recommend "objective" options and forms of pedagogy. The "act of revising" de-centers any presently construed form, and instead appreciates the flow or traversing between (Dolphijn & van der Tuin, 2012). Priscilla's pedagogy requires constant self-reflexivity. In this way, she has radically reconceived of the term "pedagogy." She re-asserts Black women's agency as subject in the college classroom, while giving herself and her students permission to constantly revise what is appropriate and necessary.

Specific Ontological Analysis

Yvetta connected her role as an academic to her role as a mother. When describing her early years in academia, she related it to the language development of her children, explaining how these experiences with her children have had an illuminative impact on her pedagogy in higher education. Yvetta stated,

> Like when my children were babies learning to speak and knowing they had something to say, they just didn't have the language to communicate it to me yet. [For me] coming into academia already knowing something, being able to say it in some way and then having people constantly tell me that I can't say that or I couldn't possibly know that unless I go cite that person, you know. And so for me that was, that's commodification. And it's not just commodification of work, its commodification of souls, meaning life. So another important piece of the art of pedagogy for me with students is to help them make that transition from simply consuming knowledge to producing knowledge, from simply consuming the theorist to ... to theorizing yourself, and to understanding yourself as capable of that kind of work ... For me writing a dissertation on African–American identity and then going back to cite white people to seek validation for whatever just didn't make sense. I was like "That's just ludicrous!" And so I tried really hard not to and when I had to I would then again do it like "bell hooks says" and then I'd put everybody else in parentheses. I'd put all the white men in parentheses because you know again it was a constant process of reasserting myself my perspective on the world and the perspective of those other women who were seeing what I was seeing, you know who were dealing with what I was dealing with.

Yvetta described another challenge she encounters regularly in academia, again naming the material circumstances that structure her interactions in the classroom:

I would say that my other big pedagogical struggle is teaching something that people don't really want to hear about all the time, most of the time … who want to refuse the knowledge. I struggle with that all the time. Some days I [think], "I could really roll down to [the local historically black college/university (HBCU)] where they are thirsty for this kind of understanding." And here I'm doing battle with people who just don't want to get it … And I don't mean get it in a "get to this one point of view." I mean get it in understand how complicated it is. Get outside of your one point of view and try to see how complicated it is.

Yvetta paints a picture of the often strenuous environment in which she works and theorizes. She also reflects on the racist mechanisms that are the impetus for these tensions. Her recognition of and response to the struggle is evident. Her pedagogy is partly an active engagement with these perennial challenges.

My original assumption was that Priscilla chose not to engage or observe the ways her raced, gendered, and cultural difference influence the college classroom. After revisiting her narrative, I recognized the ways in which I had imposed specific expectations on that observance. At the time, I expected her description of the predominantly white classroom to be more akin to Yvetta's. Revisiting her testimony after some years of intellectual growth and theoretical dexterity, I have been able to dislodge my expectations for response and resistance. I now notice that throughout the conversation, Priscilla offered numerous specific ontological analyses of the college classroom. I had simply been unable to recognize them apart from my limited frame of reference. One such example is when Priscilla posited,

It may be part of assimilation, where you're in a different environment with different rules you got to learn them (laughter), you got to learn them. When I came down here [to the U.S. South] … I was really really frustrated because I've always lived on the coast, coastal places except for [the U.S. Midwest]. And I was talking to, I was a research assistant, and so I was talking to the administrative assistants and asking them, I needed their help—see even now I'm phrasing it that way—I was asking for different things, I don't even remember what it was, but they weren't responding, or they were very very cold, you know kind of resistant. And I didn't know … why. And so [a fellow student] who's from the South … I had to ask him [why] they respond to [him] so well … What am I doing wrong? And he said, "Well you're too professional. That's not part of the culture you know when you were living [on the U.S. West Coast] it may have helped to be very polite and professional, but … you'll probably get what you want if you just take the time to ask people about who they are, about how their grandma's doing, about you know just be more social rather than efficient." And let me tell you that worked! But it's one of those social rules that vary from place to place to place so here I have two [cultural tools] now, right.

During my revisit with Priscilla's words, I recognized my knee-jerk reaction to the word "assimilation." This conceptual roadblock concealed to me how she frequently made thoughtful observations about the ways cultural difference collide in the academy; observations that did not necessarily incite frustration or criticism. Instead, she became a student of the moment, picking up new tools for negotiation and navigation in a manner that emerged in the context of her Black female migrant academic experience. She understands herself as relating to people with different cultural backgrounds in the story of her ongoing intellectual journey. During our conversations, while Priscilla agreed with the fact that being a Black woman in the academy affects personal interactions and access, she also saw her intersecting social location as an opportunity to better understand the multiple identity markers and cultural frames that concurrently influence these interactions.

Explicit Research Agenda and Pedagogical Practice

A commitment to an explicit research agenda and an analysis of how that agenda manifests in pedagogical practice was readily apparent in both Yvetta and Priscilla's narratives. Each woman expressed very specific ideals for the classroom. They both espoused deep commitments to the educative process in ways that promoted equity and justice. As both women are scholars of education, their pedagogical commitments were also linked to their research agendas.

During a discussion about her goals for the classroom, Yvetta stated,

> I try to bring my whole self to the project … [And] for me it's about, it's a lot about choice. And really ironically it goes back to something I first read in Dewey's work about the forked road. You can't do any critical thinking unless you come to a fork in the road then you have the choice of which sort of which way to go and until you have that choice you have really nothing much to think about. You just stay on the same path. So for me that's been critical, bringing students to that fork in the road … you know. So it really is to say the world is very complicated and I think when you say the world is very complicated to students it puts more onus on them to have to decide what is right rather than to having somebody to tell them what is right, you know you have to make that decision.

Later in the conversation, Yvetta shared her goals for her students:

> Because this makes sense and this makes sense depends [on] where, when, how, what, who. But you have to put your feet down somewhere. [You have to] make the decision and work from that point … I think that point of having choice having to make decisions and having to understand

your own reasons for making those decisions is a huge part of intellectual moral development.

This statement reveals an explicit decision, a specific political engagement. Yvetta asserted a pedagogical discontent with neutrality. She continued,

> So I tell students all the time be very very strategic, especially my doc[toral] students, very strategic about how you write this dissertation. So for instance, I would say things in my dissertation like, "I think that … and bell hooks agrees with me, and so and so agrees with me." You know what I'm saying? [Be]cause psychologically I had to get into the frame of mind that I'm producing the knowledge here. But also for me it was very, it's also very much a political project.

Viewing scholarship and pedagogy as a "political project" was directly related to her own marginal position within the academy as a Black woman, and by extension the marginalization of her students of color. The work went beyond philosophical debate or intellectual dialogue. Her research agenda and pedagogical practice were targeted at making those things visible that often go unrecognized or silenced in the academy.

Similarly, Priscilla makes an explicit reference to her commitment to creating an educative space where college students grow into independent, accountable thinkers.

> In terms of preparing students, you know regardless of the age, to become ethically responsible citizens, be that at a local, national, global level, I feel like my role as a teacher is to open up more ways of thinking, more you know, more questioning in terms of you know to use the cliché "doing the right thing," whatever that may be for the circumstance, for that person so that they're not blindly you know living kind of on a routine basis. And because we teach teachers you know I feel like the responsibility is doubly there for them to have an ethic towards their students. But also knowing that the work is not just for the students that they teach. It's for themselves. And so it's a double thing where you have to figure out who you are, where you stand in life, what are you about. Then how are you going to help your students achieve the same thing … so what does this [information] have to do with you being a good person, with you being a citizen in the world.

Later she made reference to how her students' cultural backgrounds influence their worldview, and how that affects her pedagogical practice:

> I've found when I was teaching in [the U.S. Midwest], when you have to teach a course like multiculturalism you know and 24 out of 25 students

[are] white you have to figure out ... they're not coming from the same background worldview perspective. How do I ... form a bridge or how do I get them to start questioning what they take for granted, which is that the way that they see the world is normal and everybody sees the world that way? [Be]cause I feel like I know that from experience and so ... one of the things that I try to do through my pedagogies [is] to get students to understand that not everybody sees the world the way you do and that's okay.

Priscilla also promotes critical sensibilities in the classroom in an effort to resist hegemony. Her pedagogical approach differs in its attention to the benefits of accommodation coupled with an assessment of the student's social development. A deeper analysis of our conversations reveals that Priscilla's research agenda and pedagogical practice is explicitly aimed at moving students, who often occupy privileged spaces, out of their comfort zones to challenge them to take seriously the realities of others. She connects this explicit pedagogical commitment to her own experiences of cultural difference.

Embodied Knowledge

Similar to an explicit research agenda and pedagogical practice, an embrace of Austin's notion of embodied knowledge was evident early on in their testimonies and my subsequent readings of both transcriptions. Yvetta and Priscilla both theorized knowledge and pedagogy in lived-experiential and complex ways. The women often described pedagogy in ways that were specifically located within the body, as opposed to cognition. They were similar in their understanding of the multiple avenues by which knowledge is disseminated and received. They each saw these multiplicities as valuable to intellectual work. For instance, Yvetta stated,

I'd like to think [pedagogy is] simply the art of teaching not just teaching in the classroom, but thinking of your life as a teaching, as a way of teaching ... thinking about it as a way of sort of teaching through your life or with your life, or as soul.

While Priscilla stated,

I lived in [the coastal U.S. South], I lived [on the U.S. West Coast], I lived in [the U.S. Midwest], and ... [the U.S. South], and all these shifts—physical shifts—have contributed to I guess probably a richer more informed, more varied worldview, and that definitely does shape the way I think about pedagogy, or who I am, my locatedness in the classroom, and my writing comes from there. And I often, I teach autobiographically. I write autobiographically because … it's important to see how I view the world for you to understand what I'm saying about it.

Similar to Priscilla's notion of movement, Yvetta also described pedagogy as,

> A learning space whether it's a classroom or some other kind of learning space is about fundamentally knowledge as communal, you know. It's to me relational it should be always sort of circulating and bouncing and not going you know always in one direction. It should always be moving and living and growing and retracting and regressing.

She went on to offer another rich interpretation of embodied pedagogy and knowledge:

> For me teaching is an act of faith through and through, through and through. I cannot get wound up in whether you get it or not in this moment [be] cause what I know is that I can tell you something today that you won't get for ten years, because you have to be having the right experience to understand it. And so many times we miss that point. We're trying to teach something that won't ever be understood in this moment in time, because that person's not having the experience they need to be having to understand it. So again, I think also that's my belief that knowledge starts within. It's not a without. It's not this thing where you just, you're just collecting stuff in your brain. That's not sort of my perception of how it happens. I think its body knowledge, there's body memory. There's something you already know and based on that you're attracting other things into your world that you need to know to grow.

Yvetta and Priscilla both conveyed a perception of knowledge as much more than cognition. Pedagogy for these women was something to be experienced holistically through multiple planes of embodied interpretation. Pedagogy did not begin or end in the physical space of the classroom. Both women drew from varied temporal and spatial lens to interpret moments of teaching and learning multi-dimensionally. Their conceptualizations extended far beyond the *rational* divides between mind and body (and spirit). Knowledge, for these Black women, is alive, sensual, in motion, physical, and understood in the soul, body, and brain.

Empowerment

Unlike embodied knowledge, Austin's (1995) commitment to empowerment manifested quite differently for each woman. This dissonance initially presented a challenge for me as a doctoral student researcher. While Yvetta's commitment to personal and collective empowerment was apparent to me in the onset; I found it more difficult to recognize Priscilla's more subtle expressions of empowerment, and then to subsequently connect those expressions to the examples of empowerment often reflected in the canonical texts of Black women writers. I begin with Yvetta's offering:

> So for me personally I try to bring me to my pedagogy. And I think for a long time I tried not to bring me. Man, I tried this whole sort of notion of you know being neutral, being this, be that. What I started to realize is that no matter how neutral I thought I was being the students were constantly pinning politics on me or pinning points-of-view on me, or you know hearing certain things that they thought I was saying that I didn't think I was saying at all. So I just got to a point where I was like, "Okay you know I'm just going to lay it all out there, because you know clearly I'm also text in here." I'm being read as text. So if I'm being read as text I want to be read as counter-hegemonic text and I want to have as much influence in that process as possible.

Yvetta asserts a direct response to the ways she is politicized in the classroom. Instead of allowing others to compartmentalize her into a Black woman stereotype, she deliberately offers them a reading facilitated through counter-hegemonic narrative.

Priscilla's narrative of empowerment becomes potent dissonance when laid beside Yvetta's comments. While describing the influence several physical moves have had on her approach to pedagogy, Priscilla told me, "But if you're open to it, if you can move across these different cultures or physical areas, you get to come up with some new things that may be even better than what you came up with at home." By consciously and thoughtfully engaging her experiences with multiple moves and shifts, she empowers the Black im/emigration dialogue and its implications for the classroom. Instead of multiple, short-term, and often difficult experiences in various cultural spaces that create wounds or lack; these shifts create not only an appreciation for what has been learned away from "home," but a potent amalgamation that incorporates elements of all. Priscilla, similarly, finds her own way to empower discourse that shapes Black women's academic experiences. As she stated, she refused to fall into the "trap" of explaining herself:

> I feel like in terms of perceptions, maybe discussing an issue in a story is more effective for me. It's more productive for me to understand how my students think about these issues rather than how they think about me or how they perceive me ... I'm sure some of it ... how they perceive me mediates how they learn, but I feel like there's no amount of talking that I could do that would change that per se, you know what I mean ... So I could ask them, but I don't feel like there's any kind of talking, it

would then become the same kind of trap of explaining myself constantly to somebody else. "No, you have it wrong." "This is who I really am." Blah blahblahblah, you know. And I'm like (laughter), let's focus on this story. Let's focus on this issue you know, and then we'll … come out of it with something … [And] I feel like … you know specifically the Black woman, how people perceive Black women in this society from the history, I feel like I'm educated enough about that to know not to take that for granted, right. But I don't necessarily feel like I'm willing to let that limit me in any way, shape, or form! I'm just not, I'm not willing. I feel like I have a job to do. I have a very specific idea I guess about education in terms of teaching … self-realization right. I'm responsible for myself. And that comes in choosing my profession, choosing to become a professor, having a certain level of autonomy, you know making decisions for myself … and not letting other people say who I can be, or what I can be … so that kind of like fierce independence.

Priscilla acknowledges that her phenotype and cultural background elicit certain responses from her students and the broader academic community, but she chooses not to expend much energy thinking about that reality. As a doctoral student I may have argued that these perceptions warrant a direct response or defense. However, Priscilla challenged my assumptions by refusing to engage and thus presenting to me an alternative approach to empowering her own autonomy in the process. She is not compelled to respond; instead she opts out of the system. She does not allow stereotypical perceptions or social expectations to force her into prescribed actions. She remains in control, deciding the level of engagement and access others have with and to her. While the actual responses are distinctly different, both Yvetta and Priscilla have found their own way to empower their subject position as Black women in the college classroom. They each have disparately, yet deliberately changed the conversation that attempts to circumscribe their lives as academics.

Commonality

The last commitment left to explore is commonality. I reserved this particular commitment until the end, because I have chosen to contend with it differently. As opposed to sharing words Yvetta and Priscilla provide that speak to the ways they find commonality with other Black women, I have instead decided to take a more purposefully autobiographical turn and discuss the moments of commonality I experience with and between the women. This particular angle of vision is important because the crux of this project is hinged on the ways canonical Black women writers' text can be used in college curriculum to either narrowly define or make room for difference among Black women academics. I am most interested in scholarship being taught and read in complicated and diverse enough ways as to allow for multiple Black women to engage and work together towards resistance and justice.

Throughout this project, I have witnessed valuable moments of convergence that were easily camouflaged under layers of rich contradiction. Some of this richness and beauty is reflected in the way both women desire for their students to develop into critical thinkers that do not accept the status quo and thus perpetuate systems of injustice, but ask questions and come to independently formed conclusions. Both Yvetta and Priscilla articulate an immense connection between embodied knowledge, lived-experience, and pedagogical practice. Finally, and potentially most interesting is how both women connect pedagogy to movement. This occurrence was quite surprising considering these women's differing cultural, intellectual, and institutional backgrounds. It is also profound to me personally, because prior to my conversations with Yvetta and Priscilla I had also related pedagogy to movement in the sense of liquid movement and large bodies of water as metaphor for the learning experience. I find these cognitive, physical, and metaphysical connections immensely intense, especially as it relates to the life of the Black woman academic.

How does the idea of movement, as understood and adjudicated between three very different Black women, provide a clearer window into the complexity of Black women's experiences as intellectuals? Further, how do these areas of commonality and dissonance potentially illuminate possible opportunities for deeper and broader connection within Black women's academic communities? How does this analysis speak back to the larger institution of higher education and its expectations for the work and role of Black women scholars?

So What Have I (We) Learned?

> [A professional Sapphire's] partisanship and advocacy of a minority feminist [theory and philosophy] should be frankly acknowledged and energetically defended. Because her scholarship is to be grounded in the material and ideological realities of minority women ... [it] must necessarily be dynamic and primarily immanent; as the lives of minority women change, so too should the analysis.
>
> *(Austin, 1995, p. 427)*

Quotes by Black women scholars like the above are often read through assumptive lens that produce limited meanings of "advocacy," frankness, and an energetic defense. How do simplistic analyses merge with Austin's call for a dynamic engagement that changes with the development of Black women academics? What I am challenging fellow scholars and curriculum workers to consider is whether or not the academy provides sufficient room in its Black-woman-lexicon to accommodate differently radicalized academic Sapphires. By extension, are multiple forms of resistance made available to developing Black women scholars?

What is necessary is an active struggle against controlling images and continued marginalization (Collins, 1990). To be clear, this project does not support discontinuing the use of well-known and read Black women writers' texts in college curriculum. Assigning these writings represent necessary first steps in recognizing the intersections of racism and sexism in the academy. With that being said, it is simply a first step. If Black women's work does not open up space for multiple Black-feminized voices, or worse restrict those voices, then they are fruitless. As hooks (1992) notes,

> Sadly, in much of the fiction by contemporary black women writers, the struggle by black female characters for subjectivity, though forged in radical resistance to the *status quo* … usually takes the form of black women breaking free from boundaries imposed by others, only to practice their newfound "freedom" by setting limits and boundaries for themselves.
>
> *(p. 47, emphasis in original)*

If literary art imitates life, how do hooks' words reflect the current state of Black female subjectivity and its implications for progressive scholarship within institutions of higher learning? If these models are not broadened or if the canonical texts are not reevaluated and rearticulated by Black women academics and other critical scholars for multiple and continuously renewed interpretations, as Black women move into the academy will they find their experiences frightfully predetermined?

For example, after performing a cursory review of the syllabi provided during my doctoral studies, specifically searching for the readings authored by Black women, another suspicion was confirmed. The few assigned texts authored by Black women were used for a particular purpose—to discuss some issue related to race, ethnicity, and gender. As a Black woman academic whose research agenda is primarily concerned with the influence of race, gender, class, and culture on college classrooms, I realize a Black woman's decision to choose such an agenda is not entirely influenced by institutional expectations. Still, I am troubled with two queries. First, as a young scholar, like many Black girls from poor/working-class (and affluent) backgrounds, I found academia extremely difficult to navigate. While it appears I have navigated successfully (i.e., degree completion and tenure-track faculty position), I continue to struggle often. Much of the academic acclimation I have acquired is the result of finding solace in the writings of canonical Black women writers. Through their textual pedagogies and testimonies, these women taught me how to be a Black woman scholar. Yet, I wonder had my textual teachers possessed different scholarly interests or had their writings been introduced to me in varied contexts, deployed to investigate varied issues beyond the intersection of race and gender, what intellectual path would I have chosen? Or as Ropers-Huilman (2010, p. 173) writes, "While individuals are clearly not powerless to shape their identities, those identities are always also situated within discourses that affect their shaping. Additionally, those discourses also affect interpretations and perceptions of others' subjectivities." Considering the above statement, what might be the effect if Collins' (1990) "Standpoint Theory" was regularly introduced as an analytical tool to examine Irish–American immigrants' experiences with education in the mid-nineteenth century; or if hooks' (1989) concept of "Talking Back" was drawn upon to develop programming for arts-based gifted education?

Second, if college curriculum is evidence that the primary way Black women find themselves within course syllabi is by offering insight into the ways race and gender influence marginalized peoples' experiences within larger social systems, how will the next generation interpret their relevance in relation to other social phenomena? As hooks (1999, p. 27) observes,

> With no acknowledged established intellectual traditions, save contemporary ones, and even those are not widely acknowledged, black women writers ... working within the cultural context of white supremacist capitalist patriarchy have historically needed the interest of white readership to gain a hearing.

As discussed earlier, there are particular ways in which Black women become consumable for white audiences in media and curriculum. Limited latitude in regards to Black women's resistance also reinforces a message to the dominant academic community, particularly students, that Black women do not have a voice in multiple areas of intellectual discourse, specifically those identified as most significant.

> [W]hites case and control blackness as a property value for the institution as faculty attempt to decide what she [Black women faculty] should teach and how she should teach without choosing to take up issues of diversity and equity in their own courses ... [Black women faculty's] blackness is valued to the extent that it furthers [higher education's] goals of appearing equitable and diverse.
>
> *(Fasching-Varner, 2009, p. 818)*

The academy outsources those messy areas such as diversity, cultural competence, justice, equity, racism, and sexism to Black women (and other women and scholars of color). Like any capitalist institution participating in the commodification of lives, the academy receives the benefits of these products without necessarily dealing with the unpleasant side effects of poverty and cheap labor.

It is true that Black women write in various genres, but one must listen carefully to hear their voices whispered in the more institutionally valued corners of academe, with their ideas often contingently relevant in diversity discussions. If the traversing of Academic Sapphires was boldly acknowledged throughout every element of the curriculum; if their diverse resistant marks were recognizable, how might that alter the pedagogical space? How would this more developed attention revolutionize institutions of higher learning? How would it expand the subjectivity of Black women in academe?

Final (or On-Going) Thoughts

I return to my original thesis, the most damaging result of singular models of Black women academics and their scholarship in college curriculum is the ways in which it limits community, communion, and multiple forms of resistance. I am reminded of a quote by hooks (1992) where she is sharing a conversation she had with other Black women concerning the development of a "radical black female subjectivity" and its implications for social progress. She states,

> Collectively, we were working to problematize our notions of black female subjectivity. None of us assumed a fixed essential identity. It was so evident that we did not all share a common understanding of being black and female, even though some of our experiences were similar.
>
> *(hooks, 1992, p. 46)*

Through working together to address the needs of domestic violence survivors and the role of Black women in that struggle, hooks and her colleagues not only acknowledge their multiple perspectives, but recognize the value of multiplicity in a collective struggle.

The present work in many ways documents the shifts in my own priorities as it relates to the work and lives of Black women academics. "I now chiefly use writing to disrupt the known and the real—writing as *simulation* … as 'subversive repetition'" (Richardson & St.Pierre, 2000, p. 967 emphasis in original). I am hoping to reject readings and engagement with the writings of Black women that support an overly prescribed notion of the Black woman academic. I am laboring to work with these texts in ways that assist in theorizing methods that disrupt forms of academic knowing and silencing. It is my hope that these efforts can be the impetus for bridge building, community, and justice.

Note

1   All participants' names are pseudonyms.

References

Apple, M. (2004) *Ideology and Curriculum* (3rd ed.). New York, NY: Routledge Falmer.

Asher, N. (2010) Decolonizing curriculum. In E. Malewski (Ed.), *Curriculum Studies Handbook: The Next Moment*, pp. 393–402, New York, NY: Routledge.

Austin, R. (1995). Sapphire Bound! In K. Crenshaw, N. Gotanda, G. Peller, & T. Kendall (Eds.), *Critical Race Theory: The Key Writings That Formed the Movement*, pp. 426–437, New York, NY: The New Press.

Baszile, D. T. (2008) Beyond all reason indeed: The pedagogical promise of critical race testimony. *Race Ethnicity and Education*, *11*(3), 251–265.

Baszile, D. T. (2010) In Ellisonian eyes, what is curriculum theory? In E. Malewski (Ed.), *Curriculum Studies Handbook: The Next Moment*. New York, NY: Taylor & Francis.

Beauboeuf-Lafontant, T. (2005) Womanist lessons for reinventing teaching. *Journal of Teacher Education*, *56*(5), 436–445.

Berkel, L. A. & Constantine, M. G. (2005) Relational variables and life satisfaction in African American and Asian American college women. *Journal of College Counseling*, *8*, 5–13.

Brooks, D. E. & Hébert, L. P. (2006) Gender, race, and media representation. In B. Dow, & J. T. Wood (Eds.), *The SAGE Handbook of Gender and Communication*, pp. 297–319, Thousand Oaks, CA: SAGE Publications, Inc.

Collins, P. H. (1986) Learning from the outsider within: The sociological significance of black feminist thought. *Social Problems*, *33*(6), S14–S32.

Collins, P. H. (1990) *Black Feminist Thought: Knowledge, Consciousness, and the Politics of Empowerment*. Boston, MA: Unwin Hyman, Inc.

Collins, P. H. (1996) What's in a name? Womanism, black feminism, and beyond. *The Black Scholar*, *26*(1), 9–17.

Connelly, F. M. & Clandinin, D. J. (2006) Narrative inquiry. In J. Green, G. Camili, & P. Elmore (Eds.), *Handbook of Complementary Methods in Education Research*, pp. 375–385, Mahwah, NJ: Lawrence Erlbaum.

Crenshaw, K., Gotanda, N., Peller, G., & Kendall, T. (1995) *Critical Race Theory: The Key Writings That Formed the Movement*. New York, NY: The New Press.

Dolphijn, R. & van der Tuin, I. (2012) New materialism: Interviews & cartographies. In G. Harman, & B. Latour (Eds.), *New Metaphysics*. Ann Arbor, MI: Open Humanities Press.

Edwards, K. T. (2014) "The whiteness is thick": Predominantly white classrooms, student of color voice, and Freirian hopes. In G. Yancy, & M. del Guadalupe Davidson (Eds.), *Exploring Race in Predominantly White Classrooms*, pp. 17–30, New York, NY: Routledge.

Edwards, K. T. & Baszile, D. T. (2016) Scholarly rearing in three acts: Black women's testimonial scholarship and the cultivation of radical Black female inter-subjectivity. *Knowledge Cultures*, *4*(1), 85–99.

Edwards, K. T. & Thompson, V. J. (2016) Womanist pedagogical love as justice work on college campuses: Reflections from faithful Black women academics. In M. Byrd (Ed.) "Spirituality in the workforce: Philosophical and social justice perspectives," *New Directions for Adult and Continuing Education (NDACE)*. *152*, 39–50.

Fasching-Varner, K. J. (2009) No! The team ain't alright! The institutional and individual problematics of race. *Social Identities*, *15*(6), 811–829.

Giardina, M. & McCarthy, C. (2008) The popular racial order of "urban" America: Sport, identity, and the politics of culture. In C. McCarthy, & C. Teasley (Eds.), *Transnational*

Perspectives on Culture, Policy, and Education: Redirecting Cultural Studies in Neoliberal Times, pp. 113–142, New York, NY: Peter Lang Publishing, Inc.

Gutierrez y Muhs, G., Niemann, Y. F., Gonzalez, C. G., & Harris, A. P. (2012) *Presumed Incompetent: The Intersections of Race and Class for Women in Academia*. Boulder, CO: University Press of Colorado.

Hawkesworth, M. E. (2006) Globalization and feminist activism. In M. B. Steger (Ed.), *Globalization*. Lanham, MD: Rowman & Littlefield Publishers, Inc.

hooks, b. (1989) *Talking back: Thinking feminist, thinking black*. Boston, MA: South End.

hooks, b. (1992) *Black Looks: Race and Representation*. Boston, MA: South End Press.

hooks, b. (1999) *Remembered Rapture: The Writer at Work*. New York, NY: Henry Holt and Company, LLC.

Hudson, S. V. (1998) Re-creational television: The paradox of change and continuity within stereotypical iconography. *Sociological Inquiry, 68*(2), 242–257.

Jean-Marie, G. & Lloyd-Jones, B. (2011) *Women of Color in Higher Education: Turbulent Past, Promising Future*. Bingley: Emerald Group Publishing Limited.

Lawrence, C. (1995) The word and the river: Pedagogy as scholarship as struggle. In K. Crenshaw, N. Gotanda, G. Peller, & T. Kendall (Eds.), *Critical Race Theory: The Key Writings that Formed the Movement*. New York, NY: The New Press.

Lincoln, C. E. & Mamiya, L. H. (1990) *The Black Church in the African American Experience*. Durham, NC: Duke University Press.

McCarthy, C., Giardina, M. D., Harewood, S. J., & Park, J. K. (2003) Afterword: Contesting culture: Identity and curriculum dilemmas in the age of globalization, postcolonialism, and multiplicity. *Harvard Educational Review, 73*(3), 449–465.

Manatu, N. (2003) *African American Women and Sexuality in the Cinema*. Jefferson, NC: McFarland.

Miller, J. L. (2006) Curriculum studies and transnational flows and mobilities: Feminist autobiographical perspectives. *Transnational Curriculum Inquiry, 3*(2), 31–50.

Ng-A-Fook, N. (2007) *An Indigenous Curriculum of Place: The United Houma Nation's Contentious Relationship with Louisiana's Educational Institutions* (Vol. 25). New York, NY: Peter Lang.

Patton, L. D. (2009) My sister's keeper: A qualitative examination of mentoring experiences among African American women in graduate and professional schools. *The Journal of Higher Education, 80*(5), 510–537.

Rhoades, G., Kiyama, J. M., McCormick, R., & Quiroz, M. (2008) Local cosmopolitans and cosmopolitan locals: New models of professionals in the academy. *The Review of Higher Education, 31*(2), 209–235.

Richardson, L. & St. Pierre, E. (2000) Writing: A method of inquiry. In N. K. Denzin & Y. S. Lincoln (Eds.), *Handbook of Qualitative Research*, pp. 959–978, Thousand Oaks, CA: Sage.

Ropers-Huilman, R. (2010) Motivated to make a difference: Student change agents' gendered framings of engagement. In E. J. Allan, S. V. Iverson, & R. Ropers-Huilman (Eds.), *Reconstructing Policy in Higher Education: Feminist Poststructural Perspectives*, pp. 171–192, New York, NY: Routledge.

Spivak, G. C. (1988) Can the subaltern speak? In C. Nelson, & L. Grossbeg (Eds.), *Marxism and The Interpretation of Culture*, pp. 271–316, Urbana, IL: University of Illinois Press.

Torres, M. N. (2002) Reflecting on the games of academia: A view from "the porch." In L. Jacobs, J. Cintron, & C. E. Canton (Eds.), *The Politics of Survival in Academia: Narratives of Inequity, Resilience, and Success*, pp. 77–94, Lanham, MD: Rowman & Littlefield Publishers, Inc.

Wallace, S. L., Moore, S. E., Wilson, L. L., & Hart, B. G. (2012) African American women in the academy: Quelling the myth of presumed incompetence. In G. Gutierrez y Muhs, Y. F. Niemann, C. G. Gonzalez, & A. P. Harris (Eds.), *Presumed Incompetent: The Intersections of Race and Class for Women in Academia*. Boulder, CO: University Press of Colorado.

5

FOR WOMEN OF COLOR WHO HAVE CONSIDERED CRITICAL SOCIAL THEORIES

When the Dominant Narrative Is No Longer Enough

OiYan Poon, Ester Sihite, Natasha Turman, Briellen Griffin, and Devita Bishundat

The goals of critical social theories are unapologetically emancipatory and radically transformative. So, what are such theories doing in a nice field like student affairs and higher education (SAHE)?[1] Historically, the student affairs profession grew out of institutional responses to student demands for colleges and universities to support their learning, psychosocial, financial, and other developmental needs more holistically (Barr & Upcraft, 1990; Thelin, 2011). Like other vocational areas in education, the field became feminized (McEwen, Williams, & Engstrom, 1991) and subsequently viewed within higher education as secondary to faculty activities, existing on the periphery of the core research and classroom teaching mission of higher education (Manning, Kinzie, & Schuh, 2014). In turn, graduate programs in SAHE have generally prepared students to work as support services professionals and rarely to challenge systems of higher education. Following the student development imperative, many graduate programs in the field encourage future professionals to facilitate the development of student growth in areas of psychosocial wellness, interpersonal skills, moral and cognitive growth (Rhoads & Black, 1995), paying little attention to empowering student affairs practitioners to be transformative social justice leaders. However, an increasing number of educators and student affairs professionals are interested in working to transform higher education to be more socially just (Rhoads & Black, 1995).

As women of color,[2] we each pursued our advanced degrees motivated by questions about systemic injustice we encountered in education both personally and professionally. Our previous roles as student services professionals and administrators had allowed us to play important roles in helping many students navigate educational access structures; however, we had continued to witness and experience the confusing and harmful ways the system reproduced unjust outcomes. Consequently, for each of us it was no longer enough for us to work *within* the system; we came to academia searching for answers on how to transform higher education to be more just.

As five women of color, we came into our Critical Social Theories (CST) course ready to engage in a different kind of classroom learning experience. In this chapter, we present our reflections on how a CST graduate seminar applied to education cultivated collective hope for a sustainable praxis toward systemic transformation. Offered through a higher education graduate program, the course represents a curricular intervention in the field of student affairs and higher education.

Authored by students and the faculty member from two cohorts of the class, this chapter illuminates the emancipatory experiences facilitated by our engagement in a range of critical social theories. The next section provides an overview of the Freirean approach to critical pedagogy which was foundational to the course. We then each present our reflective narratives as students–teachers and teacher-student on why we chose to take part in this curricular project, what we wanted to accomplish, memories from the course, and how it has affected our own development. The chapter closes with a discussion of themes drawn from our narratives and their implications for advancing emancipatory curriculum as women of color in the academy.

Critical Pedagogy

> I came to Freire thirsty, dying of thirst (in that way that the colonized, marginalized subject who is still unsure of how to break the hold of the status quo, who longs for change, is needy, is thirsty), and I found in his work (and the work of Malcolm X, Fanon, etc.) a way to quench that thirst. To have work that promotes one's liberation is such a powerful gift that it does not matter so much if the gift is flawed. Think of the work as water that contains some dirt. Because you are thirsty you are not too proud to extract the dirt and be nourished by the water.
>
> *(hooks, 1994, p. 50)*

Like bell hooks (1994), we recognize that Paulo Freire's work is imperfect. At the same time, we also acknowledge that Freire's work offers a revolutionary model of education. Freire was a radical educator whose advancement of literacy in Latin America branded him a threat to the state. Exiled from Brazil, Freire demonstrated how teaching and learning to read and write goes beyond a form of communication or skill for upward mobility within existing systems. The development of critical literacy, or pedagogy for critical consciousness, empowers people to engage in a critical analysis of dehumanizing social circumstances and to collectively transform systems of oppression (Freire, 2000).

Banned in totalitarian states like apartheid South Africa, the philosophy of teaching and learning presented by Freire's *Pedagogy of the Oppressed* fundamentally questions the traditional banking model of education and its dehumanizing, oppressive effects. In this practice of schooling, teachers are positioned as powerful knowledge bearers, who deposit information into students who are framed as empty vessels expected to obediently receive what the teacher and school deem to be valid knowledge (Freire, 2000). Banking education is a passive and dehumanizing process of learning that teaches students not to question authority and the status quo.

Promoting a humanizing educational process, Freire (2000) offers problem-posing education. This liberatory form of education undermines the traditionally hierarchical relationship between teacher and student, and advances an egalitarian teacher-student relationship. In problem-posing education, it is necessary to recognize that students bring with them a wealth of knowledge from their previous experiences, which Yosso (2005) calls "community cultural wealth." It transforms the traditional authoritarian relationship between teacher and student to one that is more egalitarian, allowing for the development of vibrant learning communities for humanistic inquiry.

Challenging hegemonic frames of formal schooling, authority, and knowledge, problem-posing education empowers students and teachers to engage in a collaborative process of co-construction of knowledge through the collective identification and analysis of problems (Freire, 2000). Critical pedagogy disrupts common expectations of formal schooling. Students, conditioned to look to the teacher for guidance and approval, may feel confused and uncertain in a learning environment that positions them as equal partners in inquiry and knowledge construction. Teachers, often positioned as authoritarian figures in the banking model, may feel a discomfort in the vulnerability required to engage in this radical approach to teaching. It humanizes the subjectivity of students who have been dehumanized as objects of the education system and society in general. It is also a humanizing process for teachers, because it acknowledges that they are not omnipotent, and allows them to also learn through the transformative praxis Freire advocates.

Praxis consists of both critical reflection and action (Freire, 2000). Reflection in problem-posing education includes critical self-reflection and a collective in-depth examination of an identified problem, inclusive of an analysis of the structures and relationships of power that serve to reproduce oppression. Through this reflective process, learning communities develop an analysis of the mechanisms leading to the reproduction of inequalities. With knowledge drawn from the process of critical reflection, communities can then act to transform oppressive systems. Reflection, deep analysis, and action are both necessary components of praxis in the process of critical pedagogy as defined by Freire (2000).

Our CST graduate seminar was intentionally structured according to Freire's framework of critical pedagogy. To begin each term, class members discuss selected contemporary and pressing issues in education and society. At the start of the fall 2013 and 2014 semesters, many were becoming painfully aware of the persistent oppressive state of anti-Black racial violence, through the cases of Trayvon Martin and Michael Brown. As such, the class focused attention on the unrelenting and troubling reality of racist state violence inside and outside of formal educational settings, recognizing that conditions external to schools and universities permeate the realities of students and others inside schools. By reading assigned texts[3] and considering their application to developing our understanding of systemic oppression, we each came to our weekly class dialogue ready to engage in a problem-posing process of education and praxis. Within our collective learning community, we considered and reconsidered our perspectives and our roles in maintaining or contesting hegemonic structures of oppression in our professional and personal lives.

What we found in our experiences was the foundational necessity of the development of a community safe enough to allow for vulnerability and personal investment in a transformative praxis. The creation of this brave and transformative space (Arao & Clemens, 2013) echoed Anzaldúa's (2015) affirmation of the need for "a reflective and passionate space for discussion by representing many of our diverse faces," and "a refuge, linking us with each other, renewing old connections among women of color" (p. 261). At times in this space, the course content and discussions drew anger, frustration, disappointment, sadness, guilt, spiritual growth, and deep self-reflection. However, it also cultivated an important sense of sustainable critical hope while class members confronted overwhelming social ills. Drawing from Freire's work, Duncan-Andrade (2009) explained that critical hope "rejects the despair of hopelessness … [and] demands a committed and active struggle" against oppressive circumstances, which can easily engender hopelessness (p. 185). Equipped with the tools of praxis, individuals can come together in a practice of collective community reflection and action for social justice transformation. As a collective practice, critical pedagogy combats the notion that the burden for change rests on a sole individual, and that we must passively wait for a hero or leader to emerge and save the day.

Instead, as a learning community, we valued each individual's perspectives as important contributions to the collective learning process. We leaned on each other for support and offered challenges in the critical reflection process. As a result, we transformed how we approached our engagement in social justice as educators and scholars, as will be seen in our narratives.

Narratives

Engagement in critical pedagogy is not new, but it can be a counter-hegemonic practice in the classroom, leading to an emancipatory experience for both teachers and students. In this section, we present our individual narratives, which illustrate how the collective praxis of Freirean critical pedagogy shaped our growth as scholars and education practitioners. In our CST seminar, each of us experienced a communal yet highly personal place for confronting imposter syndrome, reconciling our complex and intersectional identities, reconnecting with and rearticulating our commitments to social justice in the academy.

This Is What a Professor Looks Like
(OiYan, Teacher–Student)

The CST class is where I confront my imposter syndrome as an Asian–American woman who felt like my appointment to a tenure-track faculty position was made in error. Especially in the field of higher education and student affairs, where there were only about a half dozen tenure-track faculty nationwide who identified as Asian–American women, I felt an acute uncertainty about the legitimacy of my presence. Although I was also driven by my desire to introduce critical social theories to the field of higher education and student affairs, in reflecting on how I arrived in this class, I must acknowledge my insecurities as a legitimate professional scholar and teacher.

During my first semester on the tenure track, I was having a casual lunch meeting with my program chair. As we chatted, she offered me the opportunity to create an elective of my choice for my second semester. I was struck with both excitement and fear. By creating my own course from scratch, I would not have my colleagues' syllabi to serve as models, and the openness for innovation triggered my imposter syndrome and anxiety in feeling like I needed to have all the answers as a professor. I do not consider myself a theoretician. However, I decided it was time to confront the imposter syndrome that had been cultivated in graduate school, so that I could engage in theories that both intimidated me and could support my research.

In pursuing my Ph.D., I had not followed a traditional career trajectory, which set me up for feeling like an academic poser. I had worked in student affairs for several years before becoming overwhelmingly frustrated by the immense systemic inequalities that pervaded higher education. These experiences led me to graduate school as a pragmatist interested in developing and using research skills to contribute toward projects of social justice transformation. During classes, I was both intimidated and awestruck by my classmates and professors who were fluent in critical theory speak. They sounded so sophisticated in their fluid integration of citations of works by fancy-sounding scholar names like Anzaldúa, Bourdieu, DuBois, Gramsci, Foucault, Illich, and Althusser into class conversations. Reading and trying to engage in dialogues about "high theory" made me feel like an imposter. In class, I was both afraid of asking questions, which would reveal my lack of knowledge, and fascinated by the ideas to which I was exposed.

In offering a CST course, I wanted to create a learning environment where vulnerability in struggling through theoretical concepts was welcomed, so I relied on radical Freirean pedagogical principles that were radically expanded by the inclusion of women of color epistemologies (Collins, 2000; hooks, 1994; Delgado Bernal, 1998). For instance, according to principles of Pinayist praxis, the course incorporated notions of connecting "the global and local to the personal issues and stories of Pinay [and others'] struggle, survival, service, sisterhood, and strength" (Tintiangco-Cubales & Sacramento, 2009, pp. 179–180). This led me to start each semester by acknowledging my lack of expertise in critical theories and anxieties and struggles as a woman of color in the academy. Although my confession allows me a deep sense of liberation, I sometimes sense disorientation from students who are unaccustomed to a professor unequivocally stating her lack of expertise in the course topic. My intention is to set the tone for a learning environment that values and acknowledges diverse forms of knowledge that may have been cultivated outside of the walls of academia. Yosso (2005) defines this concept as community cultural wealth, which is cultivated in marginalized communities, and provides minoritized individuals with vital sources of aspiration, resilience, and knowledge often unrecognized within spaces of formal schooling. Perhaps due to the common experiences of having experiential knowledge rejected by academia, some students need time to adjust to having their wealth of knowledge validated. As the teacher-student, I also needed time to adjust to a different concept of how a proper professor should carry herself. Although I was afraid that my admission of limited expertise would encourage some students who might hold implicit biases against a woman of color faculty member to act with disrespect toward me, I have instead experienced a higher level of respect from students in this class than in others. Each year, students have expressed their appreciation for the unique experience of co-constructing a learning community that allows for deep introspection, collective accountability, and support in developing notions of social justice praxis. Simultaneously, I am thankful that my program chair allowed me the opportunity to construct a course that has provided me a place to work through my imposter syndrome and increase my self-efficacy as a legitimate faculty member. It has helped me value my own forms of community cultural wealth and combat my internalized perceptions of academic legitimacy that made me feel excluded from academia as a graduate student.

Through the course I have experienced and witnessed a transformative form of collective learning. I expect students to be co-teachers and learners with me through class activities including shared blogging and class discussions. After the first two classes of the semester, students are responsible for leading class discussions about assigned readings by presenting current news items or pop culture that demonstrate relevant concepts like hegemony and counter-hegemony. Through this co-construction of teaching and learning, community members are able to draw connections between theoretical texts, which are often hard to comprehend, and tangible, contemporary examples of concepts. Together, as Freire (2000) suggests, we read the world before reading the word, and engage in a process of critical literacy development to better deconstruct systems of oppression.

As the semester progresses, many often reach epiphanies about current events and systemic injustices. The most important realization that class members inevitably achieve is the necessity of communities of support and accountability for critical self-reflection. The connection between individuals committed to social justice and the cultivation of sustainable communities of hope, accountability, and strategic action is essential. At the end of the semester, we leave the classroom knowing we are not alone. Because systemic injustices are daunting and overwhelming, they are too much for any one individual to solve. Work for transformative change requires connection with and development of communities committed to justice, disciplined and joint analysis of problems to reveal potential solutions, and collective action for social justice.

The intentional practice of critical pedagogy in this course reminds me each year about the importance of community and helps me to confront my lingering imposter syndrome as a woman of color faculty member. It also allows me to reject dominant notions of what a professor looks like and what a professor should be like. Theories can be accessible. Academic speak should not be required as a badge of credibility in academia. Powerful theoretical concepts that deconstruct oppressive systems are tools for transformation, both personal and structural. Accordingly, CST is a place for reclaiming scholarly identities as women of color in the academy.

Resisting Dominant Discourses (Brie, Student–Teacher)

"Multiracial isn't going to work for you": Looking white and being brown in academia

When I made the decision to attend Loyola for graduate school, I knew that it would be the ninth predominantly white institution (PWI) I would have attended in my lifetime. My previous experience as a student in PWIs had shown me the voices and experiences of women of color (WOC) were often marginalized in academic and social spaces. To be a Black woman at a PWI meant being tokenized, fetishized even, in spaces where the existence of people of color (POC) was deemed unusual or exceptional. Being both Black and white, as in my case, often meant that my role as a student was connected to my identity as a border-crosser or bridge-builder; someone who lived in multiple monoracial spaces, but also pushed the limits of racial identity by living in overlapping racial spaces.

Since being a multiracial student at a PWI was not new to me, when I decided to enroll in classes at Loyola I looked for academic spaces that would allow me to explore my own identities in the context of my work in sociology of race and education. During both high school and college, I had looked for similar spaces, both academically and socially, that validated my existence as a woman of color in the academy. These spaces often took the form of a Black Student Union or courses on women in the Civil Rights Movement. Regardless of its form, I knew that having a space where my identity as a racial queer (Chang, 2010) would be embraced as a part of my academic and professional competency was integral to my well-being. The CST class, or ELPS 429 (our formal course number, turned social media hashtag), became that space as I began my journey as a doctoral student of color.

ELPS 429 created space for diving into and sorting out our identity politics in the context of our professional lives. At the core, this was made possible by the foundation of Freirean pedagogy, in which formal teacher and student roles are dissolved to make room for authentic, liberatory education. As Freire (2000) writes, "Education must begin with the solution of the teacher-student contradiction, by reconciling the poles of the contradiction so that both are simultaneously teachers and students" (p. 72). As co-educators, or educators of each other, our class community became a space of humanization, in which trust and partnership were the starting point for the critical work of understanding oppression and resisting dominant discourses that dehumanized many of us as women of color in academic spaces.

I was reminded of the grounding I experienced as part of ELPS 429 at a recent academic conference focused on justice and education. After giving a presentation on race and schooling, I was approached by another presenter who expressed her deep interest in my work. After asking for a copy of my bibliography, which I had offered to all in attendance, she closed our conversation with a comment I didn't expect. "Yeah ..." she said, looking directly into my eyes. "Multiracial isn't going to work for you." Having spent my entire life in PWIs, I came to expect challenges to my racial and ethnic identity as commonplace. What surprised me was my white colleague's willingness to challenge me in a space that was supposed to be focused on social justice and racial equity. How was it that, even in an environment that is designated as safe, which requests authenticity and reflexivity in research, dominant narratives still seep in, sometimes through the mouths of fellow critical female scholars?

Following the incident, I returned to a critical reading reflection I wrote for ELPS 429 and found it to be an apt example, not only of the work that grew out of our collective emancipatory practice, but also of my recent encounter with dominant ideologies in supposedly radical academic spaces:

> My husband and I had a casual-turned-serious conversation the other day about the intersection of my "truth," with my intellectual-activist public persona. It has been challenging for me to walk into a space and not qualify my racial background. I dislike people thinking that I am white for a number of reasons, one of which is that they have no idea who they're dealing with. (I would be remiss if I didn't say that this has often worked in my advantage. Even when they know I am multiracial, whites seem to be put at ease by the fact that I "look white," and thus say whatever they want. [Sigh]).
> My husband challenged me on this. "What if you didn't tell everyone, all the time, in every space, what you are? They are going to make their own assumptions anyway. And even when you tell them what you are, they are

going to address you like they see you. *What if you just do the work you do, fight what you fight for?*"

Even in class, the desire to "qualify my racial background" was deeply intermingled with my exploration of identity in personal and professional contexts. When I read this reflection, I was reminded that this is not new work, for me or for those with whom I interact. The struggle to understand my own complex identity and to be able to express that identity is tangled up in who I am as a scholar, researcher, and activist. As I think about my most recent interaction with a colleague who was dissatisfied, to say the least, with my racial self-identification, in the context of ELPS 429 and the commitment to a pedagogy of humanization, I am reminded that continued engagement with other women of color within and outside of academic spaces is a healing, energizing and powerful force. Women of color receive so many messages that we are not where we belong and struggle to get academia to "love [us] back" (Martinez, 2016). Echoing Freire, I would say that we cannot wait for a collective realization that academia and academics often practice dehumanizing pedagogy; rather we have to intentionally create spaces of partnership and trust, where our identities as women of color are recognized and normalized. The space that ELPS 429 created to study critical theoretical approaches in education allowed me to give myself permission to engage with the persistent internal dialogue of racial identity and the politics of academia. Consistently moving in circles that reinforce dominant discourses is weary work. It tests not only our professional personas; it also challenges the simple presence of our identities in those professional spaces. However, when education is the "practice of freedom," our identities, voices, and experiences manifest in our scholarship, our activism, and our communal struggles for humanization. By refusing to wait for others to gain critical consciousness, we can create spaces that emphasize collective exploration of knowledge and help to imbue each other with the strength to resist, even in the most dehumanizing contexts.

Claiming My Counter-narrative (Devita, Student–Teacher)

Being the first in my family to go to college, obtaining a master's degree was never a reality. It took eight years to return to higher education. As a first-generation, low-income, Guyanese–American cis-woman, I never felt a sense of worthiness or belonging within the walls of the classroom. With the love and encouragement of friends, family, and mentors, I took the plunge and knew instantly that I wanted to take a course during my first semester with Dr. OiYan Poon. As someone who has engaged personally and professionally in work around diversity, equity, and access, I wanted to challenge myself with a course taught by an Asian–American woman. This was the first time I was in a class taught by an Asian–American woman.

Our first class shook me to my core. Fearing the unknown, my nerves and imposter syndrome kicked into high gear once introductions began. Being in a class with doctoral students, a professor whom I admired from afar for months, and many second-year master's students, I felt inept and unworthy of being in the classroom with these brilliant individuals. Afraid to speak up, I entered this space with the notion that I could "get by" as I had done throughout my schooling: participate occasionally, turn in assignments on-time, and limit attention to myself. Little did I know, this mentality would not fly in this class. More importantly, I began the journey of recognizing my worth, finding my voice, and developing my counter-narrative.

This course allowed me to explore my identities and lived experiences in a way in which I had never been afforded. Almost everything we read was written by people with multiple marginalized identities. I finally saw myself and my narrative reflected in an academic space. This meant that I could form deeper connections between the words on the page and my own life. For example, Anzaldúa's *Borderlands* spoke to my experience of straddling Guyanese and American cultures while never being fully accepted by either. With each new book, I yearned for more. For the first time, I began to make sense of the education I received over the past sixteen years. My K-16 educational experiences upheld dominant—White supremacist, Christian, patriarchal, cisgender, capitalist, heteronormative—narratives, which bell hooks (1994) has described so powerfully in her work. Nowhere did I ever learn about my history nor see myself reflected in literature or standardized tests. More importantly, I never once questioned why. As a product of the banking model of education, I had been socialized to accept what I learned from teachers as right and to not question its validity. This class allowed me to examine topics of my choosing and unpack my identities in relation to systems of power and privilege. I finally held power over my own learning, revealing to me what true liberatory education can, and should, look like for every person. Through this course, I was encouraged to speak my truth, share my lived experiences, and constantly question the world around me.

As I continue to engage in social justice work professionally, intersectionality is at the crux of my approach. Recognizing that individuals navigate a society that is simultaneously raced, gendered, and classed (in addition to other forms of oppression), my interactions with students and colleagues alike must take into account the intersections of their identities and their individual lived experiences. Further, my approach as a practitioner focuses on problem-posing education which aims to develop individuals as complete beings and allows them to possess ownership of their education in order to create an authentic learning experience. Two questions that have become permanent parts of my practice are: "What kind of harm am I (and others) potentially doing" and "How can this decision or action oppress someone else"? Although I had been taught to think about the effects of decisions and actions, reframing these questions allows me to critically think about the personal impact on others in a way that centers their humanity.

ELPS 429 also continues to shape how I show up in spaces. I am unapologetically me and share my voice. I proudly say I am Guyanese–American and no longer feel shame when others do not know where Guyana is. I correct individuals when they mispronounce my name. In turn, I take time to pronounce others' names correctly. I do not assume a person's pronouns; I ask. I avoid the use of possessive language because people are human beings, not objects. While these acts may seem minor, they are acts of resistance against discrete forms of hegemony. They demonstrate care for others and the importance of our shared humanity.

In connecting with peers who had both different and similar lived experiences, I more intimately understood the complexities of institutionalized oppression and dehumanization.

Maintaining hope in the midst of oppression is an uphill battle. However, I was able to develop strategies as a direct result of this course. One such strategy is surrounding myself with individuals who share a similar critical consciousness and passion for issues of equity. Second, I must view self-care and self-love as something that is not selfish, but rather, it is "self-preservation, and that is an act of political warfare" (Lorde, 1988, p. 132). For my entire life I have been conditioned to prioritize everyone's needs over my own. I now reframe self-care as mandatory in order to be my best self for others. Further, there is always a counternarrative. Lastly, taking a strengths-based approach to this work will continue to highlight the beauty and power of marginalized communities. I refuse to use a deficit-based approach when working with communities of color and other individuals with marginalized identities because it negates their rich lived experiences and the resiliency that they develop as a result of navigating spaces that were not created for their success.

Interrogating the "Kool-Aide" (Natasha, Student–Teacher)

Having been privileged to graduate from the number one all-women, historically Black college in the nation—Spelman College—I can boldly declare that my higher educational foundation was anchored by culturally rich, historically focused, and gender empowered experiences. I was equipped with a set of tools that encouraged me to be unapologetically smart, unapologetically critical, and most importantly, an unapologetic educated Black woman. A seed of advocacy, leadership, mentoring, feminism, and a desire to evoke change was implanted within me. Learning about the historical relevance and significance of historically Black colleges and universities, and discovering the critical importance of the African Diaspora and its implications for my entire existence—socially and academically—was the first time I started to realize my positionality in this world. I didn't have the language then, but I know now, that my critical consciousness was being developed ever so intentionally and purposefully.

But it wasn't until I started this journey to the Ph.D., with eyes pressed toward the mark of becoming a woman of color scholar in the academy whose research and scholarship would center the often-absent voices of those like me, that I grew deeper in my understanding of my positionality and acknowledged that a new set of tools would be required to successfully fulfill my calling. It was for these reasons that I was intrigued by the CST course. I knew that a course like this would allow me to examine society and higher education through critical frameworks, to expose the fissures in the foundations. The course allowed students the space to problematize the systematic marginalization and inequitable practices that plague our society and educational systems.

When I reflect back to my time in CST, there was one class session in particular that resonated deeply. During this class session, we discussed culture and anti-oppressive education. The level of vulnerability and awakening that occurred during those two hours and 45 minutes was mind-blowing. It was the first time I realized how I was affected by inequitable practice in education and how I had unconsciously been navigating that reality. Growing up in the inner city of East Orange, New Jersey, I was acutely aware that depending on your zip code, your life and educational experience looked very different. Even moving to a suburban town like Hampton, Virginia for high school, I still observed the cultural and educational disparities. Critical feminist scholars Evans-Winter and Esposito (2010) validated my personal observations by positing that racism, sexism, and class oppression in the United States (U.S.) have the potential to cause negative compounding effects on African–American girls. Specifically, Black girls "are in multiple jeopardy of race, class, and gender exclusion in mainstream educational institutions" (Evans-Winter & Esposito, 2010, p. 13). One of the texts for that class session was *Troubling Education* by Kumashiro (2002), who talked about one of the many ways students respond to oppressive treatment in educational environments. One of those tactics was to overcompensate—hyper-performing in academic, extracurricular, and social activities. I had an "ah ha" moment, and quickly realized, that was me. Several women of color scholars who have examined Black girls in U.S. educational systems have described this academic and social overcompensation as resiliency; an illustration of strategic practice to survive and thrive in school (Fordham, 1993; Henry, 1998; O'Connor, 1997). Evans-Winter and Esposito (2010) posited that Black girls' resilience in school was dynamic, yet mediated by social forces in school and society; their academic success became a catalyst despite social burdens. I never considered this overachievement my response to the acknowledgement of my own oppression, nor did I think of myself as exhibiting resilience. Through high academic achievement, I thought I could remove myself from being "othered." For me, the goal was to achieve success and social mobility with each academic credential. Don't get me wrong, striving for better and excelling academically are not bad things. But it was not until that class session that I began to unpack the *why* behind my rhyme and reason.

CST helped me fully interrogate the "Kool-aid" I had been consuming from the dominant narratives all around me. What does it mean to be 'other' and who or what created this label? Why were little Black girls like me being told and telling themselves that they need to work twice as hard to make it in this world? How does one reconcile inequitable realities when you have no idea they have been your reality? As my personal lived experiences have shown, and the literature further validates, "Black female students struggle against systematic racist, sexist, and classist policies in schools," yet we are not always cognizant when these oppressive forces are at play (Evans-Winter & Esposito, 2010, p. 14). How does one ascertain what things should be unlearned and what things should become cornerstones of your life? I didn't have all the answers then, and I still don't now, but these questions served as a catalyst for my commitment to praxis that invests in the liberatory possibilities of education. In the spirit of critical race feminism, elevating counter-narratives to the dominant discourse in higher education became my new source of hydration (Evans-Winter & Esposito, 2010; Wing, 1997; Sulé, 2011).

Before taking this seminar, for example, I could explain to you why I appreciated the tenants of feminism and its ability to elevate the voices and perspectives of women. I could share how important it was for me to take a feminist lens to understand various phenomena in higher education and society. But I had not quite acquired the framework for considering *why* certain voices shape that lens, *how* I could and should use that lens within the context of my irreducibly complex intersecting social identities—because being a woman of color, specifically an able-bodied, middle-class, cisgender, Christian Black woman, wife, daughter, sister, friend, and scholar whose roots are urban and southern inspired is complicated—and *why* it matters. What I learned in CST class was far more nuanced and intentional. I was immersed in a learning environment that challenged me to scrutinize, deconstruct, and reconstruct how I viewed the world. Every conversation, blog post, and paper made me more conscious.

Although at times our class discussions were uncomfortable, a little confusing, and downright overwhelming, I truly believe I walked away with a new lens on my own life and a new take on how I want to engage with the higher education community. As I reflect on this journey to defining my voice in the academy and enhancing my critical consciousness through exposure to critical thoughts, I am reminded of the words of Gloria Anzaldúa (2012):

> Every increment of consciousness, every step forward is a travesía, a crossing ... Knowledge makes me more aware, it makes me more conscious. "Knowing" is painful because after "it" happens I can't stay in the same place and be comfortable. I am no longer the person I was before."
>
> *(p. 70)*

I appreciate the mirrors that a class like CST held in front of me—mirrors that allow me to continue to grow, question, and challenge the status quos. Even more so, I value that I will never be the same after each new lesson learned.

Liberation, Hope, and Power (Ester, Student–Teacher)

In the senior year of my undergraduate career, I distinctly recall the words of a guest speaker in a service-learning course. She was a community leader and founder of the first and only English edition newspaper for the Asian–American community in Washington state, and she left a small imprint on me when she said, "The purpose of higher education is to imagine what can be." I had rarely experienced having women of color teach in the classroom and, notably, this message felt more palpable coming from this Asian–American woman leader who looked like me and with whom I felt like I could identify. Looking back, these words affirmed and reflected a growing belief in me that higher education could serve as a positive force in the progress of humankind and social change. This timeframe also saw the nascent stages of my working in higher education as my vocation, fueled by my belief that this field served as a unique medium that could transform and liberate individuals and society.

After several years of working in and studying higher education, I began to hold a more ambivalent view toward higher education and the possibility of social change in general. In learning about academic capitalism, increasing social stratification (even in higher education), neo-liberalism and other trends of marginalization and oppression, my sense of hope for social justice was waning. Not only did I struggle to make sense of the injustices I was seeing, I also dealt with uncertainty about my role in partaking in systemic change. What could I offer the field and/or academia? Did I want to be a part of academia? Would it ever become easier to navigate the field and society at large as a woman of color? In spite of (or perhaps because of) these questions, I was thirsty for hope and a class like CST.

What I got out of the course was so much more than I imagined. If I could share three themes from the course, they would be the following: (1) that the process of seeking liberation is liberation itself; (2) that maintaining critical hope sustains the possibility of social justice; and (3) that I, as a woman of color, hold assets and power to work with others for change.

Process. Through this course, for the first time in my life, I encountered the works of Paulo Freire in *The Pedagogy of the Oppressed*. I can sincerely say that this text changed my life. One of the insights that stood out most poignantly for me was that, "the struggle to be more fully human has already begun in the authentic struggle to transform the situation" (Freire, 2000, p. 47). For so much of my scholarly and professional life, I had encountered and accepted the philosophy that only quantifiable outcomes define change or "success." I see these outcomes-centered barometers being used widely in U.S. organizational settings, including higher education institutions. But in reading and discussing Freire, I realized that what rang true for me was that change is a process; it is embodied in relationships and trust, and the process of submitting to the greater wellbeing of humankind is inextricably the start of liberation itself. I learned that my interdependence on others is what makes the work of pursuing social justice worthwhile *and* necessary to reclaiming my own humanity. While the dominant narrative has feminized and therefore deemed inferior anything other than hyper-independence, I recognize more than ever the salience of interdependence to my identity as a woman of color feminist. Notably, through having a classroom space in which other students and I could authentically share our stories, questions, and struggles with one another (even within just one semester), other students' humanity became intertwined with my own.

Critical Hope. Through my coursework and life experience, I had become increasingly affected by and witness to a number of macro-level injustices that seemed nearly impossible to fix, particularly along the lines of race-, class-, and gender-based oppression. Leading up to and during this course, I wanted to be replenished of hope that change could occur within higher education and beyond. Yet, there were so many pervasive and evidently monumental barriers to achieving long-term social change, and these dynamics impacted me directly and deeply on both a cognitive and affective level. During and after the CST course, I believe it was the awareness, pain, and indignation about the very real challenges to social justice, coupled with the steady and supported vision of better possibilities that allowed me to develop *critical hope* (Duncan-Andrade, 2009). What facilitated the building of critical hope within this course was seeing that not only was social change deeply needed but also that other people were doing this work and sparking noticeable changes in the way society is living. I took to heart the notion that while hopelessness can be debilitating, critical hope can be empowering and moving. hooks (1994) writes:

> When we only name the problem, when we state complaint without a constructive focus on resolution, we take away hope … Hopefulness empowers us to continue our work for justice even as the forces of injustice may gain greater power for a time.
>
> *(p. xiv)*

In looking back on this course, I can see that my sense of critical hope gleaned from learning about others who have so deeply wanted social justice and have embarked on journeys toward that change. Importantly, I also saw myself in their stories.

Yes, I Have Power. Prior to this course I had processed and celebrated to some degree the forms of "border knowledge" (Anzaldúa, 2012) and community cultural wealth (Yosso, 2005) that I have derived from my identity and experiences as a woman of color and daughter of working-class immigrant parents from Indonesia. My learning within this course not only affirmed these non-dominant assets but also highlighted the ways in which I have unique power in moving forward social justice. I resonated with how Anzaldúa (2012) spoke of her identity and assets as a Chicana: "Here we are weaponless with open arms, with only our magic. Let's try it our way, the mestiza way, the Chicana way, the woman way"

(p. 88). I also resonated with Freire's (2000) emphasis that it is the oppressed that are able to lead and instigate liberation. And so with my complex identities, I came to learn that I am able to both lead and be led.

Suffice to say that I did not drastically or overnight develop the belief that I possess the power to partake in social change and liberation. The work of believing this and of having my efficacy cultivated has continued long after the course ended. I continue gleaning from the work and legacies of people with whom I have interacted, both in person and through written testimonies. For myself and I believe for others, this ongoing and intentional work is what fosters the confidence, both in the head and the heart, that "we are the leaders we are looking for" (Boggs & Kurashige, 2012, p. 178).

Discussion and Conclusion

Across the presented reflections arose several commonalities regarding our experiences leading up to and during the CST course. These include dealing with and silencing the imposter syndrome both as faculty member and graduate students, the salience of being in community as we worked to reconstruct paradigms while cultivating critical hope, and the importance of marrying reflection and action in working toward sustainable social justice. Altogether, our reflections indicate that the CST course served as a sacred space for us to claim/reclaim our scholarly identities in academia as women of color and as social change agents.

Notably, academia has historically barred women of color from entry based on both race and gender. Although explicit barriers to participation are no longer legal, higher education generally continues to reproduce a culture that dismisses the valuable and diverse talents and epistemologies of women of color. Accordingly, many women of color have found higher education to be hostile and dehumanizing, a place where we are "presumed incompetent" despite our credentials and accomplishments (Harris & González, 2012). Some of us have internalized the notion that we do not belong in academia, that our contributions are not valid, and that engaging in efforts for social justice change is futile.

Part of what this course has validated is that critical pedagogical approaches to teaching and learning entail important efforts to disrupt the reproduction of persistent, hegemonic and dehumanizing cultures, such as what permeated throughout our narratives. As bell hooks (1994) explained, liberatory pedagogies incorporating Freirean and feminist ideas seek to confront and resist dehumanizing and oppressive, intersecting systems of racism and white supremacy, patriarchy, heteronormativity, and capitalism. Demonstrating that radical alternatives to banking education is possible, teaching and learning guided by humanizing principles of critical pedagogy can empower new generations of diverse scholars and educators. As our narratives illustrate, critical pedagogy serves as a powerful tool for individual transformation and as a process for building and sustaining communities of accountability, reflection, support, and action.

As women of color, we can lead the way in claiming and transforming classroom spaces through our pedagogical choices. More than ever, spaces of learning need to be redefined as humanizing, emancipatory, and empowering for women of color, people with other marginalized identities, and all those who wish to work in solidarity toward transformative social justice change. Indeed, within even such an imperfect space as higher education, critical pedagogy represents a powerful tool to cultivate what Grace Lee Boggs (2012) has called for: a long-term revolution sustained by communities courageously imagining and collectively implementing solutions to the great problems of our times (Boggs & Kurashige, 2012).

Notes

1   This question parallels the title of Gloria Ladson-Billings's (1998) article introducing Critical Race Theory to the field of education.
2   In using the term *women of color*, we do not simply refer to women who do not identify as white. Rather, the term denotes a collective and politically conscious identity. By claiming this identity, we recognize the commonalities and differences in the experiences of African–American, Asian–American, Latinx, and Indigenous women, and work in solidarity for our mutual liberation from structures that marginalize us as racially minoritized women.
3   Selected texts for the course include works on racial formation theory, Critical Race Theory, color-blind racism, and whiteness as property, hegemony, capital, and anti-oppressive education. They also included works by radical scholars like W. E. B. DuBois, bell hooks, Gloria Anzaldúa, and Grace Lee Boggs.

References

Anzaldúa, G. (2012) *Borderlands / La Frontera: The New Mestiza* (4th ed.). San Francisco, CA: Aunt Lute Books.

Anzaldúa, G. (2015) Counsels from the firing … past, present, future (Foreword to the third edition, 2001). In C. Moraga & G. Anzaldúa (Eds.), *This Bridge Called My Back: Writings By Radical Women of Color* (4th ed.), pp. 255–260. Albany, NY: SUNY Press.

Arao, B., & Clemens, K. (2013) From safe spaces to brave spaces: A new way to frame dialogue around diversity and social justice. In L. M. Landreman (Ed.), *The Art of Effective Facilitation: Reflections from Social Justice Educators*, pp. 135–150. Sterling, VA: Stylus Publishing.

Barr, M. J., & Upcraft, M. L. (1990) *New Futures for Student Affairs: Building a Vision for Professional Leadership and Practice*. San Francisco, CA: JosseyBass.

Boggs, G. L. & Kurashige, S. (2012) *The Next American Revolution: Sustainable Activism for the Twenty-first Century* (2nd ed.). Berkeley, CA: University of California.

Chang, A. (2010) Reflections of a racial queer. *Multicultural Perspectives, 12*(10), 107–112.

Collins, P. C. (2000) *Black Feminist Thought: Knowledge, Consciousness, and the Politics of Empowerment* (2nd ed.). New York, NY: Routledge.

Delgado Bernal, D. (1998) Using a Chicana feminist epistemology in educational research. *Harvard Educational Review, 68*(4), 555–583.

Duncan-Andrade, J. M. R. (2009) Note to educators: Hope required when growing roses in concrete. *Harvard Educational Review, 79*(2), 181–194.

Evans-Winter, V. E. & Esposito, J. (2010) Other people's daughters: Critical race feminism and Black girls' education. *Educational Foundations*, 24(1–2), 11–24.

Fordham, S. (1993) Those loud Black girls: (Black) women, silence, and passing in the academy. *Anthropology and Education Quarterly*, 30(3), 272–293.

Freire, P. (2000) *Pedagogy of the Oppressed*. New York, NY: Continuum.

Harris, A. P. & González, C. G. (2012) Introduction. In G. Gutiérrez y Muhs, Y. Flores Niemann, C. G. González, & A. P. Harris (Eds.), *Presumed Incompetent: The Intersections of Race and Class for Women in Academia*, pp. 1–16. Boulder, CO: University Press of Colorado.

Henry, A. (1998) Complacent and womanish: Girls negotiating their lives in an African centered school in the U.S. *Race, Ethnicity and Education*, 1(2), 151–170.

hooks, b. (1994) *Teaching to Transgress: Education as the Practice of Freedom*. New York, NY: Routledge.

Kumashiro, K. K. (2002) *Troubling Education: "Queer" Activism and Anti-oppressive Pedagogy*. New York, NY: Routledge.

Ladson-Billings, G. (1998) Just what is critical race theory and what's it doing in a nice field like education? *International Journal of Qualitative Studies in Education*, 11(1), 7–24.

Lorde, A. (1988) *A Burst of Light: Essays*. Ann Arbor, MI: Firebrand Books.

McEwen, M. K., Williams, T. E., & Engstrom, M. (1991) Feminization in student affairs: A qualitative investigation. *Journal of College Student Development*, 32, 440–446.

Manning, K., Kinzie, J., & Schuh, J. H. (2014) *One Size Does Not Fit All: Traditional and Innovative Models of Student Affairs Practice* (2nd ed.). New York, NY: Routledge.

Martinez, T. (2016, October 27) Academia, love me back. Retrieved from https://vivatiffany.wordpress.com/2016/10/27/academia-love-me-back/

O'Connor, C. (1997) Dispositions toward (collective) struggle and educational resilience in the inner city: A case analysis of six African American high school students. *American Educational Research Journal*, 34, 593–629.

Rhoads, R. A. & Black, M. A. (1995) Student affairs practitioners as transformative educators: Advancing a critical cultural perspective. *Journal of College Student Development*, 36(5), 413–421.

Sulé, V. T. (2011) Restructuring the master's tools: Black female and Latina faculty navigating and contributing in classrooms through oppositional positions. *Equity & Excellence in Education*, 44(2), 169–187.

Thelin, J. R. (2011) *A History of American Higher Education* (2nd ed.). Baltimore, MD: Johns Hopkins University Press.

Tintiangco-Cubales, A. & Sacramento, J. (2009) Practicing Pinayist pedagogy. *Amerasia Journal*, 35(1), 179–187.

Wing, A. K. (1997) Introduction. In A. K. Wing (Ed.), *Critical Race Feminism: A Reader*, pp. 1–9. New York, NY: New York University Press.

Yosso, T. J. (2005) Whose culture has capital? A critical race theory discussion of community cultural wealth. *Race Ethnicity and Education*, 8(1), 69–91.

6

BLACK WOMEN, CURRICULUM DESIGN, AND THE SUBJECT OF DISIDENTIFICATION

Maria del Guadalupe Davidson

Introduction

In one way or another, a large portion of black feminist scholarship involves (re) tracing, (re)narrating, or (re)visioning the history of black women's bodily and embodied sexual exploitation. Building one upon another, black feminist theorists—from Patricia Hill Collins, to Beverly Guy Sheftall, to bell hooks, to a new generation of scholars that include Alexis Gumbs and Jennifer Nash—continue to reveal how black women's bodies are situated within a social order structured by an oppressive race-gender axis. Consequently, it is not misleading to say that black feminist scholarship is fundamentally about the body. Given the history of race- and gender-based violence that black women have endured—violence that has invaded our mouths, our hands, our anuses, our vaginas, our backs—what else would or could our scholarship be about?

This is the reason why the scholarly framing of black women's bodies—black women's flesh and beyond flesh—is a central entry point into black women's studies for most students and readers.

To theorize black women's experience from the vantage point of the body, however, in no way limits black women's studies ability to account for relationships with others. To speak about the body is not simply to remain confined to a singular entity because, as Lisa Blackman (2008) notes, "the body is not bounded by skin, where we understand the skin to be a kind of container for the self, but rather our bodies always extend and connect to other bodies … to practices, techniques, technologies and objects which produce different kinds of bodies and different ways, arguably, of enacting what it means to be human."[1] The black female body is situated within a socio-historical *embodied system of oppression* from which there is no outside. What this ostensibly means is that most students and readers become acquainted with black women's experience and history through a study of the oppression and exploitation of black women's bodies by others. As a result, the black female body, and more broadly, the black female experience easily comes to be defined as an exploited body. And many of the narratives that belong to curricula designed around the black female body are narratives about the suffering and survival of oppression.

While I do not want to deny the urgency of our work, the unwavering commitment to black women's liberation, and its lifesaving mission—a mission to save black women from the violence visited on the (un)rapable jezebel; to resist arguments that we do not feel pain and therefore do not require as much anesthesia—I do want to pose the question of whether the standard narratives about black women's bodies and experience have narrowed the full meaning and range of black women's bodies and experiential possibilities within systems of domination. To be precise, by positioning the black female body as a site of oppression and of suffering, has black feminist theory closed itself off from the full range of black women's bodily pleasure and sexual desire? Furthermore, given the history of oppression that black women's bodies have endured—physically, mentally, spiritually—what are the distinctive challenges and complexities of thinking about black female sexuality?

Imagine, for instance, the challenge of using black women's bodies to *illustrate sexual desire and pleasure*. Doesn't this open the door to further objectification of the black female body? Doesn't it replicate the very same exploitation that black female theorists have been struggling against? To be sure, there are many historical examples of black women's bodies being used as tools or instruments for the pleasure of others. Sara Baartmaan's body (to some readers known as the Hottentot Venus) is one of the most well-known examples. During the nineteenth century, Sander Gilman observes that "the female Hottentot comes to represent the black female *in nuce*" and although "many groups of African blacks were known to Europeans in the nineteenth century, the Hottentot remained representative of the essence of the black, especially the black female" (Gilman 1985, 225).[2] Yet, even as they professed repulsion of the black female body, it is impossible to deny Europeans'—especially European men—perverse fascination with Baartman and her body.[3] Janell Hobson (2005) does an excellent job chronicling this perverse fascination in her book *Venus in the Dark*, writing: "Yet, for all the refinement and civilization of European men, Baartman's exhibition was so popular that satirists often called into question the fascination that European men did have for this African woman on display."[4] Add to this the robust trade in pornography during the nineteenth century,[5] some of which featured black women, and we begin to see the emergence of a disturbing system of exploitation and signification; a system trapping black women at the center of its violence. As I have written about elsewhere, most Europeans came to understand black women through what I refer to as *didactic pornography* where certain colonial images, "not only present the black female body as *other* but do so in a way that presents the black female body as available for sexual possession."[6] While I do not want to minimize or underestimate the objectification of the black female body, what goes beyond the confines of these examples is the question of the black female agency. By this I mean the black female body not as an object of desire or as oppressed by another but as actively desiring and finding sexual pleasure *in herself and for herself*. I contend that much black feminist scholarship has neglected this aspect of the black female body and experience.

My question, then, concerns those of us who design teaching materials on black women's liberation. In addition to positioning the black female body as broken or exploited—which for many of us may be our entry into any discussion about liberation—how might we also conceptualize the black female body as a site of sexual desire and sexual freedom? Black women scholars and professors, in my opinion, should broaden the narrative of black women's studies by designing curriculum that speaks to black women's agential experiences of sex and sexuality, a curriculum that encompasses the breadth of black women's loving and consensual sexual relationships, *as well as* curriculum that explains black women's sexual desire that is out of bounds or deviant, and which some may read as a re-inscription of exploitation.[7]

Working from within empire, if we are going to really begin to reshape the contours of black women's studies, we must also stretch beyond the prescriptive, safe sex zone—the one focusing on sexuality primarily within a heterosexual context—to discover and uncover for ourselves and our students aspects of black women's sexuality and sexual expression that reads as non-normative and unsafe. Why? I'm not sure about the reader, but for myself I want my students to grapple with black women's full and dynamic being-in-the-world *as it is*. I want to provide students with non-traditional methods of analysis that complicate the social constructions of sex, race, and gender. I want to give students the opportunity to complicate the very structure of language itself encouraging them to "think together"[8] words like *slut*, *sex-positive*, *gender fluid*, and *hoe-life* within a solidly black feminist context so that they may expand the totality of black women's experience.

To that end, this chapter adds to recent work done in the area of what I refer to here as *black deviance studies* where primarily black women scholars explore black women's sexuality as *free* and *mischievous* through such practices as Bondage, Discipline, Sadism, and Masochism (BDSM) and its subgenre *racial role play*. And, in so doing, this work opens a new way of being a black woman in the world in a way that, I hope, revolutionizes how we *teach* and *design* curriculum around black women and their sexuality. Unlike recent very good scholarship, I am not interested in the idea of black women engaging in things like kink[9] but how black women scholars can use kink culture, for example, in the classroom to help our students rethink black women's historical agency. Since deviance is a term that black women's scholars can/should reclaim, the question then, is how might such a course design effectively and ethically engage the complexities of sexual desire and agency, particularly forms of sexuality that might be called deviant within an unapologetic black female context?

My answer to these provocative questions will begin with a brief discussion of the distinctive challenges faced by discussions of black women's sexuality. To think more deeply about these challenges, I will build on earlier work I've done on Jose Munoz's analysis of disidentification, which describes a process whereby people from marginalized groups can find a *workable* balance between pleasure and pain. In this way, I am using disidentification as both a theory and pedagogy; as a *theory*, disidentification provides an interpretative lens for black women's sexuality; as a *pedagogy*, disidentification is a unique tool to expand students' thinking about black women's history and resistance. Next, I evaluate how black women scholars might design a curriculum that reclaims desire as an important site of analysis from which to theorize black women's bodies. Finally, I posit teaching about black women who practice BDSM via the lens of disidentification, which allows us to see them as engaged in a form of agential practice.

Fully and Freely All That I Am

For many students, the first introduction into the wide and diverse field of black women's studies is an iconic text like *Some of Us Are Brave* where we see the heavy hitters of black feminist thought engaging in *the work*. Among the many key discussions in this text are the systematic oppression black women live under from the Combahee River Collective and the difficulties presented by black male patriarchy from Michele Wallace. In addition to these foundational pieces, students also learn about the severe and brutal impact of racism and sexism on black women's lives. Students are likewise given resources that *Brave* readers need to further their studies in black women's critical theory. Besides *Brave*, some students may also have an opportunity to engage in black women's studies via Beverly Guy-Sheftall's (1995) anthology *Words of Fire*. Offering a historical overview of black women writing from an offensive rather than defensive position, *Words of Fire* offers students a clear and accessible entry point into black women's historical resistance and unbridled brilliance. Guy Sheftall's (1995) collection is organized topically around issues related to womanhood, feminism, and the challenges of working in the academy. The fifth section of the book, titled "The Body Politic: Sexuality, Violence, and Reproduction," introduces readers to personal/close bodily concerns[10] that some black women face, like intimate partner violence (IPV) and HIV-AIDS. It is not until the reader gets to June Jordan's (1995) essay "A New Sexual Politics" that they encounter an interpretation of black women's sexuality that marks—for that particular time—something new.

Jordan begins her essay by pushing back against the advice of a well-known child expert, Dr. Benjamin Spock. According to Jordan (1995), Spock's *A Common Sense Book of Baby and Child Care* warns nursing mothers not to "wear miniskirts or other provocative clothing because that will upset your child, especially if your child happens to be a boy" (407). Jordan (1995) talks about how she initially followed Spock's advice by dressing in "lusterless colors and dowdy tops and bottoms, self-consciously hoping thereby to prove myself as a lusterless and dowdy and, therefore, excellent female parent" (407). Years later, however, Jordan (1995) recognizes this advice as a masquerade for the oppressive and disciplining nature of patriarchal power and terms this the "politics of sexuality." Unlike many traditional black feminist scholars, Jordan (1995) points to the repression of sexuality as the fundamental "oppression," or in her words, as "the most ancient and probably the most profound area for human conflict" (407). Jordon continues:

> Increasingly, it seems clear to me that deeper [sic] and more pervasive than any other oppression, than any other bitterly contested human domain, is the oppression of sexuality, the exploitation of the human domain of sexuality for power.
>
> *(1995, 407)*

In making this bold claim, Jordan (1995) disturbs the apple cart of intersectional analysis. By this I mean that she calls for an extension of gender analysis to include a discussion of sexuality as a site of oppression and domination. Further, Jordan (1995) opens a space for exploration not only of the sexual repression and sexual shaming that women experience under men, but also the heteropatriarchy that accompanies the disciplining of gays and lesbians as well as the marginalization that bisexual people experience due to the privileging of the homo-hetero binary that excludes other sexual and gender expressions. Jordon (1995), hesitantly yet boldly (contradiction noted) comes out of the closet in the following way:

> I am black and I am female and I am a mother and I am bisexual and I am a nationalist and I am an antinationalist. And I mean to be fully and freely all that I am.
>
> *(408)*

Although Jordan's essay veers to a discussion where she rejects the notion that "it is blasphemous to compare oppressions of sexuality to oppressions of race and ethnicity," the text's embedded appeal to carefully consider sexuality (free, healthy, *explorative*[11] sexuality) provides readers with an opportunity to conceptualize black women's sexuality in a way that is different to the traditional structuring of black women's sexuality as only being exploited by others. Using Jordan's liberatory piece as a roadmap, I want to think creatively not only about how educators might present a side of black women's sexuality that transcends discussions about exploitation qua exploitation and black women's bodies as the site of difference. This does not mean that educators should not still teach about black women's bodily exploitation in all its myriad forms. What it does mean is that there is much more to the story than controlling images, black women as breeders, and the commodification of black women's wombs. We need to add breadth and complexity to the narrative.

BDSM and the Complexities of Race

BDSM is a form of interpersonal and physical engagement that involves careful negotiation by consenting adults. Scholars like Kostas Tomazos (2017) offer a broad definition of BDSM as: "a group of behaviours and lifestyle practices that include a variety of fetishes, role-playing, and other nonmainstream activities."[12] Some activities associated with BDSM include:

- Bondage: restraining with ropes, belts, other material; can also include suspension;
- CBT: cock and ball torture; restraining of male genitals;
- Flogging: refers to play involving devices used to strike usually fleshy parts on the body;
- Master/Slave: exchange of power between consenting adults.

When done correctly, those engaged in a consensual BDSM relationship agree to the following:

- relationship's power dynamics (dominance/submission);
- consent to the use of pain or punishment for the erotic pleasure of both;
- a clear negotiation of the boundaries of engagement.

With the rise in popularity of such books like *Fifty Shades of Grey*, BDSM practices have gone "mainstream."[13] For those who are not familiar with the franchise, *Fifty Shades of Grey* is the first book in a trilogy about a young woman named Anastasia (Ana) who has a relationship with a young, wealthy businessman named Christian Grey. Christian Grey introduces Ana to BDSM culture. Given the popularity of the book, we should not be surprised about conversations related to intimate partner violence (IPV), pornography, feminism, and the domination of young women by older men. Yet, we should take note of the fact that the book *Fifty Shades of Grey* and related movies created a public space for, I would argue, mainly white women to think and daydream out loud about the attractiveness of sexuality *beyond* the border of heterosexual normativity. The popularity of the novel and film is indisputable. As reported by *Variety*: "James' "Fifty Shades" trilogy has sold (sic) 125 million copies worldwide, and the movie based on the first book has grossed more than $500 million at the global box office."[14] If nothing else, these strong numbers are a public show, if not of the mainly white female audience support for BDSM, then at the very least their interest in this form of outsider sexual engagement particularly when there is a strong romantic component. And beyond purchasing the book and supporting the film, there is also circumstantial evidence to show that more Americans were engaging in border sexual activities after publication of the novel.[15]

Though thoroughly sexually engaging for some, the book and movie *Fifty Shades of Gray* cannot avoid the absence of people of color in the narrative. Professor Moon Charania (2016) makes a compelling argument for the unspoken whiteness of *Fifty Shades* pointing out not only the dearth of non-white people in the narrative but also "whiteness, as a key demonstrative site of power"[16] embodied in the antagonist Christian Grey. Charania (2016) writes, "certainly Grey plays out the fantasy of the 'great white man': he is handsome, wealthy, powerful, well-spoken, appears self-made."[17] In addition to these characteristics, Grey's character has a will to power that seeks conquest and submission in his professional and personal life. Unlike some white women fans of Christian Grey who may read his body as dangerously alluring, due to Christian Grey's embodiment as white-male-wealthy (a formidable historical triumvirate) and his overt enactment of white male power, *black* women may, however, be more reticent of engaging with his character because of the history of white male appropriation and sexual torture of black women's bodies. For example, Danielle L. McGuire's (2011) *At the End of the Street* recounts the story of 24-year-old Recy Taylor who was abducted and raped by six white men in Abbeville, Alabama in 1944. To put a finer point on the sexual violence black women faced at the hands of white men—violence that is ignored and simply erased from K-20 textbooks on American history—it is worth quoting McGuire in full:

> The rape of black women by white men continued, often unpunished, throughout the Jim Crow era. As Reconstruction collapsed and Jim Crow arose, white men abducted and assaulted black women with alarming regularity. White men lured black women and girls away from home with promises of steady work and better wages; attacked them on the job; abducted them at gunpoint while traveling to or from home, work, or church; raped them as a form of retribution or to enforce rules of racial and economic hierarchy; sexually humiliated and assaulted them on streetcars and buses, taxicabs and trains, in other public spaces. As the acclaimed freedom fighter Fannie Lou Hamer put it, "A black woman's body was never hers alone."[18]

As an aside, there is much discussion on the topic of racial fear. Oftentimes, this discussion centers on white society's fear of black men and more recently, black men's fear of random confrontations with white society that may lead to their death. What we need more of is discussion and research about black women's fear of white men—for some black women, white men are the personification of their worst nightmare. Turning back to the novel *Fifty Shades of Grey*, black women may also have a challenging time seeing themselves in Ana's character for reasons like not being down with *willingly* letting someone 'whoop your ass with belt', restrain you, or control your behavior. As has already been alluded to, other reasons are more complex and have to do, of course, with race, the genealogies of submission, respectability politics, and the historical white fetish with black flesh and the violence which typically accompanied it. For black women, being an active participant in sexual domination—particularly with a non-black partner—runs contrary to history *and* to home training.

Nevertheless, there may be black women who *are* in fact attracted to both Christian Grey, the danger his body presents, and to the practice of BDSM. On some level, there is a discussion to be had here about the science of attraction and arousal that I am not fully equipped to engage in, yet what I am prepared to complicate is our (in)ability as black and as women to separate what is personally attractive and arousing from what is historically painful. This to me is what makes introducing topics like BDSM in black women's studies so interesting, disruptive, and expansive of the discourse. I would like to submit that further developing the field of black women and deviant studies is a *creative* way of introducing topics in our classrooms about interracial dating between black women and white men, attraction between different races, and out-marriage. On the topic of out-marriage, the 2015 study "Interracial Marriage: Who is Marrying Out"[19] states:

> Among blacks, men are much more likely than women to marry someone of a different race. Fully a quarter of black men who got married in 2013 married someone who was not black. Only 12% of black women married outside of their race.

The vast differences in these percentages have to do with the complexities of gender and gender inequality; black men having more dating option and less stigma associated with dating someone who is not black; black women being perceived as unattractive by men of multiple races. From these various discussions, a skillful professor can circle back to BDSM and the novel *Fifty Shades of Grey* to relate to the students how even if black women desire to engage in what we might consider deviant sexual expression, *history is ever present*—past, present, and future literally collide the choices that black women make/don't make about our sexual engagement. Nevertheless, the fight for space within kink reveals a potential other area from which to evaluate the long "arc of the moral universe" where our understanding of rights and justice are inextricably linked to sexual choice and the freedom of sexual expression for all. For adventurous black women who fight for space specifically within kink culture as they seek to create "Ana" in their own images; and adventurous professors who are interested in expanding the canon of black feminist studies to include deviance sexual expression as form of agency, the challenges are considerable.

Eggplant: BDSM, Agency, Black Pleasure, Black Pain

In her article "When You Want to be into BDSM but it's too soon because you're black," Luna Malbroux (2016) writes:

> I don't remember a time when I didn't have fantasies about being domi-
> nated. I would imagine someone gripping my hair tightly or a sting-
> ing slap on my ass—all very exciting. But every time I would let my
> thoughts run wild, they would get rudely interrupted, like an angry
> grandmother unplugging the cord while you're sneakily watching
> TV after 2 a.m., yelling "Turn this OFF!" As soon as my brain camera
> spanned to any props—whips, chains, that sort of thing—all I could
> think about was Roots.[20]

Malbroux's (2016) words are playful and poignant. In some way, they may even be interpreted as filled with longing to be free of history; yet the fact of black-ness is that it can never be ahistorical. In my estimation, Malbroux (2016) also highlights the difficulties that BDSM, kink, and other still non-normative forms of sexual engagement present to black women. In movies like *Roots* where the chains binding black bodies, it seems, are characters themselves it is not difficult to understand why such depictions of black bodies—no criticism here of these depictions being incorrect or insensitive—would be triggering to all black peo-ple. Primarily because chains are powerful figures of black involuntary submis-sion; they are the symbol of our oppression and figure prominently throughout our collective imagination via prisons, songs with lyrics like "that's the sound of the man working on the chain gang"; and organizations that use the word "chain" to signal continued subjugation at the hands of the carceral state;[21] chains equals psychic trauma. In a sense, Malbroux (2016) does not have the freedom to disassociate, decouple, or detach objects from their historical signification dur-ing BDSM. White people are perhaps freer to give themselves over to be fully engaged; they are free to experience the chain as *an instrument of pleasure*. Adding to the sense of danger for many black women who are interested in kink is the problematic interaction with white practitioners of BDSM. These interactions can be slippages of the language that form the lexicon of the BDSM community. Words such as master/slave simply do not have—though they should—the same emotional, historical, or cultural impact on whites that they do on blacks who engage in BDSM. In her article, Malbroux (2016) relates the emotional and com-pelling story of the white man who was game with introducing her to BDSM. Malbroux and her partner follow the protocol of creating a safe word that would end the contact if she (since Malbroux was in this case playing the submissive) felt uncomfortable—their word was "eggplant." She explains how at first things were going very well until her partner said, "Call me *master*" (italics mine). Malbroux (2016) continued:

Eggplant.[22] That hurt. Immediately, all I could think about was my ancestors rolling over in their graves, breaking out like the zombies in Michael Jackson's Thriller video. All my worst fears had come alive. I thought of Harriet Tubman admonishing me: "19 times! 19 times I came back, to save our people from slavery. All for you to be here willy-nilly, calling some white dude 'master'?" Life tip: No dick is so good that it's worth being haunted by Harriet Tubman.

Malbroux (2016) goes on to explain that her partner was very open to the correction she offered. Nevertheless, words like master/slave hold real psychological and flesh level feeling for black people. In this case, Malbroux and other black women, to be sure, cannot help but recall the history of black women's sexual exploitation at the hands of white men. It is very difficult for black people to de-historicize the words master and slave. It could certainly be argued that black women engaged in BDSM, particularly with white partners that other words could be used as substitutes such as top/bottom or dominant/submissive. But, these words do not take one out of the dynamics of the situation of control that harken back to enslavement (particularly if the black person is the bottom or submissive). There is nothing that subverts the hierarchy of submission and violence between black and white; *there is simply no outside of the hegemony of history.* Replaying Malbroux's (2016) interaction with her white male partner, there is nothing about the language—master/slave—nothing about the instruments—chains—that pull him back into himself that makes him recall history. In fact, if it were not for Malbroux (2016), he seemingly would have continued as if nothing happened. The lack of awareness about how race, history, and language are intertwined in the lives of people living in the US is an essential trait of whiteness. Malbroux's (2016) fantasies about domination in a deep, existential sense are always already fraught. She is never *not* self-aware.

Pushing our exploration further into the realm of language, making black women's involvement in BDSM culture, specifically with white men, more treacherous is *race play* which is a subset of the BDSM culture. *Race play* refers to engaging in role-play with a specific emphasis on race, such that race becomes the focal point and is related to the sensual pleasure of one or both partners. *Race play* can be extreme where it can include using demeaning racial stereotypes and words such as a white partner referring to a black partner as "nigger." The use of this word acts as a turn on for both parties. It is important to note that during all forms of BDSM, sex may not even occur as language, the exchange of power, the ability to become another character is what stimulates participants. Feminsta Jones (2013) adds another level complexity to our discussion of *race play's* popularity, for example, when she explains that in the adult entertainment industry: "There are even scenes with White men wearing confederate flag attire having sex with Black women."[23] Somewhere someone may be thinking—"Jesus take the wheel."

Agency and the Black Female Subject

In her groundbreaking text *The Color of Kink: Black Women, BDSM, and Pornography*, Ariana Cruz (2016) interviews a cross-section of people working in the adult entertainment industry. Her work explores black women's experiences in the industry for the purpose of reformulating how we think about black women's sexuality and violence. In a review of Cruz's book, Roach (2017) writes the following:

> To conceptualize the relationship between black female sexuality and violence, Cruz proposes that we engage representations and performances of black female sexuality *perversely*. That is, rather than approaching representations and performances of black female sexuality from an androcentric standpoint presuming pornography and BDSM as sites of racialized sexual trauma and black women as unwitting participants in their own sexual objectification, critics should query the ways that black women practitioners and spectators apprehend pornography and BDSM as potentially radical sites of pleasure, power, and self-making.[24]

One of the most intriguing parts of the book happens when Cruz (2016) explains how "racism" is not simply "eroticized" but may also be seen as "a vibrantly imagined racial difference in which the color line between black and white is *played* with—constantly smudged, re-delineated, and traversed. Performances of racial-sexual alterity are therefore essential in race play."[25] Cruz's (2016) point is that *racial role play* cannot escape "narratives of racialized sexual violence," nevertheless, this does not preclude the possibility of walking extreme forms of BDSM into our classrooms and analyzing these forms not only as *texts* helping to elucidate the complex sexual history between blacks and whites; but also as a pedagogical *tool* to extend black women's agency. If I taught about *racial role play* in black women's studies, one question I would ask students to consider is "how might racial role play generate a space to think not only about how the antebellum south continues to overcloud the American imagination but also how we might conceptualize *racial role play* as a movement toward black women's liberation?" While I understand that linking *racial role play* to agency might seem strange to more traditional black feminist educators, I now would like to draw from my previous work on black women and agency to make the case for what I describe as *the three principle intersecting makers of agency* and how *racial role play* is, in fact, not antithetical to agency.

In my book *Black Women, Agency, and the New Black Feminism*, I argue that the first marker of agency is having the ability to *choose*. Thus, the distinction between the human agent and the non-human actor resides in the ability to be led by deliberation rather than instinct or ignorance, it is the ability to determine oneself rather than be determined by another. Being an agent, in the simplest terms, means that one has the *capacity* to choose *to do* or *not to do* something. The second marker of agency is *rationality*. To be an agent means that our choices are guided by rationality. Thus, "Rational actors always act out of a well-defined interest in their own personal welfare."[26] Rational actors are clear about their desires and have what it takes to achieve an end goal. This view of agency is significant because it understands agency as based on ability—meaning the *ability* to think in a rational way and the *ability* to use rational thoughts to one's own advantage. The final marker of agency is having one's agency recognized by others.

As a result, black women engaging in forms of *racial role play*—whether they are submissive or dominant—should be viewed as agents because they are engaging in the activity of their own freewill; they are *choosing* to be there. In playing slaves, mistresses, or engaging in *racial role play* however they see fit might be construed as a way of re-writing, re-narrating, or re-figuring history. Even if it is a history that we disagree with, I don't think that we can deny the power, intentionality, and choice embedded in either re-conceptualizing the black female body or the play which will emerge from troubling these racio-sexual-historical waters brought on by engaging in *racial role play*. Second, engaging in *racial role play* based on the freedom to choose also shows *rational* action. Black women who participate in this extreme form of BDSM do so understanding the historical underpinnings of such play; and have chosen nevertheless to participate. As such, they are engaging in what we might see as a suspension of disbelief which makes the act of *racial role play* no different from watching a fantasy or horror movie. As rational beings, black women who engage in *racial role play* can distinguish between fact and fiction; and, like a good actress they are playing a role. Finally, the *racial role play* is agential because the black woman and her partner have agreed on the parameters. In this way, her partner *recognizes* her agency and her ability to end the play at any point she feels uncomfortable. Since a submissive may end play using a *safe word* this ability alone challenges us to rethink elements of power in *racial role play* as under enslavement, black women were *not* recognized as agents and thus did not have the ability to say "no." It should be noted that not all *racial role play* scenarios involve black women as submissive. Some also involve black women dominating white men. In such cases, history is again disrupted allowing black women the ability to exhibit power over white men. Nevertheless, I certainly understand a reluctance on the part of students and educators to push these boundaries without a clear and rigorous interpretative lens from which to analyze such action. In the next section, I suggest disidentification as a robust theoretical framework that will allow us to better contextualize and understand black women who play at the margins of sex and sexual identity.

Dis-i-dent-If-i-cation

There are few theorists better at troubling normative and binary thinking and saying "yes" to questions and actions that many read as disturbing like Jose

Estaban Munoz. Munoz, I believe, offers a developed picture of disidentification as he focuses not only on gender but also on race. Munoz's examination of disidentification attempts to trouble the fixedness of identity as well as the way that social scripts overlay the body imbuing it with signification that restricts its functionality and freedom. This reading of Munoz calls to mind the way that stereotypes function. To stereotype another is to draw upon simple and often misleading perceptions that we use to paint an incomplete picture. We use stereotypes for our own convenience and for expedience since they provide a way to quickly form an opinion and response to those we deem as different. Sartre's (1946) *Anti-Semite and Jew*, for example, is as much about stereotype as it is about trying to discern the actions of those who engage in irrational racial hatred. Take for instance Sartre's account of the woman who is upset because her fur was ruined and then states "Well, they (the people who handled her fur) are all Jews." Sartre (1946) rightly asks "But why did she choose to hate Jews rather than furriers Why Jews or furriers rather than such and such a Jew or such and such a furrier" (273)?[27] In this example, we see how this woman falls back on a simple, misguided, and potentially dangerous stereotype of Jewish people. And since she is part of the majority, her perceptions about Jewish bodies have real implications for how Jewish people are treated or mistreated within society. Returning to Munoz, thus, disidentification is crucial because it allows not only another avenue to theorize the multiple pressures that marginalized bodies are subjected to but also a way to resist such marginalization by creating spaces (greyness) and pockets for new oppositional identities to form—identities that defy stereotypes and signification. Andrew Huston's (2015) work speaks to the functionality and usefulness of disidentification for marginalized identities when he sees identity formation as a "process that takes place at the point of collision … this collision is precisely the moment of negotiation when hybrid, racially predicated, and defiantly gendered identities arrive at representation."[28] In this way, disidentification is Foucaultian in that it allows for resistance to the creation of docile bodies, and it accomplishes this pushback by way of rhetoric or the force of language.

In his work, Munoz shows that terms like queer and hybrid constitute a type of rhetorical force that can be used to resist powers bent on determining bodies as marginal and non-normative. Consequently, whereas the queer body can be read (and is often read) as a place that invites violence due to its inability to orient the spectator because it does not fit neatly into a binary gender role, disidentification via rhetoric reclaims queerness as a site of radical possibility *precisely because it does not fit into binary gender roles*; its greyness functions as a form of strength and resistance and this opens up real and diverse ways of *being queer-in-the-world*. As previously mentioned, disidentification creates a space of wonder, creativity, and agency that can happen in the greys or that area created when binaries collide. In celebration of queerness as a form of hybridity, Munoz writes:

> Hybridity helps one understand how queer lives are fragmented into vari-
> ous identity bits: some of them adjacent, some of them complementary,
> some of them antagonistic. The hybrid—and terms that can be roughly
> theorized as equivalents, such as the Creole or the mestizo—are paradigms
> that help account for the complexities and impossibilities of identity, but,
> except a certain degree of dependence on institutional frames, what a sub-
> ject can do from her or his position of hybridity is, basically, open-ended.[29]
>
> *(79)*

"Queer lives" are not the only ones "fragmented into various identity bits." So
too, as I have attempted to show, are the identities of younger black women
caught between bodily pleasure and historical pain. Examples include being stim-
ulated (sexually, mentally) by the (white) male gaze of *racial role play* while at the
same time being objectified by it. Or, being comforted by patriarchal power that
can be found within kink culture, while at the same time it limits your potential. How do black women understand embracing womanist principles of loving
other women—including sexually—yet find themselves attracted to *racial role play*
where they willingly subject themselves to racial epithets?

In order to answer to such questions, we might begin by situating our analysis
into a discussion about the kinds of pleasure that black women can experience.
Speaking about black gay men as consumers of images created to commodify
them yet at the same time finding pleasure in such images, Munoz writes:

> Is a disidentificatory pleasure, one that acknowledges what is disturbing
> about the familiar practices of black male objectification that Mapplethorpe
> participated in, while at the same time it understands that this pleasure can-
> not easily be dismissed even though it is politically dangerous.
>
> *(71)*

Disidentification allows us to *recognize* and *own* the sensations and yes, the pleas-
ures that we feel in situations that our critical frameworks call us to disavow.
Munoz is correct when he argues that it is "politically dangerous" to embrace
pleasure that is out of bounds because it can be argued that we place our theory,
perhaps even our liberation, in jeopardy if we find or acknowledge pleasure in
what is simultaneously read as painful and dehumanizing. But to *not* recognize
the sometimes-twin feelings/sensations that accompany forms of objectification,
I think, limits the creative power of our theory by making it one dimensional, and
even essentialist. Munoz continues:

> Like melancholia, disidentification is an ambivalent structure of feeling that
> works to retain the problematic object and tap into the energies that are
> produced by contradictions and ambivalences.
>
> *(71)*

Through the lens of disidentification, we might be able to see how black women purposefully engaging in *racial role play* and consuming images of *racial role play* perhaps experience "a powerful validation" (71) of their bodies. I know it may sound contradictory, but there is static potential in this space. As educators and students—and those of us who are directly implicated by such meaning making—perhaps we can look at this textual play on a visceral/lived experience level and utter "freedom." We cannot and should not be blind to this radical reimagining of BDSM or border sexual experiences as a *non-thing*, nor should we deny ourselves the feeling of pleasure we too might receive by consuming such images. Munoz explains this radical reimaging or "making over" rather eloquently, writing:

> The object that is desired is reformatted so that dignity and grace are not eclipsed by racist exploitation. Disidentification is this "making over"; it is the way a subject looks at an image that has been constructed to exploit and deny identity and instead finds pleasure, both erotic and self-affirming.
> *(72)*

Designing a Deviant Curriculum

Early in this chapter, I mentioned some standard curricula that introduces students to black women's history and critical thought. Such material is important because students need to be introduced to, understand, and ultimately grapple with the history of violence that has impacted and continues to impact black women's bodies. When this history of violence is not learned, students are given an incomplete rendering of black oppression and its twin white terrorism. More troublesome, those students who do not have a complete picture of black women's violent treatment at the hands of white society may not be fully able to critically assess knowledge gaps in white feminist curriculum or even their own programs of study, for example. As the director of a women's and gender studies program, I can attest to this concern. I recently taught a course on contemporary feminism where my white students had a general sense of enslavement as destructive and immoral. They understood what I would call the contours of enslavement, but they lacked any understanding of enslavement as having real impact on the flesh of the enslaved. Consequently, it was critical to me that they were exposed to enslavement at the level of the flesh. This meant reading about the rape of black women, white women's participation in the torture of black women, and medical procedures performed on un-sedated or un-medicated black women.

Alternately—yet not contradictorily—I am also dismayed when students only see black women as survivors of violence and oppression and the "strength" with which black women can endure all kinds of atrocities. In the same course, I spent a great deal of time disrupting the image of the strong black woman. I remember students (black and white) being surprised and mildly disturbed to read bell hook's

(2002) assertion that strength in the face of brutality is not a path to liberation; rather it may supply justification for those around you to heap even more burden on you because you can *bear it*. The notion of black women as natural and resigned bearers of suffering is a false narrative. If professors are not careful we may well contribute to furthering a myth which, I believe, helps to sustain black women's oppression. While I am not arguing that we should replace such material, even the material that reifies black women's existence—these readings can provide opportunities for robust dialogue—I am suggesting that we need to expand how we teach black women's history and critical thought to include the complexity of their lived experiences beyond foundational curriculum focused on either white terrorism or black women's strength. This complexity includes the way that black women experience joy as well as physical and emotional love and closeness with others. Therefore, I am a strong proponent for introducing, for example, bell hook's (2002) work on love and affirmation[30] and novels like Toni Morrison's (2003) *Love*, which is a haunting story that illustrates *Philia* and *Eros* and the impact of the disruption of all forms of love on black girls and women. Teaching our students about black women in loving relationships and the ways that black women affirm themselves and other black women is a pedagogical practice rooted in Mariana Ortega's (2016) understanding of the "multiplicious self" where the self is layered and produced by several interconnected experiences.[31] To think of the black female self in terms of its multiplicity calls scholars to rethink how we design curriculum around black women's being-in-the-world. The point is to present students not only with a different picture of black women's experiences but also one less polar, dichotomous, and marred in pain. In addition to including the broad topic of black women and love into curriculum designed to explicate black women's experience, I want to now make a case for inclusion of what I call the edges of black women's sexuality into black women's studies.

Black women with "sadomasochistic souls"[32] have quite a bit to offer black women's studies. They introduce new ways to understand the different experiences and conflicting realities that black women because of their humanness—inhabit. Black women engaging in BDSM, particularly *racial role play*, gives black women professors an opportunity to create impactful curriculum in the vibrant field of sexuality studies; a field that oftentimes renders blackness invisible. If black women academicians are not purposeful in leading the way by designing historically rooted, critical, and engaged curriculum about black women in the space of sexuality studies; others will. And, that is a frightening proposition.

Notes

1 Lisa Blackman (2008) *The Body: Key Concepts*, 1. Oxford: Berg.
2 Sander L. Gilman "Black Bodies, White Bodies: Toward a Iconography of Female Sexuality in Late Nineteenth-Century Art, Medicine, and Literature," in Henry Louis Gates, ed., *"Race", Writing, and Difference*. Chicago: University of Chicago Press, pp. 223–261.

3 For a detailed discussion of Sara Baartman, see Janell Hobson's (2005) *Venus in the Dark: Blackness and Beauty in Popular Culture*. New York, NY: Routledge.

4 Janell Hobson (2005) *Venus in the Dark: Blackness and Beauty in Popular* Culture, p. 37. New York: Routledge.

5 For a detailed discussion of the photographing of black women's bodies from colonialism through the present see Deborah Willis and Carla Williams (2002), *The Black Female Body: A Photographic History*. Philadelphia, PA: Temple University Press.

6 Maria del Guadalupe Davidson (2016) "Black silhouettes on white walls: Kara Walker's magic lantern," in *Body Aesthetics*, ed. Sherri Irvin, Oxford: Oxford University Press.

7 The exploitation of black women's intellectual capacity can be seen in such films as *The Help* where the white protagonist exploits the lived experiences of the black maids to further her own career; while we see the black women's intellectual capacity exploited in films like *Hidden Figures* where it literally took a group of black women to show NASA how to get to the moon. As the film shows, for years the black women who worked on the space project were given no public credit.

8 The language of "thinking together" comes from Latina feminist philosopher Mariana Ortega.

9 According to Sandra LaMorgese (2017) the term *kink* means "enhancing sexual intimacy with your partner by adding new and creative elements of sex" see "The One Key Difference Between Kinky and Having a Fetish" http://www.huffingtonpost.com/sandra-lamorgese-phd/difference-between-kinky-and-fetish_b_9709874.html.

10 I understand that the personal is political, nevertheless some events that happen in our personal lives are shielded from public viewership; they are private.

11 Emphasis added.

12 Kostas Tomazos, Kevin O'Gorman, and Andrew C. MacLaren (2017) "From leisure to tourism: How BDSM Demonstrates the Transition of Deviant Pursuits to Mainstream Products," *Tourism Management* 60: 32.

13 Kostas Tomazos, Kevin O'Gorman, and Andrew C. MacLaren (2017) "From leisure to tourism: How BDSM Demonstrates the Transition of Deviant Pursuits to Mainstream Products," *Tourism Management* 60: 31.

14 Alex Stedman (2015) "Fifty Shades' Spinoff 'Grey' Copy Reportedly Stolen from Publisher" http://variety.com/2015/biz/news/fifty-shades-spinoff-grey-stolen-from-publisher-1201516843/

15 See Christian Ingraham's (2015) "Sex Toy Injuries Surged after *Fifty Shades of Grey* was Published," *Washington Post*. Retrieved from https://www.washingtonpost.com/news/wonk/wp/2015/02/10/sex-toy-injuries-surged-after-fifty-shades-of-grey-was-published/?utm_term=.b3ea8fbe3e89

16 Moon Charania (2016) "The Promise of Whiteness: *Fifty Shades of Grey* as White Racial Archive," *Intensities: The Journal of Cult Media*, 8: 77.

17 Moon Charania (2016) "The Promise of Whiteness: *Fifty Shades of Grey* as White Racial Archive," *Intensities, The Journal of Cult Media*. 8: 78.

18 Danielle L. McGuire (2011) *At the Dark End of the Street: Black Women, Rape, and Resistance—A New History of the Civil Rights Movement from Rosa Parks to the Rise of Black Power*, xviii. New York, NY: Knopf.

19 Wendy Wang (2015) "Interracial marriage: Who is 'marrying out'?," Pew Research Center, Retrieved from http://www.pewresearch.org/fact-tank/2015/06/12/interracial-marriage-who-is-marrying-out/

20 Luna Malbroux (2016) "When you want to be into BDSM but it's too soon because you're black," Fusion. Retrieved from http://fusion.net/story/281403/bdsm-while-black/

21 Shout out to the work done by Deborah Small and her organization *Break the Chains.*

22 Eggplant was their safe word. Members of the BDSM community are encouraged to use safe words to communicate their discomfort in situations. Upon the use of the safe word, all activity should stop.

23 Feminista Jones (2013) "Race place ain't for everyone," *Ebony*. Retrieved from http://www.ebony.com/love-sex/talk-like-sex-race-play-aint-for-everyone-911 #ixzz4cZ1W6TG9

24 Shoniqua Roach (2017) Book review, *Women & Performance: A Journal of Feminist Theory*, 0.0. Retrieved from http://www.tandfonline.com/doi/full/10.1080/07407 70X.2017.1315241

25 Ariane Cruz (2016) *The Color of Kink: Black Women, BDSM, and Pornography*, 50, New York, NY: New York University Press.

26 Stephan Fuchs (2007) "Agency (and Intention)." *Blackwell Encyclopedia of Sociology*. Ritzer, George (ed). Blackwell Publishing, Blackwell Reference Online. 18 May 2011. Retrieved from http://www.blackwellreference.com/subscriber/tocnode?id=g9781405124331_chunk_g97814051243317_ss1-24.

27 Sartre, Jean-Paul. *Anti-Semite and Jew: The Exploration of the Etiology of Hate*. Translated by George J. Becker. Schocken Books: New York, 1948.

28 Andrew Huston (2015) "Dis-ing the Main Drag and Walking Toward the Public Good in *Here Be Dragons* Mapping Queer, Asian-Canadian Identity in Kitchener, Ontario, "*Theater Research in* Canada, 36: 282.

29 Munoz, Jose Esteban. *Disidenfitications: Queers of Color and the Performance of Politics*. University of Minnesota Press: Minneapolis, 1999.

30 See bell hooks (2002), *All about Love, Salvation: Black People and Love, and Communion: The Female Search for Love*. New York, NY: William Morrow Paperback.

31 See Mariana Ortega (2016) *In-Between: Latina Phenomenology, Multiplicity, and the Self*. New York, NY: SUNY Press.

32 Ariane Cruz (2015) "Beyond Black and Blue: BDSM, Internet Pornography, and Black Female Sexuality," *Feminist Studies*, 41(2): 410.

7

TRANSGRESSING CURRICULUM BOUNDARIES

Nichole Guillory

A substantial body of literature exists documenting a disconnect between campus and field-based teacher education as well as calls for strengthening university-school partnerships as a way to address the divide between theory and practice (Cochran-Smith and Lytle, 1999; Darling-Hammond et al., 2005; Featherstone, 2007; Zeichner, 1995). The literature on school and university collaborations, especially in *School-University Partnerships*, the journal published by the National Association for Professional Development Schools, is replete with success stories of how university faculty and their school partners create improved programs to prepare pre-service teachers. Not enough has been done to examine the messy, complicated work of collaboration or challenge what it means to work across institutional boundaries. Building on hooks' notion (1994) of "teaching to transgress" which she says allows for "movement against and beyond boundaries" (p. 12), this paper problematizes Zeichner's (2010) work that examines newly created teacher education programs that more closely align campus courses and field experiences in schools through a "non-hierarchical interplay between academic and practitioner expertise" (p. 89).

Zeichner (2010) maintains that academic knowledge has traditionally been valued over practitioner knowledge in teacher education programs resulting in a disconnect between course work and field work that detrimentally impacts the effectiveness of teacher preparation. Drawing on Bhabha's notion (2004) of third spaces, which he conceptualizes within the discourse of hybridity theory and its rejection of binaries, Zeichner(2010) calls for the creation of third spaces that "involve an equal and more dialectical relationship between academic and practitioner knowledge in support of student teacher learning" (p. 92). Collaborations in this space, according to Zeichner (2010), require "shifting the epistemology" of "pre-service teacher preparation programs" so that academic knowledge and practitioner knowledge are "treated with equal respect" (p. 93). Zeichner's model with its emphasis on "equal relationship" suggests that third spaces are apolitical and ahistorical boundary crossings, which I maintain is a limitation of his conception of third spaces as they relate to university-school partnerships. The teacher education programs Zeichner (2010) features are all "success stories" of school-university partnerships in which teachers and university faculty come together in the third spaces in what he terms "synergistic ways" to support student teacher learning (p. 93). His model of the third space as apolitical and ahistorical does not address the inherent challenges of working across difference and across institutional contexts, specifically the ways in which power and privilege affect collaborations between school and university faculty.

Collaborations with school-based faculty raises myriad questions for me as a co-teacher and co-researcher: As we work across school and university boundaries, how do we define the space of collaboration and ourselves in it? In what ways does our collaborative teaching and research transgress existing hierarchical boundaries between university professors and public school teachers? How do we define curriculum and how do we determine whose knowledge counts as we create curriculum? In what ways do our respective institutional contexts support or hinder our collaborative transgressing? My narratives—crafted from teaching journals, course materials, transcripts of classes, and interviews with our high school faculty co-instructors—detail my attempts to answer these questions. These narratives present only partial understandings of the complex nature of collaborations between university and school faculty, and while I explain the ways in which my students and I are positively impacted by working with our school colleagues, my narratives also reflect questions, dissonances, and struggle. So, while I will reflect on the successes of collaborating with school partners across institutional boundaries, I will also expose the ways in which our collaborative work reproduces traditional epistemological hierarchies in teacher education. I intend to complicate how we define our research and teaching and how we negotiate tensions across institutional boundaries within hybrid spaces of collaboration between universities and schools.

Blurring Boundaries

I have always been drawn to working in schools with complicated histories. Arbor Heights High School was labeled "urban/at-risk/inner city"—the politically acceptable code language for an all-black school, and I named it as my first choice for a student teaching placement. I chose to go there for purely selfish reasons: I thought if I was successful there, it would increase my chances of getting a teaching job after graduation. An institution different from the mostly white, privileged, Catholic schooling with which I was familiar, Arbor Heights was a training ground every student teacher in my cohort avoided. A well-publicized murder of a high school student there the previous year and a well-known, mostly media-generated, reputation in the community as a low-achieving educational institution frightened most away. Because of my experiences at Arbor Heights, a school with fewer resources compared to others in the district, I began to shape my teaching philosophy around a commitment to teaching for educational justice. So when I was asked in fall 2009 to work as a university liaison in Woodland Hills High School, a school with a reputation in the community as "underperforming" and as having "urban school issues" even though it is suburban and shown student performance growth over time, I was eager for the opportunity. While the school has been a place too many have tried in the past to avoid for various complicated reasons, I have always felt at home there. Teachers with whom I work at the school share my commitment to improving the preparation of teachers for schools in urban communities.

Woodland Hills High School is located on the geographic margins—literally speaking—of the larger suburban school district in an unincorporated area of the county. In a district that includes some of the highest performing high schools in the state of Georgia, this school, in contrast, was a "Needs Improvement" (NI) school for not meeting "Adequate Yearly Progress" (AYP) goals for seven consecutive years before the State Superintendent received a No Child Left Behind (NCLB) waiver for all public schools in Georgia, which did away with the NI status altogether. As the oldest high school in the district, it serves a student body that is 90% Black and Hispanic and working class, almost twice the percentage of Black and Hispanic students in the district, and is located in a community with very few middle-class job opportunities. Many parents who live within this school's zoned boundaries took advantage of the district's choice option that allowed them to send their children elsewhere while the school was under NI status. Overnight—literally—Woodland Hills High went from a state-directed school to being named a "Georgia Rewards School," recognition for making "significant academic progress" under the new state accountability system, a designation that administrators at the school say more accurately measures the gains in student achievement as a result of the hard work of teachers there … The numbers do not tell the story of this school, however.

I am at Woodland Hills High School every week—teaching my classes, coordinating field experiences for interns, and working with high school faculty as well as university faculty to support a new urban education concentration in existing secondary teacher education programs. I was immediately drawn to developing a foundations course that focused on urban education, culturally relevant pedagogy, and family and community engagement in partnership with Woodland Hills High School faculty. I was equally excited to co-teach the course with Jane, my Woodland Hills colleague, after we developed it together. Since 1998, I have worked in and studied the field of multicultural teacher education, so I welcomed the opportunity to broaden my experience and learn how to more effectively prepare pre-service teachers for schools in urban communities. Over the years, every pedagogical decision I have made has been for the purpose of helping pre-service teachers to examine their own histories and beliefs and interrogate underlying systems of power and privilege and their effects on public schools. This pedagogical framework guided my work with Jane as we decided on course texts, created assignments, and planned weekly activities.

On the surface, Jane and I are an unlikely pairing. She was a math teacher and I was an English teacher; Woodland Hills High School is located in a suburban community in northwest Georgia and mine in a rural community in southwest Louisiana; she studied educational leadership in graduate school and I studied social justice education; and her teaching philosophy is focused on the individual student—building relationships and developing critical thinking skills—and mine is focused on the institutional—examining power and privilege and their effects on public schools. Despite our differences, we do share a commitment to improved teacher preparation, and in the three years of teaching together, I have learned a lot from Jane about teaching and learning in general and myself as a teacher educator in particular. From the beginning, I wanted to show Jane and the students we taught that she was as much a teacher educator as I. I never wanted her to be the go-to person for practical, school-based knowledge while I remained the real "expert" on matters of educational theory.

Important to note is that we taught "Introduction to Urban Education" once a week at Woodland Hills High School, not at the university, and we structured our course such that we took advantage of the real-time school context as often as we could. For example, when the focus of the day was on "urban students," we began class with a discussion of the required reading on urban students; next we analyzed movie clips for the ways in which urban students were constructed in mainstream films; we then reviewed Woodland Hills yearbooks—past through present—noting the demographic shifts; then we arranged a question and answer session with a panel of students from the school; and when schedules aligned, we ended class by attending a student-centered event at the school like a pep rally or homecoming parade. In another example, when the focus of the day was on national data on urban schools, we had students examine Woodland Hills student data (test scores, graduation rates, attendance rates, AP enrollment, suspension rates, etc.) with comparison data at national, state, and local district levels. When we introduced students to Ladson-Billings' conception of culturally relevant pedagogy, we created and taught a model lesson for a set of standards that teachers at Woodland Hills were required to teach. Every year, Jane arranged for a variety of guest speakers from the school for question and answer sessions that connected to course readings, including teachers, administrators, instructional coaches, parent liaisons, and family and community members.

With no previous history with the school before my college established a professional development school partnership, I was able to learn so much about Woodland Hills's culture and its community from its "insiders." Important to note is that I did depend on the "insiders" to teach me about the school and its community. While I have participated in school clean-up projects and attended a number of sporting events during after-school hours, I have not become involved in the community in ways that connect me to it and its history in more authentic ways.

Jane's long-time history (25+ years) with the school and its community as resident, teacher, and now administrator was not only beneficial to our students but to me as well. She was able to fill in gaps and provide context for everything we learned about the school and its community, and she offered a current teacher's perspective on what we learned about teaching and learning in urban schools through the course. Through our teaching together, I learned how to help math and science pre-service teachers understand how to "do" culturally relevant pedagogy in their content areas. Jane helped grow my pedagogical repertoire, helping me to model instructional strategies that might be effective in any content area classroom. I like to say that because of working with Jane, I have more "street cred" as a teacher educator with my students—both pre-service and in-service teachers—because I am able to provide examples that are current and locally familiar. Most rewarding have been those instances where I have been able to "prove" to students— most often in-service teachers—that an approach to engaging students or their families was indeed possible—when they argued it was not—because I was able to point out that it was being done by my teacher colleagues at Woodland Hills.

A Complicated Context: Successes and Struggles

While working in the field has positively impacted my work as a teacher educator, I have experienced the field—in the school on the margins—as a contradictory space. A success of my collaboration is that in many ways, the school has been a liberatory space for me as a teacher educator, one in which I feel more free to experiment with curriculum that is aligned with educational justice. This kind of curricular experimentation has rarely been possible within programs at the university that are under increased standardization because of National Council for Accreditation of Teacher Education (NCATE)—now Council for the Accreditation of Educator Preparation (CAEP)—mandates. I have created a pedagogical space outside of the boundaries of the university's traditional teacher education program where I do not have to force my teaching into a lockstep curriculum with the same textbook that other instructors use for different sections of the same course, where I am not forced to collect evidence and artifacts from students only for the purpose of CAEP accreditation, where I am not forced to only focus on best practice teaching strategies in the instructional fields to improve P–12 achievement. I have been more successful in creating a more cognitively dissonant space where my students and I wrestle with questions related to privilege and its potential impact on our identities as teachers, where we understand through careful study that there are no quick fixes—or best practice recipes—to fix everything that is purportedly wrong about (urban) education, the focus of our course together. This school allows us to examine systemic inequity alongside teachers who do what is in the best interests of their students even if their efforts are not always measurable in the bottom line of the school's performance data.

Jane has helped me to become a better teacher educator and better teacher. I do not mean to suggest, however, that working with Jane at Woodland Hills has been uncomplicated. I did have experience with co-teaching prior to becoming a co-instructor with Jane, so I was familiar with planning and dividing responsibilities in advance. What was unfamiliar and complicated—and what I was unprepared for—was working across institutional boundaries to make decisions about the course and to share pedagogical space. For example, even though I included Jane in deciding which texts would become required reading for the course, I was the one to choose the larger set of books from which we ultimately selected three course texts. Even though Jane and I came to agreement on course assignments, I was the one to draft assignment guidelines first, which she later "approved." Even though we made more deliberate attempts to share pedagogical space every year we taught the course, I still remained the clear "lead" in the class. Jane contributed to class discussions of required reading, but she has never led an analysis with students. More importantly, I have never insisted that she do so.

One poignant moment that illustrates my reluctance to give up pedagogical space was a day in the course when the focus was on "urban teachers" and Jane volunteered to do a teaching interview simulation activity that I had done with students many times before. The activity is always a pivotal moment in my classes because it helps to concretize what an "asset"—rather than deficit—model perspective is; it helps students uncover hidden assumptions they have about Black boys, and helps students understand the necessity of a teacher always having high expectations for her students. I was very hesitant to "let go" of this activity, but I did not convey my reluctance to Jane in our planning meeting. There were many times I wanted to jump in as she led students through the activity, and for the most part, I did not do so. I remember that she ended the discussion with a reminder to students: "Individuals tell the story, not the numbers," and I remember feeling more comfortable with her taking lead because in that moment she was able to capture a big lesson for students that I had not thought of before. I cannot say, however, that I completely let go so that we might really share pedagogical space. In effect, I marginalized her expertise and reified the university professor/school teacher hierarchy.

While the field has been liberating in many ways as a teacher educator, it has also been a confining space for me as a tenure-track faculty member. An important struggle to note is that the work can sometimes be time-consuming, isolating, and exhausting. As is often the case for teacher educators who work at the university and in schools, I spend a lot of time on the road alone traveling to and from the school for planning meetings with my co-instructor, meetings with collaborating teachers, and evening events at the school. Much of this work often goes unaccounted for in annual reviews, and the tangible benefit to me has not always matched the amount of time and energy—professional capital really—I have spent in working with colleagues across three colleges to sustain the urban education concentration. Yet I am bound by the same writing expectations of my colleagues who do not spend as much time in service activities in schools. A barrier to my writing life, my work at the school has slowed my productivity and my efforts at maintaining a robust writing/research agenda.

Also confining for me as an intellectual is that I am accustomed to critique as a mode of pedagogy. Helping my students develop and hone their skills in problematizing the status quo of public education is of primary importance, yet I do not always feel comfortable in questioning the practices of teachers and administrators at the school. Even though I have been welcomed at the school, I still recognize my "place" as an outsider, someone who has not earned the right to "judge" what teachers are doing against the backdrop of an accountability-run-amuck-NCLB context, so I am careful in my critiques at/of Woodlands High. Navigating boundaries between university and schools is complicated work.

Familiar Endings

The two school faculty colleagues' voices included in this section of the chapter both care deeply about students and their success in and out of school. Both are exemplary teachers with lots of experience in co-teaching situations in their own classrooms, and we all share a commitment to improving teacher preparation. When I asked our school partners to write their own narratives to include in this paper, they said they would prefer being interviewed instead, to include their quoted excerpts in the paper, and then to read and comment on the final draft. I told them I welcomed any changes they would make to the final draft before its publication. They cited their lack of time as the major reason for choosing to be interviewed rather than write their own narratives. That school partners left "authorship" to the university professor speaks to my privileged position in the collaboration, which affords me more time and formal reward structures for publishing. I outline our process of writing and interviewing here not to show that we have been successful in negotiating our positions and representing our voices in ways suggestive of the kind of the collaborative space Zeichner (2010) says is possible among university and school faculty, "third spaces in teacher education [that] involve an equal and more dialectical relationship between academic and practitioner knowledge in support of student teacher learning" (p. 92). Instead, I outline our writing process to make explicit how uneven our relationship and the representation of that relationship is when traditional research paradigms and traditional conceptions of university-school collaborations position school co-instructors as participants and me as an "expert" when they "chose," mostly because of institutional constraints, to be interviewed rather than author their own narratives. I am no expert, they are not participants to me, yet I still occupy a privileged position as university professor.

I wrote narratives after I analyzed my teaching journal and class lesson plans from our three years of teaching together before I conducted my first interview with school partners. Because my understanding of our collaborative experience was still in process, the first interview with school partners was unstructured. My only goal was to engage in a dialogue about our experiences working collaboratively, specifically our initial impressions of our respective institutions and how we defined our collaborative spaces. I then asked our co-instructors to read my narratives before I interviewed them a second time. In the weeks between the first interview and the second, I reviewed interview transcripts and developed an interview guide for the second interview, which was semi-structured. Questions focused on school partners' responses in their first interview as well as on their reactions to specific statements I made in the narratives. I then analyzed both interview transcripts for themes that repeated across interview data and narratives. I wish to acknowledge that even though school partners will read and "approve" all parts of the final draft of this paper before its journal publication and that even though I have tried to represent the complexity of our relationship, the rendering of our experiences is necessarily incomplete and unbalanced. As is typical of research in teacher education, the reader hears much more from me, as university professor lead author, in comparison to the voices of our school partners. The ways in which I narrativize experiences with our co-instructors represents a single perspective. Comments by Jane highlight this singularity:

> I continue to think that it is a privilege to be able to work with you [Nichole] and I learn something new all the time. And from reading this, I saw our classroom in a little different way than—or, I saw that you see it sometimes a little different, a different lens I guess in the fact that you think it was a struggle to share teaching space and I didn't. I didn't feel that from you.

I also know that I do not always problematize the myriad ways my own privilege prevents me from understanding my own complicity in reifying existing hierarchies between "professors" and "practitioners" and reproducing the familiar binary of "theory" and "practice" in teacher education. So why share my experiences of co-teaching across institutional boundaries if my claims are not generalizable and if my intent is to problematize the process rather than offer solutions? Like Bass (1999), I understand teaching problems as "ongoing investigations" that are not necessarily solvable, so I lay bare my experiences as a form of problem-posing inquiry (Freire, 1970) that will inform and challenge the extant literature on school-university partnerships in teacher education that tend toward solutions-based narratives. This paper joins Johnsen, Pacht, van Slyck, and Tsao (2009) who invite teachers to "break the wall of silence about our messes" in our scholarship of teaching (p. 120) and Miller (1990) who says her research group of university and school teachers is "remaining in the mess" (p. 149) of collaborative research to explore their process of becoming challengers in their respective educational contexts. She says:

> As a result of collaborative efforts, we have come to believe that any attempts to change school structures, or our relationships to them, that we find to be oppressive or stifling must originate in "the mess" of our daily work as educators.
>
> *(p. 149)*

In my narratives, I discuss how collaborations with school partners allow us to situate the authentic learning experiences of high school students with what we are studying in our courses, rather than manufacture or simulate K–12 classroom experiences as we often do in our college campus-based classes. Our teacher colleagues bring a wealth of expertise in helping us and our pre-service teachers to think more deeply about as well as problematize what the literature says about what is "best practice" in our respective fields. They have infused our courses with new ideas, helped us model for our students a shared pedagogical space, and challenged us to create alternative assignments, which all have resulted in improved teacher preparation. Jane says that our work together has not only changed her own instructional practice, but the professional learning we have done as a team at the school has impacted some other faculty at Woodland Hills:

> I think the learning curve is different for different people, for the different faculty members that have joined, from both sides actually. And so I think there have been larger gains for some than others. There's still some that are finding their way. But they're willing to work at it, so it's, you know, that's an important piece. I think I'm more thoughtful in my practice because of the things I have learned through this program. And my choices—I make different choices because of it. So, I have definitely changed. We have faculty who are looking to students first before they make classroom decisions. I'm not saying that it's the entire faculty, but we do have faculty that are doing that, new faculty and veterans. The choices that we make have made our practice more thoughtful toward the students. And I think that's there because of this program. I wouldn't have come up to that. I wouldn't have come to where I am now without it I don't think.

Natalie explains that working with a university professor gave her "new ideas" and "different perspectives on things [she] could try in the classroom." She explains further:

I've changed. And I think that it saved my career working with you all because, you know, I didn't tell anybody this, but after ten years I was like, okay now what? What do I do? So I didn't know where to go. I was bored in my teaching. So when you actually came with that theory I was like hmm, that's something to try, something to practice, and something to add to my tool belt. So it kind of saved me in a way.

While I highlight the improvements made in my practice as a result of working with school partners, which does seem to suggest that Zeichner's (2010) conception of hybrid spaces which bring together school and university-based teacher educators is indeed possible, I also point to the epistemological divide in teacher education between theory and practice that went largely unchallenged in our collaborative work together. I question whether or not an "equal and dialectical" relationship between "academic and practitioner knowledge" (p. 92) that Zeichner proposes is ever possible for school and university faculty in teacher education.

I, as the university professor, took lead in choosing required reading and developing course assignments, and Jane and Natalie explain their response to doing so:

Jane: Well, I'm going to say that I felt like I had a voice in all of our texts and what we were using. I mean we spent a lot of time looking at different options and changed and changed back. I think that was shared equally. I think you [Nichole] have more knowledge base in what's out there and so you may have brought more options to the table, but I still feel like I had a voice in what we used. I think you had the knowledge base about what was out there because I might be living some of it, but that's your job, right. But I felt like I had an equal weight in that final decision.

Natalie: For me, it was opposite because the course was already established. All the assignments were already made … At first I just went around— went along with the program, but then last summer I actually got to voice my opinion more, maybe added some assignments that I suggested. So that made me feel a lot more comfortable. I knew the unit plan assignment that we're now considering to revise—I really think that needs to be revised, the unit plan that we have the interns do. So that's the only suggestion I would make in changing the course … Well, I think we're moving towards change now. We're changing it slowly. We worked on it last year and now we're even working on it more. So we are moving towards change in the assignments and the course structure. I think that in the beginning it wasn't—I didn't see it as a problem that it was already set up. I actually preferred it that way because I wanted to know exactly what the course was about, how it looked at university level, and how we can make it fit our interns or benefit our interns. So I was okay.

While Jane says she felt like she had a voice in the final decisions regarding required reading and Natalie says she did not see the course already set up by the university professor as a problem, school partners were not invited to frame course content from the very beginning.

In keeping with course content that I took the lead in choosing, I structured courses to prepare teachers to resist the norm of standardized lessons and "teaching to the test," and as a result, we sometimes experienced the school as a confining space for our pedagogy. As we taught our teacher education classes at the school through the lens of our Urban Education (UE) program strands of culturally and linguistically relevant pedagogy and family and community engagement, we asked students to study theory and methods that were not always aligned with what they were experiencing in the field.

Natalie: But that's something that we shared with interns as well is that you can learn from things that you don't agree with, you know? You see things that you would not do in your classroom and every school has that—I'm going to assume, that in every profession there are people that really shouldn't be there and, you know, there are people that we want to embrace all the time because they are, you know, the ones I want to grow up to be like, right? And so you know you have to make each piece of that a learning experience. There's no Utopia school and interns need to know that, too. That sometimes you come in all bright and shiny and new and have all these great plans, but you have to protect yourself so that you don't get rusty like some of the others. Since I've started shiny and new, I don't know if that's the right word, but you don't want to be broken by, you know, that you can still be strong. And you have—you have the background to make change and to do the right thing and sometimes it's hard.

When our students completed observations in classrooms at the school and noted disconnects between what we were reading and what they were actually seeing, we took for granted that the disconnect in the field was a problem with the field, not with the theory we were reading. Though we created learning opportunities for students to examine disconnects between theory and practice, we did not deconstruct our own privileging of the theory we chose for students to study. Our school partners, who were successful, award-winning, veteran teachers at Woodland Hills, spent time "testing" theories in their own classrooms and rethinking their own teaching choices based on theory we were reading in our teacher education courses. Natalie and Jane point to a very familiar theory-practice dichotomy in our work together:

Natalie: At first working with [the university professor] and actually teaching a class, I thought to myself, "Oh well, these are [university] interns. I better be quiet because I don't want to conflict with what [the university] was teaching the interns. I knew the theory was there, but I didn't want to say anything against what the theory was, or what the research said, even though I was practicing different things in my classroom. So I was afraid to kind of speak up about that. It was ten years—ten years had passed since I had any kind of pedagogy or anything. So I was like am I outdated? I don't really know what's going on. Let me try to figure out what's going on in education today and see how it relates to my practice. At first, I was thinking okay, [the university professor] is the genius in this whole thing and she's, you know, the person that knows it all and that's how I felt in the beginning. I didn't really know what I had to offer the interns at first. So I didn't want to support anything that I didn't believe was true. So I would definitely try, you know, what was in the research. And I kind of felt inadequate at first because I was like, "Oh no, I'm destroying my kids because the research says don't do this and I'm doing that." But I went in my classroom and I tried everything and then I was like, "Well, this stuff can work. I kind of want to fit this in." And then that made me feel more comfortable. So I had to practice it first before I could really—I didn't really get real comfortable until the second year of our teaching, I guess. But the first year I was very concerned about how my practice related to the theory or the pedagogy.

Jane: But I think also it's not way out there fringe practices, you know? It's good, there's good foundation to the choices that are made for the content of the classes. So it's not—and that's why. But there's also sound theory in the practices that are being taught.

Much of our pedagogy is based on helping our students to rethink taken for granted assumptions, ask critical questions, and examine ideologies that frame discourses. I should have done the same as we framed our collaborative work within the context of the theory-practice split too often reified within teacher education, especially when university and school faculty work together.

Conclusions and Questions

Even though I have a lot of experience moving across institutional boundaries to co-create curriculum and share pedagogical space with school partners, epistemological boundaries in teacher education that create binaries between and privilege academic knowledge over practitioner knowledge remained largely intact. Thus, we were not always successful in transgressing entrenched political boundaries of universities and schools. However, our work in co-developing curriculum with school partners does raise important questions: What a priori assumptions about collaboration do we have, and how do those assumptions influence how we work together? In what ways might we set up partnerships recognizing that the spaces we share are always subject to the privileging of certain kinds of knowledge? How might we resist such privileging? What resources from our respective institutional contexts must be provided to ensure that school partners' knowledge is valued as we create curriculum, teach, research, and write together? What policies need to change in our respective institutions so that our time and effort are formally recognized and rewarded? While I never intended to offer solutions at the end of this chapter, I do hope that my curriculum work with school partners raises questions that prompt us all to rethink the ways in which we share pedagogical space across institutional boundaries of school and university and the ways in which we challenge and reify the epistemological divide in teacher education between theory and practice. Then perhaps we might co-construct pedagogical spaces that allow us to be more transgressive.

References

Bass, R. (1999) "The scholarship of teaching: What's the problem?" *Inventio: Creative Thinking about Learning and Teaching* 1.1. 1 March 2014. Retrieved from http://www.doiiit.gmu.edu/Archives/feb98/randybass.htm.

Bhabha, H. (2004) *The Location of Culture.* New York, NY: Routledge.

Cochran-Smith, M. & Lytle, S. (1999) "Relationships of knowledge and practice: Teacher learning in communities." *Review of Research in Education, 24,* 249–306.

Darling-Hammond, L., Hammerness, K., Grossman, P., Rust, F., & Shulman, L. (2005) "The design of teacher education programs." In L. Darling-Hammond & J. Bransford (Eds.), *Preparing Teachers for a Changing World*, pp. 390–441. San Francisco, CA: Jossey Bass.

Featherstone, J. (2007) "Values and the big university education school." In D. Carroll, H. Featherstone, J. Featherstone, S. Feiman-Nemser, & D. Roosevelt (Eds.), *Transforming Teacher Education: Reflections from the Field*, pp. 203–220. Cambridge: MA: Harvard Education Press.

Freire, P. (1970) *Pedagogy of the Oppressed.* New York, NY: Continuum.

hooks, b. (1994) *Teaching to Transgress: Education as the Practice of Freedom.* New York, NY: Routledge.

Johnsen, H. L., Pacht, M., van Slyck, P., & Tsao, T. (2009) "The messy teaching conversation: Toward a model of collegial reflection, exchange, and scholarship on classroom problems." *Teaching English in the Two-Year College, 37*(2), 119–136.

Miller, J. (1990) *Creating Spaces and Finding Voices: Teachers Collaborating for Empowerment.* Albany, NY: State University of New York Press.

Zeichner, K. M. (1995) "Beyond the divide of teacher research and academic research." *Teachers and Teaching, 1,* 153–172.

Zeichner, K. M. (2010) "Rethinking the connections between campus courses and field experiences in college- and university-based teacher education." *Journal of Teacher Education, 61*(1–2), 89–99.

8

CURRICULUM AS COMMUNITY-BUILDING, LIBERATION, RESISTANCE, AND EMPOWERMENT

Reflections from Fifteen Years of Teaching

Bridget Turner Kelly

I teach, in part, because I am a Black female. It is out of my most marginalized identities that I find the courage and motivation to teach. Being a visual learner, I could not imagine my career as a college teacher until I was in my first year as a doctoral student and saw a Black female in front of the classroom, commanding a presence and in her very being transgressing what it means to be a professor. When I saw Dr. Sharon Fries-Britt, this Black female, cisgender, Christian, heterosexual, middle-class professor teaching graduate students about higher education, I was transfixed and a light bulb went off in my head: Dr. Fries-Britt and I share so many salient identities and she is a professor. If she can do this, then so can I. If I did not see her in this role I may have missed what I believe I was made to do for my career. How many other females and people of color might miss seeing college professor as a career if they do not have models? Sharon Fries-Britt and I documented how we retained each other in the academy (Fries-Britt & Kelly, 2005), and how that helped me visualize what I wanted to do with my career. I wanted to be that person in the front of the room, designing and teaching courses in a body that transgressed (hooks, 1994) from the dominant White, male professor. What motivated me to be a professor was embodying that person that walked into a university classroom and challenged students' ideas about what professors looked like as well as provided examples for students of color of what they could do with their education. I used Dr. Fries-Britt and others to mold my career as a faculty member. As a faculty member, I am determined to shift the center to give voice to my marginalized existence as a Black female as well as to others marginalized in the academy.

In this chapter, I chronicle my fifteen years of designing curriculum and teaching in the area of higher education. As I describe curriculum design as spaces of community-building, liberation, resistance, and empowerment, I also weave in how my own intersecting identities shaped the curriculum I designed and delivered. The chapter concludes with sharing the contexts in which this curriculum was developed and the success I have experienced, in large part, because of the development of my salient identities that run counter to being a tenured associate professor (Black and female) and ones that provide privilege and power in academia (Christian, middle-class, temporarily of able mind and body, heterosexual, native English speaker, U.S. citizen, cisgender woman).

Curriculum Design and My Racial Identity Development

In graduate school I was on my way to realizing my vision of being a professor in a body that ran counter to the dominant narrative of who teaches in a research university. My very first time teaching a class on my own was a liberating experience. As a doctoral student with a graduate assistantship with a Black female supervisor who was the campus coordinator of the Racial Legacies and Learning (RLL) initiative, a project of the Association of American Colleges and Universities (AAC&U), I was given the freedom to design and teach a year-long course to undergraduate and graduate students that focused on race. This was back in the 1990s when then President Bill Clinton created the President's Initiative on Race, which supported organizations such as AAC&U's RLL with funding for 50 universities to design programs and curriculum around race. Was it because I was Black that I was asked to create this course? Was it because my supervisor was Black that she was charged with delivering such a course? We did not ask these questions, at least not out loud to each other. Instead, we relished the opportunity to create a course with funding. We dreamed big in creating The Racial Dialogue and Action Project (RDAP). We asked students to apply to be in this course so that we could ensure there was diversity of sex, race, religion, class, and other identities we would focus on in the course. We designed it to run from August until May so we would have time not just to introduce and learn concepts, but to also apply them in real-world settings. The funding enabled us to have an orientation day before the semester began so the students could get to know each other, build trust and begin to understand how they came to understand race and racism. We consulted with a national organization, National Conference for Community and Justice (NCCJ), to come in monthly to the class in the fall and work with the students on intergroup dialogue and conflict mediation. In the spring, we partnered with NCCJ and had funding to send the class to a weekend-long retreat where they facilitated dialogues with high-school students, facilitated dialogues with middle-school students in an after-school program, and facilitated dialogues in NCCJ's Cinema and Conversation series they held throughout the city. The chance to work with community partners and actualize much of what was in the research at the time about best practices in pedagogy was inspiring and propelled my desire to be a teacher that transgressed curricular boundaries.

The curriculum for the RDAP changed as I learned more about teaching and partnered with other academic departments on campus to institutionalize the course beyond the year of funding from AAC&U and the President's Initiative on Race. My experience designing a course that met outside the confines of an academic semester intentionally brought students from different backgrounds together, and invited collaborators in to co-teach, gave me a different perspective for how I could design curriculum, even before I became a full-time faculty member.

Teaching the RDAP as a doctoral student inspired me to create courses that sought to transform students' understanding about race and racism. I understood my identity mostly in terms of my race and was inspired by Janet Helms being a faculty member at the university where I earned my PhD. Helms (1990) created the Black Racial Identity Development theory, modeled after Cross' (1971) psychological Nigrescence theory. While I was learning about these theories in my own doctoral courses, I was teaching the RDAP, and going through my own racial identity development. I approached the course from the perspective of Immersion/Emersion. Immersion is defined as Black persons seeking to surround themselves with visible symbols of their Blackness and to avoid White people and Emersion is the leveling off from the anger about racism and the recognition that there are different models of Blackness (Helms, 1990). Immersion was a fun stage for me, as I was in love with things I associated with being Black—growing out my relaxer and wearing my hair natural for the first time since I began perming it back in middle school, dating Black guys for the first time in my life, and listening to Black recording artists such as Lauren Hill, Maxwell, and Jill Scott. The salience of race and racism in my life infused into my curriculum. I designed the RDAP to be an antiracism intervention through the content of the course, the focus on interracial dialogue, creating a "safe" classroom environment, and promoting positive interracial contact in class (Tatum, 1992). The RDAP was the focus of my dissertation and the process of analyzing and writing my dissertation helped me move into the Emersion status because I closely examined the Black students' racial identity development in my study and came to understand different models of Blackness. Examining the White students' racial identity development also propelled me to let go of anger toward White people in particular and see that there were White allies in antiracism work. The following reflection from my study highlights how my own racial identity development impacted my teaching:

> As the facilitator of class discussions, interactive exercises, and racial dialogue sessions, I found it difficult at times to keep my opinions to myself. Every now and then a student would say something in class or write something in a journal that I found offensive to me as a Black female. It took a lot of energy to respond to students in a way that validated their voice but challenged their language or perspective. I tried hard to mask my feelings of hurt or anger and remember that rebuking a student would not engender an open classroom environment. Often, in these instances, one student or another would challenge the classmate I found offensive or disagree

so vehemently with what had transpired that I was able to stay out of the fray of the conversation and compose myself before responding. It became necessary for me to debrief each class with the teaching assistant or with the NCCJ facilitator. We recognized that venting our frustrations or, many times, sharing our excitement from the class, helped us put students' comments and the class into perspective. We reminded each other that these students were in the process of discovering and examining their racial identity, attitudes and interactions in full view of the other classmates and instructors. These reflections helped me to understand more about my own racial identity development journey and how a journey is a continuous process with no clear beginning or end.

The process of analyzing RDAP for my dissertation research unearthed more about my own racial identity development journey and how I interacted with the Black and White females in the study:

> During the interview phase of the data collection I was moved by the Black students' stories of experiences they had with race at home, school and in the RDAP. Their stories took me back to memories of my childhood and schooling. I relived times when I was discriminated against or denied a position because of my race. When I followed up the interview questions with specific probes into the what and why in an effort to secure descriptive detail about how the students characterized their racial identity and what accounted for any changes they identified, I could relate to their responses. Consequently, the individual case narratives of the Black students seem to almost write themselves because their responses resonated so much to my own racial identity development journey. During the interviews with the White students I found myself struggling at times to elicit information on how the women felt about their own racial group, other racial groups, and race in general. I had to use multiple probes to secure one or two stories about their racial identity development. At the time it appeared that I obtained descriptive data from both the Black and White students. However, when I sat down to write the White students' individual case narratives, there was very little information that addressed the students' racial identity, attitudes or interactions. I also discovered that I was hesitant to portray the students as racist or completely unaware of their racial identity because I did not want to appear to be unfair to the White students.

Thus, my own racial identity development of Immersion/Emersion during my time as a doctoral student teaching RDAP impacted my teaching and research on race. I was empathetic with the White students in the class because I realized I focused so much on my target identities of race and sex that I had paid little attention to my privileged identities, which encompassed everything else about me—religion, nationality, socioeconomic class, sexuality, ability, and language. At the time I wrote:

> I examined my own racial identity development more than I anticipated and realized I needed to be patient with people because people are at different places with their identity development. I could not expect my students to be fully aware of their prejudices and biases when I was not even fully aware of mine. I remembered the work I put in examining my own attitudes and became more patient as I watched the students doing similar work.

As I finished graduate school and my dissertation on women's racial identity development, which was based on students who completed the first year-long RDAP, I did a post-doctorate where I taught Social Foundations courses. I went into later stages of Helms (1990) identity development model and became more cognizant of my intersecting privileged identities, such as being heterosexual. When asked by a White female faculty member during the end of my post-doctorate if I would come into her class and do an hour session on diversity, I said, "Sure, an hour is not much time, what aspects of diversity would you like me to cover?" She replied, "Just talk about diversity and that will be fine." I tried again, "Would you like me to talk about race, sex, class, and sexual orientation?" She quipped, "Yes, those are fine, but do not talk about sexual orientation." I looked at her and tried to decide in a split-second whether it was worth it to say what was on my mind. Would she still give me a recommendation letter for faculty positions I was applying to? If not, would I be able to secure a job anyway? I decided it did not matter and answered her by stating, "If I cannot talk about sexual orientation then I do not want to do a session on diversity because that is an important area and one that needs to be discussed on this campus." She looked at me and walked away. This was a university that took out sexual orientation in their non-discrimination policy while I was on campus. Watching such blatant heterosexism impacted how I designed diversity courses when I became an assistant professor. I could not expect White students to face their White privilege and racism, and male students to face their male privilege and sexism, if I was unwilling to face my sexual privilege and heterosexism. The way I had designed curriculum up to that point was about getting students to be angry. Jane Elliott of "Brown Eyes, Blue Eyes" and "Color of Fear" were some of my favorite video clips to show in class. When I finally began to confront racism after being in the early stages of Helms' (1990) Black racial identity theory for most of my k–12 and college days, I was so angry that I thought the way to get students to stop being racist and sexist was to get them to be angry enough about injustices that they want to do something about it. While I knew I should be more intersectional in my approach and true to my core nature of being optimistic and positive, this is not how I developed curriculum in my early days teaching diversity courses as an assistant professor on the tenure-track at a public university.

Curriculum Design as Community-Building

Being isolated in a university as the only person of color in my program, one of two Black female faculty members in my department and college, I felt lost at times in terms of how to show up in the classroom, how to teach required diversity courses to primarily White, middle- to upper-class students, and how to weave in other salient parts of my identity. Teaching Race and Culture, a one credit course required for undergraduates, provided me a community of other faculty of color and White allies who were committed to tackling racism. We met once a semester to construct the syllabus, learning outcomes, assignments, and more importantly for me at the time—to talk about how we showed up in the classroom.

My teaching evaluation comments from teaching Race and Culture the first time demonstrated how students saw my identities as not impacting the course. They wrote that I, "Never disagreed with anyone. I often wondered where she stood on some topics," "Very knowledgeable about topic. Respectful of other's opinions. Really made you think," "Bridget was extremely nice, very open, encouraged our comments and was never judgmental," and "I enjoyed the class and learned a lot from it. I felt well respected in this classroom with my own thoughts and ideas." While the great majority of students experienced me as not having an agenda based on my marginalized identities as a Black female, there was one comment that I held to as truthful, "Seemed to have a very opinionated and one sided point of view."

Despite the majority of testimonials that I was unbiased as a teacher, and my laundry list of privileged identities as highly educated, Christian, heterosexual, middle-class and temporarily of able mind and body, I still believed the students largely saw me for my only two targeted identities of Black and female. I perceived them as not taking me seriously in the classroom because I was so closely affected by racism and sexism. The class was designed from a position of defense where I tried to prove to students that racism existed, racism needed to be challenged, and they had, by no fault of their own ingested the racism in our society into their beings. As Beverly Daniel Tatum (1997), author of *Why Are All the Black Students Sitting Together in the Cafeteria: And Other Conversations on Race*, said, our air is polluted with racism and we cannot help but to breathe it in every time we breathe. The White educators in the Race and Culture planning meetings would share how they feared they also would not be taken seriously because they had not experienced racism firsthand. This helped me realize that, despite the dominant narrative that people of color should be the only ones teaching diversity courses, there is no perfect type of person to teach about racism, oppression, privilege, or power—only people who give a perfect effort. Designing curriculum in a community, whether it was as a doctoral student with my Black female supervisor who had lived through civil rights battles I had only read about in books, or as an assistant professor with White and faculty of color who were teaching the same course as me but coming from different lenses, helped me feel less isolated and alone as a teacher.

Curriculum Design as Liberation

bell hooks' book *Teaching to Transgress* (1994) challenged me to break out from under some of the imposter syndrome and internalized oppression tapes I had playing in my head. Some of the greatest hits from those tapes were, "You are not smart enough to be a professor," "You are lazy, incompetent and do not know this material well enough to teach it," "People will not take you seriously as a Black female who looks young, and smiles too much to be serious about oppression," and "You hold too many privileged identities and have never worked in the field so you cannot teach people anything about diversity."

Instead of giving those messages power and approaching teaching from a place of defense, I worked to design diversity curriculum from a place of liberation where I was free to be all of myself and students were free to bring all of themselves to class. This was when I decided to research more. Who am I? What is out there in terms of best practices for teaching diversity? I read as much from people like Parker Palmer, Ximena Zuniga, Sylvia Hurtado, and Mitch Chang as I could get my hands on at the time. I attended diversity sessions with Jamie Washington, Kathy Obear, and worked with Centers for Excellence in Teaching at multiple universities to find my own way of being a diversity educator. I went back to my roots from my dissertation and infused intergroup dialogue into a graduate course I taught during my first assistant professor position and I have incorporated dialogue into every cultural pluralism, multiculturalism, and social justice class I have taught.

The lessons I took away from all my reading, training, and teaching helped me to quiet these tapes and see that I had something unique to offer to students. I could show up as myself, a complex being of intersecting identities, beliefs, experiences, and knowledge, and give students the space and freedom to do the same. Not being the expert or smartest person in the room was liberating and scary all at the same time. When I was a student I looked to the teacher as the authority figure with all the right answers, and I felt naked entering a classroom in my twenties teaching graduate students who had decades on me in terms of work experience and age. There was no way I was going to win the "experience" game, so I switched the rules and tried to create as level a playing field as I could by noting we all had something unique to contribute to the learning environment. My role would be to design and implement the curriculum by picking the readings, developing learning outcomes, creating assignments, and structuring the course to meet those outcomes, and theirs would be to come to class having read but also having personally and professionally interacted with the content so they could bring it to life. What did it have to say to them as an educator? What unique lens could they bring to the content from their mix of intersecting identities, beliefs, experiences, and knowledge? Since I did not have to perform as the expert, but rather as a facilitator of learning, that liberated students to not have to show up as someone who would just receive and regurgitate what I taught. They got to bring their whole selves into the classroom—intellect, heart, and body.

The curriculum I designed was also liberating because it freed students and myself from misconceptions about who we were, not marginalized or privileged people in our individual acts of oppression or social justice, but a complex mix of intersecting identities with power within our sphere of influence to change and challenge inequities. My curriculum documents oppression so that students can see we are not in a post-racial environment or that just because same-sex marriage is now legal in the U.S. that we have rid our society of heterosexism and homophobia. My courses link past policies and practices to the present so students can view the larger, systematic cycle of oppression, privilege, and social justice and learn how to not repeat inequities of the past. The readings that I select are purposely diverse and inclusive of scholars and practitioners from varying sexualities, genders, races, ethnicities, abilities, and socioeconomic classes so students can both see themselves in the literature and learn from people who have different experiences in the world than they do. This curriculum liberates students and myself from dominant paradigms about what knowledge is, how it is socially constructed, and provides avenues for social change, whether it be in an office policy on gender inclusive language or a waiving of an application fee for students who find the fee cost prohibitive to accessing education.

Curriculum Design as Resistance

As I became liberated to teach about oppression, privilege, and social justice from a role of facilitator rather than "sage on the stage," I got resistance. My department chair during my first three-year review as a tenure-track assistant professor observed my class and later told me he did not see me doing any teaching. I was hurt because I had spent hours designing the content and facilitation of learning in preparation for his visit. As we unpacked why he believed I did not teach, he said I did not lecture, but rather guided the students in small group and large group discussions of the readings and facilitated an in-class activity. I explained how my teaching was largely in the choices I made about what material to present, the lens from which I presented it, and in inviting their critical and personal lens on the material. Later, in my three-year review documents, he wrote about my facilitation in a way that demonstrated he understood my teaching looked different than a dominant paradigm of lecture, "Her skill in guiding the learning process continues to impress me."

Another form of resistance I received was from students who preferred the "banking model" (Freire, 1970) of education whereby I deposited knowledge into them and then they withdrew it to tell me what they had learned from me. Many students came to class hoping to soak up knowledge from me without having to bring anything other than a listening ear to the classroom. They resisted having to view readings from their own personal and professional experiences, critically examine what they thought and felt about the reading, and uncover what their lens revealed about messages they had internalized from parents, media, friends, or faith traditions. Students were more interested in hearing from me and wanted me to tell them how to interpret the reading or what the answer was so they could pass the class.

Early in my career, I resisted offering my own voice and critical lens to the dialogue because of those old imposter tapes that whispered, "They are not going to take you seriously as an educator because they see you as a self-interested Black female who is only interested in supporting students of color, females, and denigrating White males." I focused more on students' voices and neglected mine. As one student commented on my course evaluations, "Would really love to hear more of your ideas on the table—you were scrupulously neutral and purposefully so, but we really crave your opinion more!" I also resisted being the dominant voice in the classroom and believed my presence was felt through my choice of the readings, my creation of the assignments, and class activities. Instrumental in my design of courses was resisting the dominant narrative that teachers were the most important voice in the classroom. A quote from an early anthology I utilized in teaching Race and Culture stuck with me as I created curriculum:

> Shifting one's center of thinking so as to include previously silenced voices is a starting point for analyzing the complex interrelationship of race, class, and gender in society and for thinking about social relationships, actions, experiences, and institutions in new ways.
>
> *(Anderson & Collins, 2004, p. 15)*

It is my belief that by shifting the center from exclusion to inclusion, one can thoughtfully and critically analyze the role power and privilege play in maintaining systems of inequity in education. Students' voices have been previously silenced in the college classroom, particularly in diversity courses where students are fearful to talk and be ridiculed, or refuse to talk and be tokenized for their marginalized identities. My voice, particularly as a Black female body in the role of professor in the college classroom, had also been silenced. Finding a way to bring my voice and my students' voices into the center of the dialogue was my challenge. Including my voice as not a dominant one, but as one that is valuable in facilitating students' learning, was an act of resistance to the old tapes of not being seen as credible, and at the same time it was resistance to the dominant narrative that the professor is the only important voice. Balancing these two competing acts of resistance has enriched my curriculum because my mind is always on inclusion of everyone's voice, as powerful wisdom to bring ourselves and others in rather than to exclude and diminish. The focus on inclusion is intended to help students see their role in creating a more equitable educational system.

Curriculum Design as Empowerment

To facilitate students becoming knowledgeable and empowered to create change in the educational system, I utilize critical thinking and reflective analysis, social justice education, and personal interaction with knowledge. In each of my classes, students are invited to approach the readings from a critical perspective that searches for personal biases, seeks to find value in their ideas, and looks for connections to other authors and ideas we have discussed. In addition, all of my students write reflection papers on readings, class discussions, and exercises that stood out for them as meaningful. Students relate ideas from the course to their own personal experiences in schools and colleges in order to affirm or refute key concepts and theories. The reflections also serve as a chronicle of students understanding and growing knowledge of the central ideas in the course. These efforts to foster critical thinking and reflective analysis align well with goals for all of education, but specifically work to empower students to see wisdom in their own thoughts and experiences. In a course I taught in my first tenure-track position entitled, "Seminar in Educational History: Struggle for Equality," I received this comment on my teaching evaluation,

> I rave about this course to other people for a number of reasons. First, Bridget is a highly skilled and thoughtful teacher. Her course builds in such a way to challenge our thinking through reading, discussions, and assignments that promote deep understanding and compassion for self and others. Second, the course material is profound and compelling. Third, the course really does the job of relating one's own history and self to themes in history of education. I could go on. All teachers should take this course.

Whether it is a course on historical inequality, or research in higher education, embracing a social justice perspective is the focal point of each of my courses. Perhaps because of how my marginalized identities as a Black female intersect with my privileged identities I both experience systemic oppression and see my power to affect my spheres of influence. I design curriculum for students to see their own power to affect change as well. As students analyze various readings on systematic oppression, personal and social identity, power and privilege they are becoming knowledgeable about the terminology, language, and experiences of various cultural groups. Students simultaneously examine personal values and attitudes about their own and other cultural groups. Through various written assignments, students formulate personal philosophies about themselves and about the type of practitioner they hope to become as it relates to being a change agent for social justice. Some students fully embrace the role of change agent and others are more skeptical about how they want to exercise their personal and professional power. I recently had a student who expressed to me that he understood he is privileged by almost all of his social identities and he sees how they benefit him in higher education and at work. He left the class with knowledge of his power, but without any motivation to use it toward empowering others. Regardless of students' overall path, I believe it is my responsibility to provide all of my students with the knowledge base and practical skills to engage in equitable educational practices. Thus, in each of my classes, I offer students a framework in which to discuss issues of social justice.

This framework is largely centered on students' personal interaction with knowledge. More than understanding multiple viewpoints and theories of education, I encourage students to relate theories to their personal lives and practice. Students have a wealth of experience ranging from elementary or secondary student teaching and assisting faculty in college courses, to advising students in campus clubs or organizations and oftentimes parenting their own children. I ask students to draw on these and other personal experiences with education to dialogue with the theory introduced in class. When students can see theories and ideas "at play" in their everyday interactions with friends, family, and co-workers, ideas become meaningful and understandable in a way that often causes them to rethink and modify current practices.

In the absence of other shared classroom experiences, students in my online classes interrogate readings and often write about how theories help them examine their current practices. For example, a student shared that she had been socialized to view males as better teachers than females. She came to this realization after examining her own family dynamics and the relationship she had with her own mother. Becoming aware that she as a female had internalized sexism from actions she saw her mother taking was an eye-opener as she now wants to be an educator and has to rethink her own credibility in that role. Students in my online classes often reveal more about their internalized biases around race and sex, two of my target identities, in ways that my face-to-face students often do not. Reading how a student was socialized to be racist based on messages they received at home and got reinforced through media is always exciting and hurtful. Exciting because if students are getting in touch with how their espoused beliefs of racial or sex equity do not align with their internal thoughts, this can lead to a realignment. I also find it hurtful to read how students were socialized to distrust and not believe someone like me, a Black female. Yet, it is this type of active engagement with educational theory and ideas that I desire for all of my students. If there is something about typing on a computer screen and not having my body physically in front of students that enables them to be more open and honest about their privileged and marginalized identities than I have seen in my face-to-face classes, then I have to examine that. Often in my face-to-face classes it takes us a long time for students to stop trying to censor what they say and be "politically correct" to get to what we really need to be talking about—their honest feelings and thoughts. My goal is to empower students to examine inequities whether it is online or in a face-to-face setting.

Conclusion

I have taught undergraduate and graduate students, face-to-face and online in schools and colleges of education for the past fifteen years. These schools have been housed in large, public universities (25,000 or more), medium-sized public and religiously affiliated private universities (7,000–11,000), and a religiously affiliated private university with 16,000 total students. My teaching evaluations from students, tenured faculty, and department chairs have all been consistently high, with one tenured faculty member noting that she was impressed with not only my skills in class, but with the care in which I prepare my syllabus, utilize my teaching assistant, and set a tone of mutual respect and critical thinking with the students. Each item in each of the evaluation instruments used by institutions where I taught were rated on a five point Likert scale, with five being the highest rating, one being the lowest, and three being average. There is one outlier course with average ratings, but otherwise my ratings have consistently been in the three point five to five range on the scales. As a graduate student, I received the Distinguished Teaching Assistant award from the Center for Teaching Excellence and the Graduate School. Over ten years later, I received the Outstanding Contribution to Student Affairs through Teaching by a professional association in my field. Just two years ago, I was awarded the Distinguished Faculty Award for Excellence in Teaching from my School of Education. I believe I am an excellent teacher and curriculum designer. Not because of the awards, teaching evaluations, or observation reports from my colleagues, but because it is what I am meant to do on this Earth. I have not mentioned my faith or religious identity much in this piece, but it is one of the most salient identities I hold. I believe I have been called to educate, but more specifically, to help others see the light inside of them. Marianne Williamson (1992) captured this sentiment in her poem, Our Greatest Fear:

> Our deepest fear is not that we are inadequate.
> Our deepest fear is that we are powerful beyond measure.
> It is our light not our darkness that most frightens us.
> We ask ourselves, who am I to be brilliant, gorgeous, talented
>   and fabulous?
> Actually, who are you not to be?
> You are a child of God.
> Your playing small does not serve the world.
> There's nothing enlightened about shrinking so that other people won't
>   feel insecure around you.
> We were born to make manifest the glory of
> God that is within us.
> It's not just in some of us; it's in everyone.
> And as we let our own light shine, we unconsciously give other people
>   permission to do the same.

As we are liberated from our own fear,
Our presence automatically liberates others.

This calling has been made manifest as a college professor, but it could have happened in another arena. For me, it is not in spite of who I am, but because of my social identities as a Black, female, cisgender woman, heterosexual, temporarily mind and able-bodied, U.S. citizen, English language speaker, and Christian, that I have embraced curriculum design as a space for community-building, liberation, resistance, and empowerment. It is because I bring my whole self, unapologetically to my teaching and invite my students to do the same that I have found myself embraced in this profession. Yes, I have met resistance from students disrespecting me in the classroom by taking their concerns directly to my department chair or dean without first coming to me; yes, I have met resistance from students questioning why we are reading works by so many marginalized groups in a course not labeled "diversity," or most recently I was questioned by students why they have to engage in online discussion forums rather than a face-to-face environment. These instances pale in comparison to the joy I get from students seeing themselves in literature and theories, or introverted students engaging deeply in an online format where they have time to process their thinking before sharing, or when students who are deeply privileged see that they have been viewing the world largely from one or two of their marginalized identities rather than from an intersectional lens. I will continue to design curriculum from my whole self in order to build community, liberate, resist, and empower.

References

Anderson, M. & Collins, P. H. (2004) *Race, Class and Gender: An Anthology* (5th edition). Boston, MA: Wadsworth.

Cross, W. E. (1971) "The Negro-to-Black conversion experience: Toward a psychology of Black liberation," *Black World, 20*(9), 13–27.

Freire, P. (1970) *Pedagogy of the Oppressed.* New York, NY: Herder and Herder.

Fries-Britt, S. & Kelly, B. T. (2005) "Retaining each other: Narratives of two African American women in the academy," *The Urban Review, 37*(3), 221–242.

Helms, J. E. (1990) *Black and White Racial Identity: Theory, Research, and Practice.* Westport, CT: Greenwood Press.

hooks, b. (1994) *Teaching to Transgress: Education as the Practice of Freedom.* New York, NY: Routledge.

Tatum, B. D. (1992) "Talking about race, learning about racism: The application of racial identity development theory in the classroom," *Harvard Educational Review, 62*(1), 1–23.

Tatum, B. D. (1997) *Why Are the Black Kids Sitting Together in the Cafeteria? And Other Conversations on Race.* New York, NY: Basic Books.

Williamson, M. (1992) *Return to Love.* New York, NY: Harper Collins.

9

DE DONDE TU ERES

Pedagogies of a Puerto Rican Academic

Mirelsie Velazquez

When a Puerto Rican, no matter what position in life they occupy, meets another Puerto Rican in the Diaspora, the inevitable question is, *de donde tu eres?* Where are you from? It is more than just a question of geography, but one of belonging. To where and who do you belong. *De donde tu eres?* Four simple words that carry a lot of weight. Words that when you are living, writing, thinking, and surviving within the ivory tower, weigh heavily on you. To belong implies a sense of power and ownership, but for a working-class Puerto Rican woman in academia, neither power nor ownership is ever implied and very seldom known. To teach in Predominately White Institutions (PWIs) is to contemplate and internalize feelings of isolation, not only in the halls, classrooms, and faculty meetings, but in the lack of curriculum interventions that would place us, our ideas, and histories, within larger curriculum settings. Who we are and what we teach is always in question. This chapter seeks to contextualize the experience of a Puerto Rican woman's (and other women of color) position within academia, as both a teacher and scholar. Borrowing from Critical Theory, Chicana Feminism, and Black women's intellectual thought, I speak to what it means to be in the very spaces that have denied us our humanity both as women and as women of color, and how as women of color we continue to serve as a bridge, a terrain that seeks to look to the past to create a better future for not only ourselves, but similarly to aid and honor our communities. Our survival, both physical and theoretical, is not guaranteed. As a Puerto Rican woman in academia, my teaching, research, and very presence become sites of constant negotiation, where battles are fought, and the only alternative is silence. But as Naomi Littlebear Morena reminds us, "complacency is a far more dangerous attitude than outrage" (Morena, 2015, p. 166). Silence and complacency within academic spaces, whether it be in our classrooms or the pages of journals, do not guarantee our survival, but instead our participation within these spaces highlights the inconsistency in which we are viewed or the double consciousness of our existence within these spaces. As a Puerto Rican woman, living, writing, and thinking in the diaspora, I cannot deny the weight of coloniality as it informs my view of the world, but similarly, it informs the ways in which I maneuver my way through my teaching and scholarship. I carry it with me. As the late Chicana Queer scholar Gloria Anzaldúa tells us:

> Before turning our eyes forward let's cast a look at the roads that led us here. The paths we've traveled on have been rocky and thorny, and no doubt they will continue to be so. But instead of rocks and the thorns, we want to concentrate on the rain and the sunlight and the spider webs glistening on both. And yes we know the origins of oppression; but do we have to dwell forever on that piece of terrain, forever stuck in the middle of that bridge? This land of thorns is not habitable. We carry this bridge inside of us, the struggle, the movement toward liberation. No doubt all of us have found by now that you don't build bridges by storming walls—that only puts people's backs up.
>
> (Anzaldúa, 2015, p.xxvii)

As a first generation, working-class Puerto Rican woman learning to survive the spaces that continue to push me to the margins, my back is up, the path is filled with rocks and thorns, but learning to clear the terrain, if not for me but for others, is part of the healing. Teaching and writing in many ways become part of the healing process. However, it is in our teaching and writing that we at times continue to be questioned and denied a sense of belonging. But similarly, our works, bodies, histories, and knowledge become sites of consumption by those who relegate us to the academic margins, as we become theorized while simultaneously terrorized. As Jo Carrillo writes, "and when our white sisters, radical friends see us in the flesh, not as a picture they own, they are not quite sure they like us as much" (Carrillo, 2015, pp. 60–61). Our very presence within academic spaces is made to feel counterproductive to those in power, as does our survival. But yet we continue to work to navigate the terrain through our daily interactions within the academy as well as our scholarship, even when we understand the ways in which our lives are at times co-opted or commodified for someone else's gains. As Aurora Levins Morales (2001, p. 29) beautifully reminds us, "I watch my life and my theorizing about it become the raw materials of someone else's expertise." Our experiences and participation within academic spaces is not or ever understood as being removed from our experiences as not only women, but women of color, who enter these spaces with not only our understanding of our own positionality but the intersecting relationships with our research, community, and our bodies. For as Anzaldúa (1987, p. 41) told us, "I am a turtle, wherever I go I carry 'home' on my back." For the Puerto Rican woman, attempting to both simultaneously survive and dismantle the hierarchies within academic spaces, carrying home becomes both healing and tumultuous in our quotidian practices.

Literature

I both borrow from and align myself with Chicana feminists to understand and contextualize how my research, teaching, and curriculum design (and life in the academy) means to "deconstruct the historical devaluation" of our lives, and how our lives are "at the center of these struggles against cultural domination, class exploitation, sexism, and racism" (Delgado Bernal, 1998, p. 562). Dolores Delgado Bernal (1998) reminds us "traditional research epistemologies reflect and reinforce the social history of the dominant race, which has negative results for people of color in general and students of color in particular" (Delgado Bernal, 1998, p. 563). For the woman of color in the academy, we occupy and internalize a tense space in which not only are we situated within the very spaces that reinforce the social history of the dominant race and gender, but we are expected to reinforce and perpetuate the intellectual contributions that continue to silence us and devalue our lives and experiences, including in the ways in which we design our curriculum and engage in our teaching. When we enter the classroom, our very presence and ideas come into question, and are challenged, including by students. But as Chicana feminists remind us, we must move to radicalize our identities, be it within or outside of the classroom or academic spaces, as a means for survival. Telling our stories become part of that process. The use of *testimonios*, and more specifically my own *testimonio* in this text, allow the Latina/Chicana researcher the space in which to counter not only the narratives regarding our own lives, but the methodological tools necessary to speak to our realities under our own terms within academic spaces. Testimonios, a form of counter-storytelling from the field of Latin American studies that honors and affirms the sources of knowledge often overlooked or delegitimized within the master-narrative (Delgado Bernal, 1998). Jason Irizarry (2011, p. 12) reminds us, "Testimonios are narratives of life experiences that pay special attention to the injustices one has suffered and the ways in which the narrator has made meaning and responded to them." With my testimonio, I turn to the work of the Latina Feminist Group and their writings in *Telling to Live*, to reimagine the ways in which our stories can facilitate a deeper understanding of how our bodies and scholarship can convene to challenge our subjectivities. As the women write, "seeking to contest and transform the very disciplines that taught us to recover our subjugated knowledge, we reclaimed *testimonio* as a tool for Latinas to theorize oppression, resistance, and subjectivity" (Morales et al., 2001, p. 19). Our stories matter, and we must continue to push to legitimize them within academic spaces.

Our identities as women of color, or more specifically for me a Puerto Rican woman, should not and could not be removed from our identities as scholars. And that identity is not only in question, but fluid and at times situational, as part of our survival. Jose Esteban Muñoz (1999, p. 8) argues, "the processes of crafting and performing the self … are not best explained by recourse to linear accounts of identification" (p. 8). Further, "the various processes of identification are fraught, those subjects who are hailed by more than one minority identity component have an especially arduous time" (Muñoz, 1999, p. 8). Our bodies and our scholarship, as Puerto Rican women, straddle the space in which our race, gender, and colonial identities come into fruition as we negotiate what space we will occupy within the academy. But it is in those very intersecting spaces in which we find ourselves contending with the vestiges of colonialism, sexism, racism, and at times classism, that has fraught our identities and our lives for so long, and which permeates our scholarship and every day within academia. Our work becomes intimately and intricately linked to our survival. But it is within our work and workspaces that we come to be questioned or seen as questionable, and must continue to work through the thorns and rocks as Anzaldúa reminds us, and learn to survive.

"What do you do?": Defending Our Positions as Professional When People Seek to Discredit Us

"Oh you're a professor? Do you teach Spanish?" Library clerk.

On a weekday morning, I convinced my daughter, who is a student at the same university I teach at, to walk with me to the library to pick up some books and films for the history of race and education course I was teaching that semester. It's one of the perks of the profession, especially for someone who is a first generation college student, the ability to share the space with the daughter I had when I myself was an undergraduate student. As we walked from my campus office to the library it gave us the opportunity to catch up on her classes and friends, something I readily do, not just with her but with other young Latina/o students on campus. We arrive at the library and I inform the young woman that I was picking up items I requested. I hand her my I.D. which she looks at suspiciously as it has the words faculty/staff on the bottom and disappears to retrieve my pile of books and film. The film, *Tulsa is Burning*, and texts on historical legal cases affecting African–American education, become a pile on the desk. The young woman looks at my name and asks, "Oh, you're a professor? Do you teach Spanish?" I look at her, and look at the collection of items on the desk, and look over to my daughter. The shock, anger, and sadness on my face is difficult to mask. I look at the clerk and inform her, "No, I'm a historian, I teach history of education … why would you assume otherwise considering the items you are holding?" She replies, "because, you know, your name." I sigh heavily, and with the help of my daughter, I gather my materials, and leave. I know the sadness came from having my daughter, a young woman of color, witness yet one other incident in which our position and presence is questioned, and made even more difficult by the fact that it was her own mother. To the young, white, library clerk, what else but Spanish, would this

Latina in front of her be qualified to teach, despite the narrative that the books and films she holds in her hand convey. My daughter and I walk away in silence, but with a seemingly mutual understanding of the situation and exchange, and unfortunately, with an understanding that this is not a unique incident, nor the last time either one of us would be read in a particular way. This is a lesson she is already very familiar with, and one I have never attempted to shield her or her sister from. But what I do regret was my silence in that moment; what did my silence towards my daughter tell her? Defeat?

I turn to Audre Lorde's words, and how "we find ourselves having to repeat and relearn the same old lesson over and over that our mothers did because we do not pass on what we have learned, or because we are unable to listen" (Lorde, 2012, p. 117). In this case, we are sometimes unable to speak (both physically and theoretically), and our silence can be equally if not even more detrimental than the actions of those imposing or inflicting particular identities or violence on us, such as the young library clerk. Even I, an educator, engaging with scholarship and teachings that focus on resistance, feminist theory, and social movements, was silent. But more so, I was her mother, someone that she expects to have the answers she needs, and I had none. I should have turned to Lorde (2012) in that moment and remembered that "your silence will not protect you" (p. 41). Our positions within these institutions will similarly not protect us. In speaking of the experiences of Latina faculty members, Alyssa Garcia (2005) reminds us that "silence is often a result of oppression and the role that power and politics plays in the production of knowledge … Shame, guilt and oppressive exclusionary forces can induce silence." And when we are not fully included in the production of knowledge, we perpetuate our own silencing. Our bodies are similarly excluded as producers of knowledge, or at times read through the racialized views and assumptions of others, as was the case with the library clerk mentioned earlier. We are silenced in multiple ways, whether verbal silence or the silencing of our scholarship and bodies, and we deal with how to react or engage within our teaching and scholarship, in order to resist the violence of silence. When we speak or react, we hope to have that pain validated, although instead it becomes a new site of oppression, as was the experience I had my first year as a tenure-track faculty.

What Are You Doing Here: When Our Work and Words Put Us In Danger

For me as a Puerto Rican woman, and others like me, my success and survival are at times contradictions that I live with everyday in academic spaces. We are part of institutions that institutionalize our silence. When our presence is questioned within faculty meetings, classrooms, (or even libraries), it becomes clear how the devaluing of our bodies and scholarship has been internalized by those we share these spaces with. To those we teach or work alongside, we become suspect. We work within systems that have historically worked against us, as is evident in the low numbers we represent as both students and educators. Similarly, our work is evaluated by the same system that devalues us, affecting our stability within academia as some of us face challenges in obtaining tenure. But more so, when we speak to our experiences and that of our students, we are targeted. Borrowing from a conversation between Gilles Deleuze and Michel Foucault (1977), "Those who act and struggle are no longer represented," nor are they given the power to speak and challenge the system that seeks to silence them. Alyssa Garcia (2005) argues, "opportunities and constraints impact issues of race and gender in the academy," constraints that impact the experiences of Latinas and the ways in which they negotiate their identities within these spaces (p. 261). Similarly, speaking to our experiences within these spaces, especially through our scholarship, creates new challenges for us.

When your work is intertwined with your lived experiences, as is the case for me as a Puerto Rican woman in the academy, the overlap could be daunting and at times fraught with danger. I write about the very communities I am a part of, both through my work on schooling inequalities and writing on Puerto Ricans in Chicago. I do not, nor can I, separate my own lived experiences from my writing and teaching. It is very personal even if not a personal narrative. Our scholarship at times speaks to the violence and inequalities that permeate the lives of our community and our students, and we attempt to use our position as a platform to bridge not only these lives but also our responsibility to both. When many of us speak against both the structural inequalities that permeate our lives (in and outside the academy), or the actions directed towards us in these spaces because of our identities, we become targets. My position as a faculty member at a research institution will not and cannot protect me. When the campus communities in which we live, write, and teach in become inhospitable places, and engage in racial-sexist violence, many of us dare to speak up, at a cost. In the spring of 2015, members of our campus community at my institution engaged in hateful language targeting African–American students, and was well documented and disseminated across the country.[1] As public intellectuals who engage in scholarship on race, racism, and community activism, we at times take on the task of facilitating conversations on how to best react and act on these incidences, and are also contacted by the media to respond. Similarly, our classrooms become spaces in which to engage in conversations on the inequities some experience and witness, and we cannot escape those conversations. Being one of the few Latina faculty members on campus whose work focuses on issues of social inequality, I was contacted for an interview for a national newspaper to respond to the campus climate following this particular incident.[2] In the article I talked about what it means to walk into a classroom at a PWI and not know if any of the students sitting across from me engage in the same behavior exhibited by the students in the video, especially as my class that semester discussed challenging material. Students at times did not feel comfortable engaging in conversations on white privilege and the everyday experiences of students of color in urban schools, prompting my response to the journalist who contacted me. Soon after the newspaper article went public, I became the target of white supremacist groups, bloggers, and alumni unhappy with my truth and speaking publicly of my experiences. Mind you, at no point did I speak negatively of the institution or a group of people, but instead spoke to the ways in which these actions and people's views manifest themselves within higher education settings. But that was the problem; I did not remain silent. I spoke to the everyday reality we face as women of color within PWIs, teaching and designing curriculum against privilege, and seeking to guide conversations on social inequalities. When we walk into these classrooms, everyday, we contend with a history that seeks to erase us. My words for this interview were a manifestation of these experiences. Instead of situating these experiences as a platform to engage in meaningful dialogue and serving as a teachable moment, my family and I had to sleep at night with police protection outside our home, and left the community for a short time unsure of whether I wanted to return and face the uncertainty that awaited me when I reentered the classroom and our home. As someone who works tirelessly to create safe spaces for students in my teaching, I myself was confronted with how dangerous higher education can be for me.

But no matter, as was evident in the number of email messages, online comments, and opinion pieces written on me regarding my interview, we risk more than our positions when we utilize them as academics to engage in rhetoric that contextualize our experiences and reality. Just like Lorde (2012, p. 40), "I have come to believe over and over again that what is most important to me must be spoken, made verbal and shared, even at the risk of having it bruised or misunderstood." Every day, I stand there as a Puerto Rican woman and speak to the violence, or even the threat of violence, not as necessarily a site or form of resistance but as an affirmation of my own life. Or telling to live as the Latina Feminist Group reminds us in their title of their collective book. Even if what we dare to say further complicates our day-to-day life, the alternative is silence and that silence is violent. To us, those who speak up and resist the silence, "our writings represent an effort to name and understand the resources we were given as well as the pain that oppression produce for us" (Morales et al., 2001, p.14). But once we name that pain and our oppression, we must work to counter the effects, and survive not just for ourselves, but also for our communities. This constant negotiation becomes part of our daily lives in academia, and for the woman of color academic, many of us engage in this type of conversation in our writing and curriculum. Returning to Lorde (2012, p. 128):

> So we are working in a context of opposition and threat, the cause of which is certainly not the angers which lie between us, but rather the virulent hatred leveled against all women, people of Color, lesbians and gay men, poor people—against all of us who are seeking to examine the

particulars of our lives as we resist our oppressions, moving toward coalition and effective action.

We utilize that anger, and the threats we face within our new intellectual communities to write to resist, and resist the urge to remain silent.

But our writings, and the writings of women who have dared to write before us, such as Gloria Anzaldúa, bell hooks, Patricia Hill Collins, are not well represented, accepted, or canonized within our fields, and instead these works are seen as contentious and at times unfounded and existing outside of traditional or normalized scholarship, except within our own intellectual (and marginalized) communities. Our works, stories, and lives should be valued and disseminated across our fields and institutions, as we similarly see the works of those who continue to Other us and our scholarship valued across our fields and institutions. But until that occurs, we must focus on our own survival.

Why and How To Remain Here: What Our Positions Mean for Others

When we enter our positions within institutions of higher learning, we assume we will not only be protected but also empowered. However, as we find ourselves negotiating with or seeking validation from the very power structures that at times deny us our humanity, or as we work to create institutional change within these spaces, our day-to-day life is complicated and fraught with danger. Similarly, the ways in which we come to be evaluated and read by our peers and students reinforces the racial and gendered hierarchies that we write and teach against. Silencing our experiences and scholarship, as well as scrutinizing our curriculum, becomes part of the narrative and is normalized within higher education. We live in constant in-betweeness, and when we speak against the very structures that seek to reinforce and maintain our marginalization, our bodies and scholarship are targeted. But we remain in these spaces, and learn to re-conceptualize our lives and work in order to survive and build on, whether through our scholarship, mentoring, teaching, or in the ways we speak out. Especially as a Puerto Rican woman, I must find ways to negotiate my responsibility to my position, and align that somehow to my responsibility to those who came before me and those I hope will follow. A responsibility that for the woman of color academic could be quite taxing. We work not only for ourselves or toward security (in the form of tenure), but many of us take on the added responsibility of mentoring and advising students (more often than not, informally), something that becomes central to our *sobrivencia* in academia but not valued or understood by others. Not only do we speak and teach against the myriad of inequalities that silence our experiences, our bodies, and our scholarship within higher education, but we all engage in this intellectual labor on behalf of the students we share a history and a space with. My survival is tied to theirs, and those relationships cannot be quantified nor theorized, and therefore not valued under current structures. Speaking on the burden and taxation of women of color faculty as they take on multiple roles within academic spaces, Laura Hirshfield and Tiffany Joseph (2012, p. 223) maintain, "the emotions that such interactions generate for faculty and any service obligations that are part of and parcel to these cultural stereotypes add an unfair and unequal load of time and emotional energy" to our experiences. Further, "current structures of tenure and promotion do not acknowledge these burdens of identity taxations" (Hirshfield and Joseph, 2012, p. 223). That is, we are expected to fulfill our roles and responsibilities, through service and publications (and where to publish becomes another layer that needs to be unpacked) under traditional structures and understanding of what our roles are, with no attempts by our colleagues to understand the multiples spaces in which we must be present and fulfill other roles and responsibilities. Merging these conversations and understanding how we occupy multiple spaces must be a conversation we begin to engage in. However taxing, at least for me, working outside my prescribed role as a faculty member at a research institution and in those relationships and collaborations with students, at times become the only space I feel most understood, valued, and loved.

To be sure, speaking to these experiences as faculty of color in higher education is not new nor are they isolated occurrences, nor is it revolutionary. Although my presence within PWIs (previously as a student and now as faculty member), is directly related to the revolutionary acts of those before me who paved the way. Their trauma and the violence they faced in order to confront our invisibility as people of color, or as Latinas more specifically, within academic spaces is part of my genealogy. But what I must return to and engage in is a praxis of revolutionary love in order to *sobrevivir* (survive) within these spaces, and also engage in transformative scholarship, pedagogy, and curriculum that seeks to dismantle the ways in which our communities and our works are erased. Love, according to Natalie Havlin (2015, p. 78), "naming both affection and an expression of ethical commitment, is often considered foundational to feminist and queer frameworks of collective change." "To truly love," as bell hooks (2000, p. 5) reminds us, "we must learn to mix various ingredients—care, affection, recognition, respect, commitment, and trust, as well as honest and open communication." In academia, we at times have to re-learn how to love ourselves, and at times that love serves as a form and site of resistance in our quotidian practices and our scholarship. As Chela Sandoval (2000, p. 130) eloquently reminds us, "this rhetoric of love is identified as a means of social change." We must write, teach, and work to resist through this lens of love, for ourselves and others, as a site of resistance and change.

Conclusion

"Nosotrase stamos jodidas, pero también somos jodonas." *Telling To Live.*

In the preface to the 2015 edition of the groundbreaking collection *This Bridge Called My Back*, Cherrie Moraga writes:

> in the underbelly of the "first world," women of color writing is one liberation too at our disposal. History is always in the making; while women of color and Indigenous peoples remain worldless in the official record. The very act of writing then, conjuring/coming to "see," what has yet to be recorded in history is to bring into consciousness what only the body knows to be true.
>
> *(Moraga, 2015, p. xxiii–xxiv)*

For the woman of color, the Puerto Rican woman, our bodies are consistently and unjustifiably read under someone else's terms and within particular moments. We write to live. And our presence within higher education continuously works toward forcing others to see us, understand us, and cease erasing us. Our bodies are tied to our work, and our works serve as a bridge between and across our communities. For the woman of color academic, "we carry this bridge inside us, the struggle, the movement toward liberation" (Moraga and Anzaldúa, 2015, p. xxviii). But we need to do more than just survive within our academic spaces and identities. Our curricular and scholarly work has to be intentional and strategic in insisting that our academic homes change both with us and for us, by engaging in transformative practices that will not only include us (especially our scholarship) but similarly protect us.

Notes

1 See https://www.youtube.com/watch?v=tudyRn6HGps
2 http://www.latimes.com/nation/la-na-ff-oklahoma-racism-20150311-story.html

References

Anzaldúa, G. (1987) *Borderlands: La Frontera* (Vol. 3). San Francisco, CA: Aunt Lute.

Anzaldúa, G. (2015) Acts of healing. In Moraga, C., & Anzaldúa, G. (Eds.) *This Bridge Called My Back: Writings by Radical Women of Color*, xxvii–xxviii. New York, NY: SUNY Press.

Bernal, D. D. (1998) Using a Chicana feminist epistemology in educational research. *Harvard Educational Review*, 68(4), 555–583.

Carrillo, J. (2015) And when you leave, take your pictures with you. In Moraga, C. & Anzaldúa, G. (Eds.) *This Bridge Called My Back: Writings by Radical Women of Color*. New York, NY: SUNY Press.

Foucault, M., & Deleuze, G. (1977) Intellectuals and power. *Language, Counter-Memory, Practice*, 205–17. New York, NY: Cornell University Press.

Garcia, A. (2005). Counter stories of race and gender: Situating experiences of Latinas in the academy. *Latino Studies*, 3(2), 261–273.

Havlin, N. (2015) 'To live a humanity under the skin': Revolutionary love and third world praxis in 1970s Chicana feminism. *WSQ: Women's Studies Quarterly*, 43(3), 78–97.

Hirshfield, L. E., & Joseph, T. D. (2012) 'We need a woman, we need a black woman': Gender, race, and identity taxation in the academy. *Gender and Education, 24*(2), 213–227.

hooks, b. (2000) *All About Love: New Visions.* New York, NY: William Morrow.

Irizarry, J. (2011) *The Latinization of US Schools.* Boulder, CO: Paradigm.

Lorde, A. (2012) *Sister Outsider: Essays and Speeches.* Berkeley, CA: Crossing Press.

Moraga, C., & Anzaldúa, G. (Eds.) (2015) *This Bridge Called My Back: Writings by Radical Women of Color.* New York, NY: SUNY Press.

Morales, A. L. (2001) Certified organic intellectual. The Latina Feminist Group, Telling to Live. Latina, Feminist Testimonios, Durham, London, Duke University Press.

Morales, A. L., Zavella, P., Alarcón, N., Behar, R., del Alba Acevedo, L., Alvarez, C., & Fiol-Matta, L. (Eds.) (2001) *Telling to Live: Latina Feminist Testimonios.* Durham, NC: Duke University Press.

Morena, N. L. (2015) Dreams of Violence. In Moraga, C., & Anzaldúa, G. (Eds.) *This Bridge Called My Back: Writings by Radical Women of Color.* New York, NY: SUNY Press.

Muñoz, J. E. (1999) *Disidentifications: Queers of Color and the Performance of Politics* (Vol. 2). Minneapolis, MN, University of Minnesota Press.

Sandoval, C. (2000) *Methodology of the Oppressed* (Vol. 18). Minneapolis, MN, University of Minnesota Press.

10

IN THE SPACE BETWEEN *ARGO* AND *SHAHS OF SUNSET* IS WHERE I TEACH

Roksana Alavi

Finding oneself on the bridge between two radically different cultures gives epistemic privilege to contribute to knowledge production. Traditional Western philosophical inquiries regarding knowledge are not personal. Feminist episte-mologists have argued that those in the margins of society see things that the dominant group does not. This perspective gives us a standpoint by which we can add to knowledge inquiry (Collins, 2000; Harding, 1991, 2004, 2004a). This is not to say that knowledge is relative or subjective, instead the particularities of the experiences of the oppressed provide other elements through which we gain knowledge; "People of color, immigrants, exiles, border dwellers, those at the margins, have paid attention to those particularities and have told their sto-ries and described their struggles" (Ortega, 2016, p. 1). It is through these stories that we can begin to understand the challenges of the marginalized within the dominant culture, as well as the power relations between them and the social structures in which they live. This idea lends itself to the standpoint theory, which aims to "study up" which "starts out from the daily lives of oppressed groups, but do not settle for merely conventional ethnographies, valuable as they can be in standpoint project" (Harding, 2009, p. 192). This chapter seeks to offer ways that personal narratives can guide us in developing curriculum to address social injustices.

Social Position of Women of Color in Academia

Similar to most, the experience of women of color in academia is both reward-ing and exhausting, but not the same way that the dominant culture experiences those challenges and rewards. As Grillo (1997) puts it, the system of academia is "crazy for everybody" and it is more so for women and minorities. Women of color have to overcome the society-wide stereotypes and biases against them, before really gaining the trust of the students, and perhaps even colleagues (Lazos, 2012). Since these stereotypes accompany students in the classroom, it makes it harder for them "to respond to the other person's own particular characteristics, making accurate, differentiated, and unique impressions less likely" (Heilman, 1983, p. 272). Beside the behavioral expectations of the professors, the expectations of minority professors is that they are not as competent as their white male counterparts (Harlow, 2003; Lazos, 2012). I am not exempt from this judgment. I am a woman of color and a faculty member at a predominantly white institution (PWI), and I experience the negative stereotypes against me. When I walk into a classroom, or when a student clicks on my profile photo on my online class, there is a history, stereotypes, expectations, and curiosity that appear with me. The students wonder if I can be smart enough, if I am an expert, if I am going to be partial to a particular group of people, or whether I am really a person that should be in an authority position in really anything (Easton, 2012; Lazos, 2012; Moore, 1996; Onwuachi-Willig, 2012; Yuracko, 2006). If I teach about women, women of color, race, religion, ethics, or other sensitive issues, which I do, it is automatically assumed that I am being biased. Women of color talking about race issues are biased. Being a woman of color and professor of ethics, I am considered biased. Talking about issues outside of the United States (U.S.), I am considered biased. In my Women and Leadership course, I often hear that women writing about women's issues are biased, or the authors of the articles that we are reading are biased. I have been told both in online class discussion and teaching evaluations that my Ethics in Leadership course "has a liberal agenda" and my course should be called a "Social Justice course instead of Ethics in Leadership." I do not believe that inclusivity is liberal or conservative, and I do aim to teach leaders who are social justice minded. Further, social justice is a subcategory of ethics. Ethics and justice cannot be separated. So, my only "agenda" is teaching how to create just environments.

Unlike my white male counterparts, the university space is not granted to me. When they earned their doctorate degrees, by default they gained access. They walk into the classroom with a history, the history that tells them that they belong, and this place is their place. I have to earn my place every day that I walk into the university. Women of color have to earn their respect, dignity, value, as well as their doctorate degrees each day that they walk into a classroom (Moore, 1996). We must keep earning our degrees repeatedly. When interviewed, 76% of African–American faculty believed that "students question their intellectual authority," and 55% believed that "they had to prove their competence and intelligence" (Lazos, 2012, p. 183). We are not assumed competent just because we have doctorate degrees, publications, give presentations, live the issues that we write/talk about, and even when we advise students. Actually at times, it seems like our lived experiences deem us biased in what we teach. Anderson (2017) argues that it is exactly from this standpoint that we, as women of color, can contribute to social epistemology that helps us create change. It is through the study into "how the social location of the knower affects what and how she knows" that places us in an epistemic advantage. White male faculty are often unaware of these struggles and biases and the explicit or implicit racist experiences has to be explained to them (Change and Davis, 2010). If we are going to make our community, and especially our classrooms, a safe space, this is a perspective that needs to be heard. Our social position adds to construction of knowledge in the university.

The next section discusses the boundaries of identities that women and minorities have to navigate. I also briefly situate myself in the dialogue of women of color in academia.

The Narrow Boundaries

> *Women have to navigate within narrow boundaries set by cultural stenotopic expectations. In workplace leadership settings, they must be sufficiently assertive to be listed to and take seriously, and yet not be viewed too assertive or overly masculine.*
>
> *(Lazos, 2012, p. 177)*

The space that Lazos talks about is even "narrower" for women of color. African–American women have to navigate the space between being "mammy (the caregiver)" or the "angry black woman" (Allen, 2000; Bonner, 2001; Collins, 2000); Native women between the "friendly squaw" or "hostile Injun" (Jacob, 2012); Asian–American women between the "model immigrant" and "exotic beings" (Cheng, Chang, O'Brien, Budgazad, & Tsai, 2017; Cho, 1997). I am an Iranian born naturalized citizen. I, too, have to navigate the "narrower" space with the history of the Iranian hostage crisis as the wallpaper to my existence. The Iran hostage crisis happened nearly three decades ago, but it continues to be a part of our culture in a very significant way, more recently through Hollywood via the movie *Argo* and the *Bravo!* television series *Shah of Sunset*.[1] *Argo* told a whole new generation that Iranians are not the nice people you see in America: they are the crazy, uncivilized people that you see in *Argo*. The *Shahs of Sunset* is just the other side of the coin of *Argo*. It perpetuates the same kinds of stereotypes in a different environment, where there is room to express one's individuality. The series depicts my community as being materialistic, shallow, emotionally unstable, judgmental, sexually promiscuous, self-absorbed, and obsessed with appearances. It is in this space between *Argo* and *Shahs of Sunset* that I live. It is in this space where I put down my roots, create my identity, raise my daughter, eat, sleep, teach, and feel ashamed all the while. These two stories create the boundaries that I have to navigate. As brown and black in America, we don't get individual stories. We get generalized stories, and stereotypical images. When there is a stabbing, shooting, mass murder, we secretly hope that the perpetrator is not one of our people.

People of color in America know that we face the danger of speaking for our whole race. We face the danger of, what Chimamanda Ngozi Adichie (2009) calls, "the danger of a single story."

Since the 1979 Islamic revolution in Iran, and the strained relations between the U.S. and Iran, Iranian–American men have been stereotyped as being uncivilized, barbaric, untrustworthy, abusive, aggressive, and fundamentalist while women have been stereotyped as either submissive victims who need help, or fundamentalist lunatics. I was born in Iran and have lived most of my life in the U.S., since 1988. After nearly 28 years of living in the U.S., and never visiting my home country of Iran, I still feel ashamed telling someone I am from Iran. I am not alone. This feeling of shame is due to the negative stereotypes against me, and those with whom I share a common identity. It is from that space that I walk in the classroom.

In the next section, I explore my teaching experience as a woman of color in academia and the challenges and expectations that I have to overcome, or meet, respectively.

My Teaching Experience

Academic institutions serve as integral components of anticipatory career socialization. As students obtain degrees, they learn about their prospective fields, as well as begin to share perceptions of their professional roles in those fields.

(Glenn, 2012, p. 136)

It is during that socialization that we learn what to expect as we become a part of that institution. In a study, female students of color report that not only they do not get much mentorship and discussion of future ambitions, the professors actually have lower expectations of them (Bowen 2010, 2012). After finishing my undergraduate years and applying to graduate schools, I asked a former (white male) professor for a recommendation letter, and his response was "you are a nice person, but you are not cut out for Philosophy." Glenn's words resonate with me here, when he says, "Instead of being socialized into our careers, college and universities can socialize us *out* of desired occupations" (2012, p. 136). Shorty after that time, in 1998, I started graduate school. During my first year of teaching, which was also my first year of graduate school, a respected mentor told me that I should not tell anyone that I was Iranian. This idea that I should hide my identity came almost exactly one decade after my initial arrival to the United States in 1988, when I was told I should try to pass as Greek. My colleague told me that if my nationality were revealed, my students would not take me seriously. So, I went on for nearly a decade, awkwardly telling my students that I couldn't tell them about my country of origin, when they asked me—I will call that "racial hiding" for my use. He, a white male professor, told me that Philosophy is objective and if I told people about my nationality, they would not trust my judgment regarding philosophy. I would be completely discredited, and would become an ineffective instructor. Of course, this implies that Iranians, especially Iranian women, could not possibly be perceived to be objective and perhaps even rational agents. I carried those thoughts all the way through graduate school. The humiliation imposed on me was not accidental, nor was it done in a vacuum. Quite the contrary, it was overt and a part of systematic oppression that foreign-born immigrants experience in the U.S. higher education system. According to M.K. Eskay et al., (2012, p. 241),

> There is no doubt that many foreign-born immigrants feel fortunate to be involved with America's higher education [and admittedly, I was and still am], however, they also feel unwanted and unneeded in it. For example, some of them sometimes see America as a Canaan land that is full of milk, honey and freedom, and blindly see it as a paradise where [gender,] racial, political, economic and social problems seldom exist. As they get entrenched in the system, they begin to see that America's higher education does not practice what it preaches to the outside world.

Most, if not all, educational institutions have laws against racial or ethnic discrimination, but social justice requires much more than making laws, and creating visibly diverse environments. Our commitment has to be to create inclusive environments where people (in our case faculty, students, and staff of color) who are recruited can flourish. Otherwise, we have not solved anything in our institutions, and injustices will continue.

Many women in academia report struggling with imposter syndrome. Our fears and insecurities are further confirmed when the university does not value our research, teaching, or the unseen emotional labor that we undertake with the under-represented students in our communities. Easton (2012) reports the high number of students visiting her class and asking for her advice not only about the class, their future plans, but also on many issues that are not school related, such as family issues, abortions, financial struggles, among other things. This kind of mentoring is not only time-consuming, but also bears significant emotional labor. On the flip side, it is also the time that we gain privilege into their social positioning and perspective. It is then our job as those with more power (faculty) to address them in our institutions.

Our students come to us with their social identities very much developed. They know the social stereotypes against the people of their race, class, gender, religion, and so on, even if they don't think those stereotypes apply to them.[2] It is important for their growth and development that we understand and acknowledge this and create an environment where they do not feel threatened. The next section will briefly discuss the effects of stereotypes on our racial identity and how that can hinder our progress.

Racial Identity, Passing, and Stereotype Threat

As a woman from the Middle East, I am assumed to be a practicing Muslim. At professional (university) events, I have been asked if I can find something "halal" to eat. While being a vegetarian, I often looked for food at the dinner table, and it had nothing to do with my spiritual commitments. I have been asked if I am fasting during Ramadan even though I do not identify as Muslim, nor do I wear Islamic attire. That does not typically affect me in negative ways, but I am well aware that my classification creates feelings of hatred and hostility on those that have stereotypical images and understandings of Muslim populations. Students have asked about my religious commitments. Given that I live and teach in the Midwest, I wonder which weighs more negatively for them, the fact that I do not have any spiritual or religious commitments, or that they think I am Muslim. Teaching philosophy, I challenge their views of God, religion, and morality. Philosophy asks whether it is logical to believe in God; what does it mean to believe in God, and if we ever have epistemic certainty about God's existence, or really any belief that we hold. Most of our students have learned about morality through God and religions. Philosophy challenges the connections between morality and religion. Can I be effective since I do not share their beliefs, and never have? I have been told that I could pass as a believer in order to avoid potentially hostile environments. I have also been told that I could racially pass since I am this particular "shade of brown." Passing is not an option for me. It does not really address the social injustice or my self-understanding of the body that I live in. It enhances the feeling that I do not belong. It brings to the forefront the realization that my people are stereotyped to embody one of the most unacceptable ways to be human.

During my time in racial hiding, my pedagogy was to be "objective." Philosophical objectivity was drilled into me during my years in graduate school. I provided every view as though it stood regardless of people's experiences. These views were entirely from White men's philosophical theories, most of whom were already dead. I designed curriculum as far away as possible from my own views. The curriculm was impersonal and mostly a philosophical investigation only from one single perspective. In that space of hiding, I did not even talk about my views, or covered them quickly. It was uncomfortable for me to discuss my own views becaue I felt like I couldn't really be objective. I often worried that I was crossing boundaries of proper distance from myself and my philosophical commitments. Although my choice to study philosophy was personal, I didn't think that I could bring that into my teaching, because of the perceived notion that my person was not accepted in the field—and that my mentor told me that it was not. There is also a worry that the views being presented were really emotionally, and spiritually challenging to students, but I was oblivious to those challenges, and perhaps was not as nurturing to students as I could or should have been.[3] So neither racial passing, nor racial hiding really helped me grow individually or professionally, or made me a more objective instructor.

Because most of the racialization of people is done in order to classify, categorize, or stereotype them, whether a person is passing or not, the negative or positive stereotypes will affect them. If someone identifies with the oppressed race, whether or not they are passing, this identification can and often does lead to self-oppression (Bartky, 1990; Jost & Banaji, 1994; Reynolds, Oakes, Haslam, Nolan, & Dolnik, 2000; Steele & Aronson, 1995). Those who are passing could be victims of psychological oppression due to stereotyping, and their own racial or ethnic identification. They might avoid the external forces of oppression but they internalize the society's stereotypes about them. The psychologically oppressed internalize the social understanding and implications of race, gender, class, nationality, religious affiliations, and so on, along with all the historical and current negative stereotypes that go along with it, and become their own oppressors. Even if I can pass as a believer, and Christian at that, I do not believe that is a healthy state of being, nor do I believe I should live a hidden life of pretense. Although I don't agree with Appiah (1990, p. 498) that passing is a moral offense, I believe passing takes away my identity and what makes me feel human and connected to a community with authenticity and wholeness. Regardless of all the stereotyping against my people, my preference is visibility. My invisibility does not shield me from the internal struggles, including stereotype threat. Even if I pass as some other person, I am not immune from stereotype threat and self-shame. Internalizing the inferior social status, one feels ashamed to be of that kind of person. Self-shame is certainly a hindrance to one's life options. It leads to low self-esteem and as a result limits one's development of capabilities, which as a result, perpetuates the stereotypes.

My Experience as a Woman of Color Faculty Member

Looking into how I am situated in the university and my involvement within my department and the rest of the university, it looks good. For the most part, I have had good experiences as a faculty member. The challenges that I have experienced have not been overt. They have been subtle and when I voice my feelings about the situation, the white faculty seem to be shocked either about my treatment by others, or by that I "felt" that way. I will share a few of the experiences with faculty and students here. As many other women faculty of color have reported, we are asked to serve in the university committees. I often feel tokenized when I am asked to serve. More than once I felt that, (1) I was ill-prepared to serve in that committee, but I didn't know how I could step out or say no when as a new faculty member, my supervisor(s) asked me to serve. Further, I was not given any guidance as how to go forward in my role. (2) I was given no tasks or unimportant tasks in the committees. Both of which set me up for failure as a committee member. These situations have happened to me in every institution that I have served as a fulltime faculty member. It feels as though I am invited to serve one purpose, to have a brown face, and that I accomplished. As a single mother in a new position, this is quite unsettling.

My experience with students has been a mixed bag. My first full time job was at a Hispanic-serving institution in south Texas. It was a teaching position and research was not expected, although my chair supported my endeavors. The students were mostly first generation college students, with 98% Hispanic backgrounds. The college had an open-admission policy. My students were grateful that I was there. My experience as a first generation immigrant really motivated them to aim higher. When they said to me, "I didn't speak English until I was 10," I responded, "well, I didn't speak English until I was 15." The students could really relate to my experience. However, that was not the case when I moved into my next job, a predominantly white institution, which was in an affluent part of town in Oklahoma, where my kindness was taken as weakness. White male students ignored my instructions in class, wore headphones, and one student often loudly argued against my grading of his assignments, and at one point he said to me, "I need to stop, because you are making me really angry." Admittedly, I was ill-prepared to deal with these sorts of behaviors. My expectation was that people were respectful to one another; that included student toward faculty, and faculty toward students. I had assumed that so long as I treated them with respect, I would get that back. That has not always been the case in the classroom. Candidly, I felt embarrassed by being treated this way. It created a sense of inadequacy that at the time I didn't know how to overcome. I didn't want to be angry at them because I didn't want to perpetuate the image of "angry" Iranians. My job always comes with the extra responsibilities of humanizing the Iranian–American community, and dismantling the stereotypes about us.

Negative stereotypes about a group of people can lead to stereotype threat. Stereotype threat is, "the existence of such stereotypes means that anything one does or any of the one's features that conform to it make the stereotype more plausible as a self-characterization in the eyes of others, and perhaps even in one's own eyes." (Steele and Aronson, 1995, p. 797). Both self-shame and stereotype threat have many undesirable consequences. First, it is limiting, it thwarts the development of one's capabilities, and aims to mold people in shapes that they might not fit. Second, stereotype threat keeps some minorities in the position of power overlooking their communities needs and challenges in the fear of being stereotyped. Immediate situational threat is "the threat of the possibility of being judged and treated stereotypically, or of possibly self-fulfilling such a stereotype." This stereotype threat,

> can befall anyone with a group identity about which some negative stereotype exists, and for the person to be threatened in this way he need not even

believe the stereotype. He need only know that it stands as a hypothesis about him in situations where the stereotype is relevant.

(Steele & Aronson, 1995, p. 798)

Research shows this threat can and (and often does) result in poor performance in intellectual tests. Stereotype or situational threat works in different ways in different people. People either internalize inferiority or blame others for their problems and "underutilized available opportunities," both of which lead to their second-class status (Steele & Aronson, 1995, p. 798). Self-blame could lead to people seeing themselves as not having the capability to succeed, and so they would not even try. I suppose we all suffer from this to some extent. Some of those do not hinder our life-options, or quality of life, nor would they leave us in an oppressed social status. But self-blame could lead to low quality of life. If we blame our lack of success on our own inabilities, it would be difficult to recognize and fight against institutional injustices. Self-blame is the final and key ingredient in perpetuating oppression. On the other hand, one can blame others to the extent that one would not take any chances because she believes that she would be kept from succeeding anyway. Therefore, she would "underutilize" the resources she has to succeed. Self-blame and blaming others can both end in situations that diminish one's abilities, and consequently lower one's quality of life.

Experiences of Iranian–American Students

A short while ago my daughter was invited to a little girl's birthday party. As typical for birthday parties for little kids, the mothers bring the children and there are often few or no fathers present. Sitting at a picnic table with other mothers, the conversation shifted to a discussion of their experiences as college students. All these women are Iranian immigrants. They are non-traditional students and have not been well-assimilated in the "American" culture. Language and cultural barriers makes integration into the mainstream society very difficult for them. Since most of the women I met do not work, they have few non-Iranian friends and acquaintances. In relating their college experiences, the women lamented about the discrimination they experienced in the classroom.[4] One woman reported that she often visited her biology professor during her office hours regarding the course material. The professor was always welcoming. However, this changed once her professor asked her about her nationality. Being a pre-nursing student she was hesitant to confront her because this course was very important. Another described how her history professor ranted about the "barbaric" Middle-East culture. She tried to argue against this during the classroom discussion but quickly realized that she might be jeopardizing her status in class. So she remained quiet in the duration. A third felt marginalized by her classmates due to her racial background, which created an unwelcoming learning environment for her. Others shared similar stories.

As I sat there listening to them I thought they needed to assimilate more. I have mostly assimilated. Why can't they? Why won't they? I thought to myself, perhaps they are paranoid, or untrusting of the culture that they do not understand. I thought they needed to start thinking and acting as if they were "white middle-class Americans," but then they are not. Perhaps I should have said what Claude Steele's father told him, "lighten up on the politics, get the best education you can, and move on" (1999). Then I thought this is my call to action. I am going to call their colleges since they aren't willing to do it for themselves, but then I realized that's not the solution. Calling the college might backfire since there were so few Iranian students in the biology class that the instructor could know who had complained. They too worried about that. Then I wondered why they wouldn't stand up for themselves. Feeling humiliated, they lost the ability to navigate their society as a full participating member. They experience themselves as the *Other*. This experience has an adverse effect on one's action. As Charles Joseph Meinhart (2007, p. 395) puts it, "Beliefs have practical consequences that affect how people understand themselves as well as how they relate to others and the world around them. Beliefs reflect and shape one's vision of life." It is perhaps needless to say that learning a new language as an adult, becoming admitted to a university after taking exams that are hard for most native English speakers, successfully completing college-level coursework in a foreign language, balancing one's life as a mother, wife, and student, are not indicators that point to an imposter. These are intelligent women with strength and determination, who have become victims of the social structures that bind them. These structures systematically work together. Marilyn Frye's (1983) famous birdcage analogy illustrates this phenomenon.[5]

As Cudd (2006, p. 181) points out, "It is not that they [the psychologically oppressed] will prefer oppression to justice, or subordination to equality, rather they will prefer the kinds of social roles that tend to subordinate them, make them less able to choose, or give them fewer choices to make." All these women voiced concerns about their future job prospects and what they might have to do in order to overcome future possible hostility. Will they have to change their career goals? Change university? What if their future boss displayed discriminatory behavior towards them? They wondered about what they could do in order to fit better? The last question was specially telling. It boils down to the balance between the question of my role in my victimization, and the structural social injustices.

Concluding Remarks

Each individual has the right to live in a society that does not degrade or humiliate her or him. Social justice demands that one is not ashamed of one's identity, does not suffer the threat of stereotypes and is not intellectually degraded. Self-shame is a hindrance to one's life options. It leads to low self-esteem and hence thwarts the development of one's talents. Stereotyping through media, poor education, lack of health care, or other services together leads to one's negative self-image, and that is oppressive. If nothing is done to stop this cycle, it will only result in perpetuating the stereotypes.

The colleges and universities keep introducing new programs or ideas to "help."[6] However, these are often symptom removers and do not really address the oppressive social structure. If we understand race theory and race within the social and historical perspective in the U.S., we are led toward, "action that has sapped valuable energies and resources working on fruitless programs" (Van Dyke, 1993, pp. 82–83). We need to see the situation of racial minorities from an institutional perspective. A capabilities approach to justice is helpful if our aim is to create a society that everyone can function as a full participant where they are treated with respect and granted their dignity.

The capabilities approach to justice considers each individual's wellbeing. The basic idea of capabilities approach is that there are certain human capabilities that ought not be destroyed, undermined, or deterred. Capabilities are things that people are, "actually able to do and to be" (Nussbaum, 2000, p. 5). Among these capabilities are capabilities of *Life, Bodily Integrity, Political Reason, Thought, Emotions,* and so on. Naturally not everyone will develop all his or her capabilities but everyone ought to be able to develop his or her capabilities if one so chooses. Martha Nussbaum (2000, pp. 70–71) proposes these capabilities, "as a foundation for basic political principles that should underwrite constitutional guarantees." Further, in order to have a fully good human life, individuals should have the opportunity to develop each of these capabilities; that is, each person must have the opportunity to go beyond the threshold of making these capabilities a part of one's life. The protection and promotion of capabilities should be a part of what justice requires. Negative stereotypes can and often do lead to not attempting to develop one's capabilities, which limits one's life options, and further perpetuates the group's oppressive status.

I suggest that we look at our higher education institutions as Nussbaum (2000) has us evaluate our society. We should ask ourselves are we creating an environment that students can develop their capabilities? Can they physically, emotionally, culturally, politically, intellectually, and personally flourish with dignity? Do the stereotypes against a group of people hinder student/faculty relationship? How are under-represented students and faculty supposed to flourish in their classroom if they are not taken seriously? What are the universities doing to overcome these obstacles, to ensure that everyone can achieve the threshold of functioning of their capabilities in and out of the classroom? By the time the student comes to our classroom, they have been well-socialized in their social, racial, and gender roles. It is our job as faculty and mentors to help them plan their future, and develop their individuality. In order to create the space, I present class material that present both a diversity of topics from diverse groups of thinkers. Since I was trained in male-dominant white tradition, it required extra time and effort to create a curriculum that is inclusive. Often when non-traditional views are offered, they get their own week or unit of discussion. This is exclusionary. It sends the message that this is a *special* topic that we are covering. If we are going to create an inclusive environment, we don't have a special topic section of "Iranian women leaders" or "Black feminism," we include writings by Iranian women, or Black feminist writing when we discuss women's leadership, or feminism—that is what I do when I develop my syllabus. In addition, I require students to attend outside of class events mostly developed by the Center for Social Justice at the University of Oklahoma, which is affiliated with the Women and Gender Studies program.[7] These events discuss issues of race, class, gender, disability, queer identity, and other social justice issues. Some of the events are organized to bring out the student's voices and their struggles within the university, be it social or personal. Others include faculty voices and challenges; some are a mix of both voices, as well as other community members, including the law enforcement. Students typically dislike the idea of attending campus events as a requirement. However, they often report that they were pleased to attend the events, and they are glad that I required it. In these events all students gain an understanding of their own challenges, and the possible challenges of their fellow classmates. Sometimes students hear a perspective for the first time in these events. The students who are struggling can find a community of others who are also challenged by the same issues. Giving extra credit is good, but does not assure that the voices are heard. Those voices help take the blame off ourselves (or others), and recognize the social barriers. Once those social barriers are recognized, then we can aim at implementing programs that can change that.

As the environment of equality is being established, we must ask what can be done to make people's choices independent of their negative social stereotypes that might affect their identity, and hence the perception of their abilities. My first full time position was teaching at a Hispanic-serving institution in South Texas, where I also advised students. One student said that she wanted to know what major she could study that did not require math. When I asked her why that was the case, she responded, because, "Hispanics are bad at math." This might seem trivial, but that is just one instance of the internal limitations.

We ought to rebuild people's capabilities that have been destroyed. A positive perception of self would open many possibilities for an individual that might not be there otherwise. The approach to these issues has to be derived from the communities of color with an open pedagogy of the oppressed. In the words of Freire (2007, p. 183), "The oppressor elaborates his theory of action without the people, for he stands against them." Let us be wise and engage in a dialogue as equals. We do not need salvation, borrowing from Rawls (2003), a social basis of respect would be a great start.

Notes

1   The movie *Argo* "begins in November, 1979, with the storming of the American Embassy in Tehran. A crowd breaks into the compound, taking more than fifty Americans hostage. Six escape through the back of the building and take refuge in the

residence of the Canadian Ambassador" (Lane, Anthony. *Film Within a Film: "Argo" and "Sinister"*, October 15, 2012. Retrieved from: http://www.newyorker.com/arts/critics/cinema/2012/10/15/121015crci_cinema_lane). The movie is the tale of how these six Americans were able to escape Iran. Regardless of whether the movie was factual, it gave the post-1979 generation the hostage crisis and fear of Iranians all over again. About the same time, the *Bravo!* television series, *The Shahs of Sunset*, aired for the first time. Internet Movie Database describes the series as, "a group of affluent young Persian–American friends who juggle their flamboyant, fast-paced L.A. lifestyles with the demands of their families and traditions." Internet Movie Database. (*Shahs of Sunset*, Retrieved on June 20th, 2016, from: http://www.imdb.com/title/tt1997999/).

2 Serena Easton talks about her upbringing as a middle-class African–American woman who grew up with many privileges in a predominantly white neighborhood. It was not until college that she realized that the stereotypes are also directed at her even though she does not fit the stereotypes of African–American women.

3 I still received mostly good evaluations, and had a good relationship with students, but looking back, I could have done a much better job of recognizing that challenging core beliefs of people can be really difficult for them. If nothing else, I could have at least acknowledged that.

4 I should note that none of these women attended the institution where I teach.

5 Frye asks us to imagine a birdcage that arrangements of its wires keep the bird in. The wires do not seem to be related as a structured whole to cage the bird. The "cageness of the birdcage is a macroscopic phenomenon" (Frye, *Oppression*, 1983, p. 86) as are the lives of the oppressed people. If we look at the birdcage at the microscopic level, we see only one wire and will not know how these tiny wires can keep the bird in, but once we step back and look through a wider lens, it will be clear how this one wire is intertwined with all the others to do so. It is "a network of forces and barriers which are systematically related and which conspire to the immobilization, reduction and molding of women [as well as other oppressed groups] and the lives we live" (Frye, 1983, p. 87). The bird is physically closed in by the wires that are analogous to the forces we find in the world of oppression.

6 When there is a racial incident on campus, the universities typically hire a diversity person. The diversity person might or might not really be able to accomplish much, due to the racist structure of universities, or society in general. Students of color might not find a community that they feel welcomed. That could be due to their major, the low number of students of color in the predominantly white institutions, absence of faculty of color, difference in socio-economic class between the faculty and students, or even among students, lack of family resources to help them only concentrate at their school, or the implicit bias that the white faculty bring into the classroom. The University of Oklahoma has mandatory diversity training for all incoming first year students, but there should be training for the faculty as well. Some faculty and staff have volunteered to participate in these trainings, but we need to do more. The training also has to go beyond a surface understanding of race issues, and in order for them to be effective, they ought to be ongoing.

7 Although I have not had a disabled student unable to attend events, we should be mindful of the challenges of those students. One student panel that I attended, a student in a wheelchair shared her challenge of getting to the events in the evening, given the bus schedule and rides from others, as well as access to some parts of the campus.

References

Adichie, C.N. (2009) *The Danger of a Single Story*, taped lecture. Retrieved from http://www.ted.com/talks/chimamanda_adichie_the_danger_of_a_single_story

Allen, B.J. (2000) Learning the ropes: A black feminist critique. In *Rethinking Organizational and Managerial Communication from Feminist Perspectives*. Ed. P. Buzzanell. Thousands Oaks, CA: Sage.

Anderson, E. (Spring 2017) Feminist Epistemology and Philosophy of Science. In *The Stanford Encyclopedia of Philosophy*. Ed. Edward N. Zalta. https://plato.stanford.edu/ archives/spr2017/entries/feminism-epistemology/

Appiah, A. (Oct. 1990) "But would that still be me?" Notes on gender, 'race,' ethnicity, as sources of 'identity'. *The Journal of Philosophy*, Vol. 87, No. 10, Eighty-Seventh Annual Meeting American Philosophical Association, Eastern Division.

Bartky, S.L. (1990) *Femininity and Domination: Studies in the Phenomenology of Oppression*. New York, NY: Routledge.

Bonner, F. (2001) Addressing gender issues in the historically black colleges and university. *The Journal of Negro Education*, 70, 176–191.

Bowen, D. (2010) Brilliant disguise: An empirical analysis of a social experiment banning affirmative action. *Indiana Law Journal*, 85, 1197–1255.

Bowen, D. (2012) Visibly invisible: The burden of race and gender for female students of color striving for an academic career in sciences. In *Presumed Incompetent: The Intersection of Race and Class for Women in Academia*. Eds. G. Gutierrez y Muhs, Y.F. Niemann, C.G. Gonzalez, & A.P. Harris. Boulder, CO: University Press of Colorado.

Change, R.S. & A. Davis. (2010) Making up is hard to do: Race/gender/sexual orientation in the law school classroom. *Harvard Journal of Law and Gender*, 33, 1–57.

Cheng, A.W., Chang, J., O'Brien, J., Budgazad, M.S., & Tsai, J. (2017) Model minority stereotypes: Influence on perceived mental health needs of Asian Americans. *Journal of Immigrant Minority Health*, 19, 572–581.

Cho, S.K. (1997) Converging stereotypes in racialized sexual harassment: Where the model minority meets Suzie Wong. *The Journal of Gender, Race and Justice*, 1, 178–211.

Collins, P.H. (2000) Black feminist thought: Knowledge, consciousness, and the politics of empowerment, 2nd ed. New York, NY: Routledge.

Cudd, A.E. (2006) *Analyzing Oppression*. New York, NY: Oxford University Press.

Easton, S. (2012) On being special. In *Presumed Incompetent: The Intersection of Race and Class for Women in Academia*. Ed. by G. Gutierrez y Muhs, Y.F. Niemann, C.G. Gonzalez, & A.P. Harris. Boulder, CO: University Press of Colorado.

Eskay, M.K., Onu, V.C., Obiyo, N.O., Igbo, J.N., & J. Udaya. (2012) Surviving as foreign-born immigrants in America's higher education: Eight exemplary cases. *US–China Education Review*, 236–243. B2.

Freire, P. (2007) *Pedagogy of the Oppressed*, 30th Anniversary Edition, Translated by Myra Bergman Ramos. New York, NY: Continuum.

Frye, M. (2005) Oppression. In *Feminist Theory: A Philosophical Anthology*. Eds. A.E. Cudd, & R.O. Andreasen. Boston, MA: Wiley-Blackwell.

Glenn, C.L. (2012) Stepping in and stepping out: Examining the way anticipatory career socialization impacts identity negotiation of African American women in academia. In *Presumed Incompetent: The Intersection of Race and Class for Women in Academia*. Eds. by G. Gutierrez y Muhs, Y.F. Niemann, C.G. Gonzalez, & A. P. Harris. Boulder, CO: University Press of Colorado.

Grillo, T. (1997) Tenure of minority women law professors: Separating the strands. *United States Federal Law Review*, 31, 747–754.

Harding, S. (1991) *Whose Science? Whose Knowledge?: Thinking From Women's Lives*. New York, NY: Cornell University Press.

Harding, S. (2004) Socially relevant Philosophy of Science? Resources from standpoint theory controversiality. *Hypatia, 19*(1), 25–47.

Harding, S. (2004a) *The Feminist Standpoint Reader* (ed.). New York, NY: Routledge.

Harding, S. (November 2009) Standpoint theories: Productively Controversial. *Hypatia, 24*(4), 192–200.

Harlow, R. (2003) Race doesn't matter, but…: The effect of race on professors' experiences and emotion management in the undergraduate college classroom. *Social Psychology Quarterly, 66*, 348–363.

Heilman, M.E. (1983) Sex bias in work settings: The lack of fit model. In *Research in Organizational Behavior* (vol. 5). Eds. B. Staw, & L. Cummings. Greenwich, CT: JAI Press.

Jacob, M.M. (2012) Native women maintaining their culture in the white academy. In *Presumed Incompetent: The Intersection of Race and Class for Women in Academia.* Eds. G. Gutierrez y Muhs, Y.F. Niemann, C.G. Gonzalez, & A.P. Harris. Boulder, CO: University Press of Colorado.

Jost, J.T. & Banaji, M.R. (March 1994) The role of stereotyping in system-justification and the production of false-consciousness. *British Journal of Social Psychology, 33*(1), 1–27.

Lazos, S. R. (2012) Are students teaching evaluations holding back women and minorities?: The perils of "doing" gender and race in the classroom. In *Presumed Incompetent: The Intersection of Race and Class for Women in Academia.* Eds. G. Gutierrez y Muhs, Y.F. Niemann, C.G. Gonzalez, & A.P. Harris. Boulder, CO: University Press of Colorado.

Meinhart, C.J. (2007) Must 'real men' have sick souls? *Philosophy of Education*, 395–403.

Moore, V.A. (1996) Inappropriate challenges to professional authority. *Teaching Sociology, 24*, 202–206.

Nussbaum, M.C. (2000) *Women and Human Development*. Cambridge, MA: Cambridge University Press.

Onwuachi-Willig, A. (2012) Silence of the lambs. In *Presumed Incompetent: The Intersection of Race and Class for Women in Academia.* Eds. by G. Gutierrez y Muhs, Y.F. Niemann, C.G. Gonzalez & A.P. Harris. Boulder, CO: University Press of Colorado.

Ortega, M. (2016) *In-between: Latina Feminist Phenomenology, Multiplicity, and the Self*. New York, NY: SUNY Press.

Rawls, J. (2003) *Justice as Fairness: A Restatement*. Ed. E. Kelly. Cambridge, MA: The Belknap Press of Harvard University Press.

Reynolds, K.J., Oakes, P.J., Haslam, S.A., Nolan, M.A., & Dolnik, L. (2000) Responses to powerlessness: Stereotyping as an instrument of social conflict. *Group Dynamics: Theory, Research, and Practice, 4*, 275–290.

Steele, C. (August 1999) Thin ice: stereotype threat and black college students. In *The Atlantic*. Retrieved from http://www.theatlantic.com/magazine/archive/1999/08/thin-ice-stereotype-threat-and-black-college-students/304663/

Steele, C.M. & Aronson, J. (1995) Stereotype threat and the intellectual test performance of African Americans. *Journal of Personality and Social Psychology, 69*(5), 797–811.

Van Dyke, S. (September, 1993) The evaluation of race theory: A perspective. *Journal of Black Studies, 24*(1).

Yuracko, K.A. (2006) Trait discrimination as race discrimination: An argument about assimilation. *George Washington Law Review, 74*, 365–438.

11

TEACHING TO TRANSGRESS

Africana Studies Curriculum as a Support for Black Student Activism

Danielle Wallace

The killing of 18-year-old Michael Brown and 43-year-old Eric Garner in the summer of 2014 sparked a wave of protest across the country. Spurred on by the killings, protests about racist and violent policing tactics were frequent, and the phrase, "Black Lives Matter," the rallying cry of this new movement, was on the lips and minds of college students nationwide. Student activists took Black Lives Matter onto their campuses, using it to inspire programs, community service, and most commonly, on-campus protests in the form of die-ins, marches, and protests.

In the months to follow, additional names would be added to the list of Black men and women to die in police custody or when stopped by police (most notably, Freddie Gray,[1] Sandra Bland,[2] and Walter Scott[3]). During this time, student activists on my campus looked to faculty members to help them understand the growing movement by providing them with a sociohistorical understanding of how and why Black Lives Matter came to be. Initially, this happened via informal conversations with students in club meetings in which they expressed their confusion and frustration with the current social climate. Then, in Spring 2015, I began to explicitly address police violence in each of my courses, but specifically used the course *Seminar in Africana Studies* to explore the theme, "The New Racism: Racial Violence, Criminality and Blackness," to help provide students with a context for their own activism. The next year (Spring 2016), I taught the same course, this time with the theme, "The Black Radical Tradition: Activism and Resistance." Teaching this seminar course served as a way that I, as a Black woman faculty member in Africana Studies, could help to support students in their political activism by providing them with curriculum that was timely and relevant to the social climate. In doing so, students had an opportunity to understand the roots of the "new Civil Rights Movement," (Day, 2015; Demby, 2014) and to explore the sociohistorical background which can be used to frame and undergird a discussion of modern-day Black activism as represented by the Black Lives Matter movement.

What I describe in this chapter are my experiences with, and approach to teaching student leaders and activists in two seminar courses in 2015 and 2016. The students enrolled in these courses were juniors and seniors majoring in Africana Studies. In the following sections, I will summarize my pedagogical approach, the courses' objectives, the topics covered in these courses, and finally, provide general reflections on how Africana Studies curriculum guided by Black feminist pedagogy can be used by Black female faculty as a way to inform and support the work of student activists.

Pedagogical Approach—Education for Liberation

As a scholar trained primarily in the discipline of Black/Africana Studies, I approach education as a fundamentally transformative process designed to encourage students to think critically about—and challenge—societal norms. The establishment of Africana Studies as a formal academic discipline is rooted in challenge. Africana Studies arose out of a need for a decolonized education, which places marginalized identities and experiences at the center of inquiry and de-centers the dominant narrative (Samudzi, 2016). The goal of Africana Studies is to help students to critically use the knowledge and information they gain in Africana Studies courses to change the conditions of Black people around the world. This goal can be realized through knowledge production (research), transformation of consciousness (teaching), and motivated action (service) (Carroll, 2008).

Africana Studies provides pedagogical grounding for teaching about race, culture, and class, but it does not provide as strong a foundation for teaching about gender and sexuality. Therefore, I also draw from Black feminist pedagogy to help ground my teaching. It is the "responsibility of Black women academicians to develop the meaningful content of a pedagogy that makes rigorous academic demands and the political aim of liberating working people, especially Black women, from ignorance and powerlessness" (Omolade, 1987, p. 38). For that reason, in line with Black feminist pedagogical beliefs, I see education as a liberatory process; one that encourages students to think critically about their lives and the intersecting racial, gendered, sexual, economic, and political systems that shape them (Collins, 2000; Crenshaw, 1989; Freire, 2000). The classroom, then, serves as a "liberatory environment" in which all members of the classroom community, myself included, are encouraged to share their experiences and realities through dialogue and continual reflection (Shrewsbury, 1987) with a particular focus on the significance of acknowledging and critiquing intersecting privileges and oppressions.

A holistic, engaged pedagogy necessitates that as a teacher-student, I must allow my students to be vulnerable—and allow myself to be vulnerable with my students—to disrupt traditional power dynamics in the classroom (hooks, 1994). I encourage students to connect the lived experience to academic material through confessional narrative, to move the information from the abstract to the concrete. For example, in a discussion about employment discrimination, students often share their own experiences, sometimes highlighting the ways in which their race has helped or hurt them in attaining employment. In creating a space for my students to share with one another, I also aim to create a space in which they can begin to put a face on the experience of privilege and oppression. Often, in students' end-of-the-semester reflections, they refer back to the aforementioned moments in which their classmates shared their experiences with racism, sexism, and heterosexism. In one such reflection, a white female student explored how our discussion of employment discrimination raised her awareness of the issue. She wrote,

> At eighteen I was hired at Hugo Boss, a high-end retailer, with no experi-
> ence in sales whatsoever. Soon I was making very good money off com-
> mission. At my job, there was an African American cashier who had been
> waiting for a position in sales for the two years he worked at Hugo. He
> knew the brand like the back of his hand, he wore only BOSS suits, and
> was loved by all. However, he was declined the position on our sales team
> because he didn't "fit the image," and had a lack of "knowledge of the
> brand." Meanwhile he could name every line of BOSS there is, and I don't
> even know how to tie a tie. This was blatant racism in front of my eyes and
> I had no clue. I was so blinded by my own success I didn't do anything to
> help this man's lack of it.

These moments stick with students, pushing their understanding of various forms of oppression from something that happens "out there in the world" to name-less and faceless people, to something that happens regularly to people that they know and respect—their friends, co-workers, and classmates. Through sharing and confessional narrative, oppression becomes less abstract, particularly for those students who do not have direct experience with racial, gendered, sexual, or class oppression.

When using dialogue in the classroom, my hope is that students reach a deeper understanding of themselves, each other, and the world they live in. My identity as a Black, heterosexual, woman faculty member allows me to model the explo-ration of intersecting identities for my students, and through dialogue, reflection and confessional narrative, I use my own experience as a way to help students in the process of analyzing and confronting the social order. For example, when dis-cussing racial privilege, I make the choice to initially approach the topic using the voices and works of white scholars such as Peggy McIntosh (1988) and Tim Wise. I have found that students, especially white students, are more open to examining white privilege when the ideas are presented by a white person. After we read their essays, watch them speak, and discuss their ideas, I then ask my students,

"How do you think you would have reacted to these ideas if I had presented them to you? Would you have been as open to it? Would you have accepted my argument or been resistant to it? How would my race and gender have shaped your reaction?" Most often, this sparks a surprisingly honest discussion about students' willingness to accept a white male and female's ideas in a way that they would not have accepted mine. I also share with them the ways in which I have been characterized by students as not "liking" white people, and as intolerant of "alternative" views on race. By sharing my motivation to allow white scholars to do the heavy lifting of broaching the discussion of racial privilege, I help students to explore how their racial biases shape their perceptions of trustworthiness and expertise in the classroom.

My primary goal is that, through learning, students will take the next steps toward informed, direct action through service to community and increased political involvement that challenges oppressive social systems and brings about their own liberation (Shrewsbury, 1987). I used this pedagogical grounding, drawn from Black Studies and Black feminism, to undergird my approach to teaching about Black Lives Matter and the current socio–political climate, all of which served as a support for my students' activism on and off campus.

The Courses

Seminar in Africana Studies, "The New Racism: Racial Violence, Criminality and Blackness" is an upper-division capstone course for Africana Studies majors. Although the students taking this course are in their final semesters at the university, are more advanced, and have a wide, general knowledge base from which to draw, they do not have specific, specialized knowledge about the topic(s) that may be chosen as the theme for this course. Therefore, my objectives when designing this course were, in part, to help students develop an understanding of the historical legacy of racialized violence in America; to develop an understanding of how the criminal justice system functions as a racist structure within American society; and to identify how the "new racism," or gender-specific racism affecting Black men and women (Collins, 2005), has manifested in relation to perceptions of criminality and in violence toward Black men and women. All of the students enrolled in this course were involved in activism on and off campus at varying levels. Some had served as local organizers for a statewide Black Lives Matter student protest, and others were active in clubs and social groups on campus that were holding forums and discussions on police violence. Given their social and political interests, I was especially concerned with exploring the roots of Black Lives Matter, the movement of which they were a part, to provide their current activism with a social, political, and historical framework.

Black feminist pedagogy suggests that the instructor in the liberatory classroom is to serve as a consultant, not a controller of the learning process. As a consultant, it is the job of the instructor to provide student leaders with "windows, out of which possible angles of vision emerge from a coherent ordering of information and content" (Omolade, 1987, p. 39). As such, in the developing curriculum, I place an emphasis on what the students need to achieve their specific goals, in this case, their desire to understand the social moment. To meet these needs, I purposely consult with the students on the first day of class by asking what they want to learn about the topic at hand in addition to what I have already put in place for the course. Using their feedback, I focused on answering the most common question I encountered from my students, "How did we get a point where police officers could avoid prosecution for the murder of a civilian?" by placing an emphasis on taking a sociohistorical approach to understanding the current socio–political moment.

As my initial task, I saw the need to trace the trajectory of the issue of violence against Black bodies in two ways. First, I wanted to explore how the belief that Black life is less important than white life, and therefore less protected, emerged. Second, I wanted to explore how and why race-driven violence is seen as a normal and regular part of life in the United States. To achieve these aims, I broke the course into four sections: the evolution of race and privilege, the historical roots of racial violence, criminality and the new Jim Crow, and racial violence in the modern day.

The Evolution of Race, Racism, and Privilege

We began by tracing the evolution of race in the United States, and in doing so, I gave prominence to helping students reevaluate how race, as a social construct with lived consequences, developed. In this portion of the course, we spent time defining "whiteness" and "blackness" as social markers with the ability to shape one's life chances and access to privilege (Harris, 1993). Building upon these definitions of race, we also interrogated gender by defining "manhood" and "womanhood" and then exploring how race and gender intersect to form specific racialized gender categories. In addition, I have found that it is also important to provide more timely discussions of systemic racism using a Black feminist framework of racism guided by Patricia Hill Collins' (2005) argument about gendered racism. Collins' (2005) concept of the "new racism" helps to support my pedagogical aim to get students to explore the intersectionality of oppression as they learn how to identify and discuss modern-day manifestations of racism and racial privilege.

The Roots of Racial Violence

In the next portion of the course, we turned our attention to the history of racial violence in the United States. Beginning with chattel slavery, we explored gendered racial tropes such as the jezebel, mammy, buck, and brute that justified the enslavement of Black men and women in the antebellum period (White, 1999).

Additionally, we looked to these tropes to help further explain the creation of gendered racial identities typically assigned to Black men and women. For example, the jezebel figure positioned Black women as hypersexual temptresses, and the brute and buck figures positioned Black men as violent, destructive, sexual predators. These characterizations served to support the idea that African men and women were incapable of controlling themselves without the structure and monitoring provided by enslavement, thereby justifying their oppression.

These figures also provided a rationale for the gendered forms of violence historically endured by Black men and women. Specifically, they justified the use of rape and lynching as a form of social control over Black women and men, respectively. Rape and lynching continued to be used in the Jim Crow era to intimidate formerly enslaved people and their descendants, particularly those who challenged the racial status quo. These forms of gendered racial violence can be traced to the present day, as represented by Daniel Holtzclaw's[4] predatorial policing of Black women which illustrates the lasting nature of sexual violence experienced by Black women.

Racial Violence in the Modern Day

Utilizing the previous historical analysis as the "window" out of which students can look to gain insight on their lives, we turned our attention fully on the present state of racial violence in the country. First, we looked to incidents of civilian violence in which Black men and women were targeted for death. Since Trayvon Martin's murder, a number of instances in which civilians shoot and kill Black men and women have been brought to national attention (examples include the killings of Jordan Davis (2012), Renisha McBride (2013), and Darius Simmons (2013)). These killings, which took place primarily because the shooters feared harm at the hands of an imagined Black threat, can be explained in the context of American perceptions of Black criminality. Here, students made the connections between the historical gendered racial tropes covered in the beginning of the course, and racialized perceptions of criminality and violence in the present. These realizations helped to solidify the lasting nature of these tropes in students' minds and also made the arguments about the new racism more salient.

Next, we explored legal policies that allow for the restriction of Black movement, such as "stop and frisk"[5] law enforcement policies. Browne-Marshall (2013) argues that these policies are a continuation of the practices of slave-catching patrols and "Black Codes" which were created specifically to control, monitor, and limit the movement of Black men and women. The New York City Police Department's stop and frisk policies have allowed police to detain and search hundreds of thousands of Black and Latino people since their increased implementation in 2002. In discussing "stop and frisk" with students, I provided them with the following general definition:

An officer may not stop a person without having a reasonable suspicion that the individual has engaged or is about to engage in criminal activity. Frisking someone is legally permitted only when the officer has a reason to suspect that the person is armed and/or dangerous.

(Center for Constitutional Rights, 2012)

Once this definition was given, I asked them to think about it in the context of the racial tropes and perceptions of criminality we had previously discussed. In addition, I pushed them to think about what it means in the larger context of police-community contact with the following questions: Of what race, gender, and class are the people that we expect police might see as "reasonably" suspicious, and why? How might police respond to these individuals based on common notions of criminality? Who may experience high rates of contact with police? And who, then, might experience high rates of force in their interactions with police? Given these questions to think about, students invariably made the connections between current police practice and historical precedent. Then, they drew conclusions between their own lives and experiences (or the experiences of friends and family), police practices, and ultimately, Black Lives Matter.

For example, Ashley[6] saw a clear link between racial tropes, lynching, and present-day police violence. She wrote,

> The myth of the Black rapist was drummed up and used to justify lynching. These lynchings were tools for White supremacy during, and immediately following, slavery. Today, the most common outlet for White supremacist tactics is police brutality. Police brutality is a form of systematic lynching that occurs as police, or modern day slave-catchers, unjustifiably and unprovoked take Black life due to fear for their own life. The threat of police violence itself is an instrument of the political and social control of Black people just as lynching once was in the South.

Ashley also argued that the sustained use of violence against African–Americans, undergirded by a belief in the inherent criminality of Black people, has also maintained the need for Black men and women to "suppress and manage" their personal behavior in order to avoid being targeted by police.

Finally, as we discussed the establishment of and rationale for Black Lives Matter, I pushed the students to think critically about the movement itself. In particular, I asked them to evaluate how the movement is dealing with issues of sexuality and gender as they relate to police violence. In particular, I encouraged students to think about gendered police violence in regard to the history of rape and lynching and how that history might inform Black women's experiences with police in the present day. Next, I asked them to think about "#SayHerName," a campaign which developed in response to the lack of mainstream attention paid to Black women and girls killed by police, such as Aiyana Stanley-Jones (2010),

Rekia Boyd (2015), Sandra Bland (2015), and Korryn Gaines (2016). In particular, I pushed them to examine what it means about intercommunity relations for Black women's experiences to be left out of mainstream discussions about police violence, despite the clear proof that this is an issue also affecting their lives. This discussion of sexism in regard to the focus of the mainstream Black community outside of the Black Lives Matter organization is important because during the class, as in all of my classes, I place an emphasis on intersectionality (Crenshaw, 1989), pushing students to think about the ways in which race, gender, sexuality, and class impact one's experience of various phenomena. Instructors should not hesitate to interrogate how the Black community addresses intersecting identities and oppressions in relation to police brutality and racial violence, and as a Black woman scholar, I believe that it is my duty to raise these questions in class when and where necessary. The students, who were all Black women,[7] were open to having this discussion, and shared their own frustrations with the seeming unwillingness of members of their student and home communities to address sexism relating to the level of attention and importance given to cases of police violence.

It is important to note that the national Black Lives Matter organization has articulated a position guided by anti-sexist and anti-heterosexist positions. The Black Lives Matter webpage provides some guiding principles that outline the organization's position on gender and sexuality. The webpage states, "We are committed to building a Black women affirming space free from sexism, misogyny, and male-centeredness." It continues, "We are committed to embracing and making space for trans brothers and sisters to participate and lead. We are committed to being self-reflexive and doing the work required to dismantle cis-gender privilege and uplift Black trans folk, especially Black trans women who continue to be disproportionately impacted by trans-antagonistic violence." Additionally, it further states, "We are committed to fostering a queer-affirming network. When we gather, we do so with the intention of freeing ourselves from the tight grip of heteronormative thinking or, rather, the belief that all in the world are heterosexual unless s/he or they disclose otherwise." (Black Lives Matter, "Guiding Principles")

Black Lives Matter's commitment to creating and maintaining a space that is safe for Black women and Black Lesbian, Gay, Bisexual, Trans. and Queer (LGBTQ) men and women is of great significance and importance. Students are often aware that the activists credited with founding the movement, Alicia Garza, Opal Tometi, and Patrisse Cullors, are Black women, and that two of the founders identify as queer. However, although the students were comfortable with addressing gender and sexism within communities on the fringes of the Black Lives Matter movement, they were less comfortable with, and sometimes less willing, to interrogate heterosexism and transphobia amongst themselves and how that then might impact the larger movement. However, I pushed them to think about the ways in which one's sexuality and gender identity might shape one's experience with police. Here, we again fall back on the framework provided by Black feminism that argues racism, sexism, and transphobia intersect to form a unique experience of oppression and violence at the hands of police and society at large.

In addition, I also asked that they think about the lack of critical attention paid to the murders of Black transgender women in police custody, such as Nizah Morris[8] (2002) and Mya Hall[9] (2015). Here, we returned to Collins' (2005) framing of the new racism, a defining feature of which is gender. However, taking that further, I encouraged them to think about the intersecting identities that shape one's life, and in doing so, reflect on whether or not sexuality and gender identity should be considered another feature of anti-Black racism. I believe that the students' reluctance to address heterosexism and transphobia in more local discussions about Black Lives Matter may be reflective of the reluctance of many cis-gender Black men and women to engage gender, sexuality, and police violence in a way that is fair and inclusive.

Autobiography and Activism: Highlighting the Lived Experience

Over the next year, although much of the activism around Black Lives Matter died down on our campus, the students were still eager to discuss the activism that continued to take place around the country. The moment of action that they had taken part in motivated them to keep going in their organizing activities. They began reinstating campus organizations, such as the Black Student Union (BSU), and were seeking out connections with local community organizations and other BSUs in the area. In the next iteration of the seminar course in Spring 2016, I chose to move past tracing the history of racially motivated violence in favor of examining the tradition of Black resistance to dehumanization and discrimination. In doing so, I found that a discussion of the tradition of Black activism in the Americas served as a complement to the sociohistorical analysis of Black Lives Matter. The primary objectives for this course were: to understand the historical tradition of radical activism in the Black community; and to explain how the tradition of Black grassroots and political activism connects to and influences the "new Civil Rights movement."

The Black Activist Tradition

The focus on Black activism in the Spring 2016 Seminar course allowed for a new way to understand and interrogate Black Lives Matter. In this course, when discussing the Black Lives Matter movement in conjunction with the tradition of Black activism, I proposed an idea to my class: What if Black Lives Matter is not a new movement, but a continuation of the long arc of Black activism that has taken place over time? I then asked them to develop a timeline of Black activism up to that point, allowing them to determine some parameters in regard to time and geographic location. The students chose to confine their timeline to the

Americas (specifically North America and the Caribbean), and began with the year 1804. As a group, they determined that the Haitian Revolution was one of the earliest articulations of Black Lives Matter, as its goals were to illustrate the value of Black life in the face of a racist and dehumanizing system of oppression. They went on to provide other points on the timeline such as Nat Turner's rebellion (1831), the abolitionist movement (ending in 1865), anti-lynching campaigns (1890s–1930s), the mid-century Civil Rights Movement (1954–1968), and the Black Power Movement (1960s–1970s). They developed the argument that all of these moments of activism had laid the foundation for Black Lives Matter, which was not a new movement, just a modern-day articulation of the continued fight for Black civil rights.

In helping to support this point, we read two autobiographies, *Assata* by Assata Shakur (2012), and *Revolutionary Suicide* by Huey P. Newton, to discuss the evolution of an activist. These two texts were chosen for three specific reasons. First, both Newton and Shakur encountered their first glimpses of activism through their involvement in the student movements to establish Black Studies on the West and East Coast, respectively. As Africana Studies majors, the students in this course have already studied the role of student protest in establishing the discipline of Africana Studies. Reading about Shakur's and Newton's own experience in these movements serves as a touchstone for student activists in Africana Studies, establishing a meaningful connection between them and these leaders.

Second, these first-person narratives were particularly useful for my students who have an interest in the Black Power Movement, but do not have extensive knowledge of the leaders within the movement. Both texts illustrate for the reader how Shakur (2012) and Newton developed their political viewpoints and came to their activism. By giving students a full description of their lives and activism, these texts provided a clear demonstration that activists do not emerge from a cocoon fully formed, but are shaped by a variety of circumstances that push them toward a movement.

Last, these books are both geographically and socially significant. Assata Shakur was accused and convicted of shooting and killing a New Jersey State trooper, and William Paterson University is located in New Jersey. The literal closeness of the events of Shakur's life is directly relatable to students as they have often personal knowledge of the towns and counties in which her story unfolds. Additionally, in 2013, Shakur's name was added to the FBI's Most Wanted Terrorists List, which drew renewed local attention to her case and her eventual escape to Cuba. Then, in 2015, the relationship between the United States and Cuba began to thaw, prompting New Jersey governor Chris Christie to demand her return from the island.

Shakur's and Newton's membership in the Black Panther Party also made reading these texts socially significant. In conjunction with the Black Lives Matter movement, there seems to be a resurgence of interest in the Black Panther Party, embodied by Beyoncé's Super Bowl Half-Time performance in which she and her dancers wore outfits and black berets reminiscent of the Black Panthers and held their fists in the air, a symbol directly associated with the organization. This performance resurrected questions about whether or not the Panthers were a terrorist group comparable to the Ku Klux Klan, and prompted some police-man's associations to view the singer as promoting anti-law enforcement attitudes. Given the political significance of these issues, students exhibited a growing inter-est in learning more about the organization and its members.

Both Shakur (2012) and Newton vividly describe their own experiences with policing, police profiling, and with imprisonment, harking back to many of the issues covered over the course of the class. Their descriptions of the ways in which their activism made them targets of police and government scrutiny is eye-open-ing for students. However, what is perhaps most useful for a discussion of Black Lives Matter was Newton's telling of the establishment of the Black Panther Party in 1966 in the chapter entitled, "Patrolling." Newton describes the hostile polic-ing conditions facing the Black community in Oakland, California, laying out one of the primary functions of the activist group: monitoring police-community relations, and ensuring that community members were not mistreated, abused, or exploited at the hands of Oakland police officers. Here, it was helpful to take a look at the Party's platform and program, better known as the Ten Point Program. In it, Newton and Black Panther Party co-founder Bobby Seale directly address the issues of police violence. Point seven reads:

> We want an immediate end to POLICE BRUTALITY and MURDER of Black people. We believe we can end police brutality in our Black commu-nity by organizing Black self-defense groups that are dedicated to defend-ing our Black community from racist police oppression and brutality. The Second Amendment to the Constitution of the United States gives a right to bear arms. We therefore believe that all Black people should arm them-selves for self-defense.
>
> *(Newton, 1973, p. 124; emphasis his)*

The Black Panther Party's platform and the resulting community patrols were an initial articulation of one of the primary concerns of Black Lives Matter. A discus-sion of the Party's goals served to illustrate the current movement's connected-ness to historical activist groups for students. I believe that looking to the Black Panther Party's program can be a useful tool for teaching about the development of Black Lives Matter as a movement, and for teaching about the continuity of the issues addressed by the movement.

Conclusion

The aforementioned courses were designed with the intention that students would not only increase their political awareness, but also possibly take what they learned in class and use that knowledge to help them move to take action in a meaningful way, fulfilling the third goal of Africana Studies, inspiring students to motivated direct action. Through the realization of this goal, students are turning their education into a useful tool for bringing about radical social change. As many of the students in these courses are embarking on the next steps in their careers (often graduate programs in law, education, or social work), they felt that the course and the research that they had conducted while in the course would be useful in their chosen fields.

As a Black woman faculty member, I am often asked to provide support and guidance to Black students when they encounter racial injustice both on and off campus. Rightfully, many scholars of color have discussed the burden this places on faculty members of color. Using curriculum to help students learn how to address these issues and find their activist voice may be helpful in alleviating that burden. In the discipline of Africana Studies, I am provided with a variety of opportunities to tailor my courses to address social and political issues. By using my *Seminar* courses to teach about the sociohistorical roots of Black Lives Matter and the Black activist tradition, I noticed that the student leaders in the class were incorporating the course information into their club programming and activities on campus, and continue to do so. This has been encouraging, as it illustrates their desire to raise their colleagues' consciousness about the circumstances shaping the current political and social climate.

Africana Studies and Feminist scholars argue that education should move students to act in the interest of social justice in their communities. As a Black feminist scholar in Africana Studies, I use curriculum to help students make the linkages between current social movements, the historical efforts to disempower Black people, and Black people's continued resistance to their dehumanization. By positioning ourselves as subjects as we actively engage with the materials being studied and in the exploration of the specific ways in which race, gender, sexuality, ability, and class shape our past, present, and future, Black women faculty are able to provide students with the academic grounding to take the first steps to using their education as a tool for transgressing and challenging the systems of oppression which casts their shadows on our lives.

Notes

1 Freddie Gray was killed in Baltimore, MD on April 19, 2015. For more on Gray's murder see David A. Graham, "The Mysterious Death of Freddie Gray," *The Atlantic*, April 22, 2015, https://www.theatlantic.com/politics/archive/2015/04/the-mysterious-death-of-freddie-gray/391119/, and John Woodrow Cox, Lynh Bui, and DeNeen L. Brown, "Who was Freddie Gray? How did he die? And what led to the mistrial in Baltimore?," *The Washington Post*, December 16, 2015, https://www.washingtonpost.com/local/who-was-freddie-gray-and-how-did-his-death-lead-to-a-mistrial-in-baltimore/2015/12/16/b08df7ce-a433-11e5-9c4e-be37f66848bb_story.html?utm_term=.82ec81264738

2 Sandra Bland died in Hempstead, TX on July 13, 2015. For more on Bland's life and death, see "What Happened to Sandra Bland?", *The Nation*, April 21, 2016, https://www.thenation.com/article/what-happened-to-sandra-bland/

3 Walter Scott was shot and killed in North Charleston, SC on April 4, 2015. For more on Scott's murder see Matt Ford, "Shot and Killed While Running Away," *The Atlantic*, April 7, 2015, https://www.theatlantic.com/politics/archive/2015/04/shot-and-killed-while-running-away/389976/

4 Holtzclaw, an Oklahoma City police officer, was convicted in 2015 of multiple counts of rape, sexual battery and forcible oral sodomy. Holtzclaw methodically targeted poor Black women with previous criminal histories and/or warrants, using his power as a law enforcement officer to detain and sexually assault at least thirteen women over a period of seven months.

5 In the United States, these stops are also known as "Terry stops," deriving their name from the U.S. Supreme court case, *Terry v. Ohio* (1968).

6 The student's name has been changed.

7 Though it is not uncommon for my seminar course to be comprised of more women than men, it is not common for all students in this course to be women.

8 Nizah Morris died in Philadelphia, PA on December 24, 2002. For more on Morris' death see Mari Haywood, "Philadelphia LGBT community asks what - or who - killed transgender woman Nizah Morris 10 years ago," *GLAAD*, April 23, 2013, https://www.glaad.org/blog/philadelphia-lgbt-community-asks-what-or-who-killed-transgender-woman-nizah-morris-10-years-ago

9 Mya Hall died in Baltimore, MD on March 30, 2015. For more on Hall's death see Peter Hermann, *The Washington Post*, April 3, 2015, "Baltimore's transgender community mourns one of their own, slain by police," https://www.washingtonpost.com/local/crime/baltimores-transgender-community-mourns-one-of-their-own-slain-by-police/2015/04/03/2f657da4-d88f-11e4-8103-fa84725dbf9d_story.html?utm_term=.74b4f16295c2

References

Browne-Marshall, G. J. (2013) Stop and frisk: From slave-catchers to NYPD, a legal commentary. *Trotter Review*, *21*(1), 98–119.

Carroll, K. K. (2008) Africana studies and research methodology: Revisiting the centrality of the Afrikan worldview. *The Journal of Pan African Studies*, *2*(2), 4–27.

Center for Constitutional Rights (2012) *Stop and Frisk – The Human Impact.* Retrieved from https://ccrjustice.org/sites/default/files/attach/2015/08/the-human-impact-report.pdf

Collins, P. H. (2000) *Black Feminist Thought.* New York, NY: Routledge.

Collins, P. H. (2005) *Black Sexual Politics: African Americans, Gender and the New Racism.* New York, NY: Routledge.

Crenshaw, K. (1989) Demarginalizing the intersection of race and sex: A black feminist critique of antidiscrimination doctrine, feminist theory and antiracist politics. *University of Chicago Legal Forum*, 139–167.

Day, E. (2015, July 19) #BlackLivesMatter: The birth of a new civil rights movement. *The Guardian*. Retrieved from http://www.theguardian.com/world/2015/jul/19/blacklivesmatter-birth-civil-rights-movement

Demby, G. (2014, December 31) The birth of a new civil rights movement. *Politico Magazine*. Retrieved from http://www.politico.com/magazine/story/2014/12/ferguson-new-civil-rights-movement-113906

Freire, P. (2000) *Pedagogy of the Oppressed.* New York, NY: Continuum.

Harris, Cheryl. (1993) Whiteness as property. *Harvard Law Review, 106*(8), 1707–1791.

hooks, b. (1994) *Teaching to Transgress: Education as the Practice of Freedom.* New York, NY: Routledge.

McIntosh, P. (1988, July/August) White privilege: Unpacking the invisible knapsack. *Peace and Freedom Magazine,* pp. 10–12.

Newton, H. P. (1973) *Revolutionary Suicide.* New York, NY: Penguin Classics.

Omolade, Barbara. (1987) A Black feminist pedagogy. *Women's Studies Quarterly, 15*(3/4), 32–39.

Samudzi, Z. (2016, March 29) We need a decolonized, not a 'diverse', education. *Harlot Magazine.* Retrieved from http://harlot.media/articles/1058/we-need-a-decolonized-not-a-diverse-education

Shakur, A. (2012) *Assata: An autobiography.* Chicago, IL: Lawrence Hill Books.

Shrewsbury, C. M. (1987) What is feminist pedagogy? *Women's Studies Quarterly, 15*(3/4), 6–14.

White, D. G. (1999) *Ar'n't I a woman?: Female slaves in the plantation south.* New York, NY: W. W. Norton.

LIST OF CONTRIBUTORS

Roksana Alavi is Assistant Professor of Interdisciplinary Studies in the College of Liberal Studies at the University of Oklahoma. She is a core affiliate faculty at the Women and Gender Studies program, Center for Social Justice, the Iranian Studies Program, and department of Philosophy. She received her Ph.D. in Philosophy at the University of Kansas, as well as a Graduate Certificate in Women's Studies. Alavi's general area of research is social and political philosophy. More specifically, she focuses on race, gender, stereotyping and oppression. Her most recent research has focused on three main areas: (1) leadership, (2) human trafficking, and (3) critical race theory.

Devita Bishundat is Director of the Community Scholars Program and Assistant Director of Academic and Student Support Services in the Center for Multicultural Equity and Access at Georgetown University. Her work focuses on increasing educational equity, access, and success for historically marginalized communities within higher education. Her current research includes retention for first-generation college student success and cultivating critical hope within leadership. She graduated with her M.Ed. in Higher Education from Loyola University Chicago, and earned her B.A. from Goucher College.

Altheria Caldera is Assistant Professor of Curriculum and Instructor in the College of Education and Human Services at Texas A&M University-Commerce. She earned her Ph.D. in Curriculum Studies and certificate in Women's Studies at Texas Christian University. Her research and teaching center on ways that teacher educators can better prepare candidates to teach students who are minoritized and poorly served because of their intersectional identities. She is also interested in the professional identities of African–American female teachers and the schooling experiences of African–American girls.

Catherine John Camara is Associate Professor of African Diaspora Literature and Culture in the English department at the University of Oklahoma. She earned her Ph.D. in literature from the University of California at Santa Cruz. She is affiliated with African and African–American Studies as well as Film and Media Studies. Her research area is the Black Atlantic with a specific focus on the philosophy of culture that emanates from the African background. She published *Clear Word and Third Sight: Folk Groundings and Diasporic Consciousness in African Caribbean Writing* (2003). Her current book in progress is entitled, *Afro-Indigenization: Internal Power as Cultural Practice*. She has published articles on various subjects including the work of Zora Neale Hurston and Black independent cinema. She has an article forthcoming on Hip Hop culture.

Maria del Guadalupe Davidson is Associate Professor and Director of the Women's and Gender Studies Program, and Co-Director for the Women's and Gender Studies Center for Social Justice at the University of Oklahoma. She earned her Ph.D. in Rhetoric from Duquesne University. She researches in the areas of rhetorical theory and criticism, black feminism, and Africana philosophical thought. Her most recent publication is *Black Women, Agency, and the New Black Feminism* (2017). She has co-edited several volumes including: *Our Black Sons Matter: Mothers Talk about Fears, Sorrows, and Hopes* (2016); *Exploring Race in Predominantly White Classrooms* (2014); and *Critical Perspectives on bell hooks* (2009). She is currently working on a book about the artist Kara Walker.

Kirsten T. Edwards is Assistant Professor of Adult and Higher Education and Women's and Gender Studies affiliate faculty at the University of Oklahoma. She earned a Ph.D. in Higher Education Administration with cognates in both Curriculum Theory and Women's and Gender Studies at Louisiana State University. Her research merges philosophies of higher education, college curriculum, and pedagogy. More specifically, Dr. Edwards is interested in the ways that socio-cultural identity and context influence faculty, teaching, and learning in post-secondary education. She is co-editor (with Denise Taliaferro Baszile and Nichole A. Guillory) of *Race, gender, and curriculum theorizing: Working in womanish ways*.

Briellen Griffin is adjunct faculty member and doctoral student of Cultural and Educational Policy Studies at Loyola University Chicago. Her research focuses on the social, historical, and political contexts of racism and inequality in American education. Currently, Brie is studying the implicit bias in teacher-student relationships and the impact of interpersonal racial discrimination on educational outcomes. In the future, she hopes to use her findings to support anti-racist curriculum and pedagogy in teacher education programs.

Nichole Guillory is Professor in the Department of Secondary and Middle Grades Education and an Interdisciplinary Studies affiliated faculty member at Kennesaw State University. She currently teaches diversity courses in teacher education and hip hop feminism in interdisciplinary studies. Her scholarship focuses on the identities of black women faculty in predominantly white institutions and the intersections of hip hop studies and curriculum theory. Her published articles have appeared in various journals, including the *Journal of Curriculum Theorizing*, *Journal of Curriculum and Pedagogy, Teaching Education*, and *Multicultural Education*. She also has published chapters in key texts, such as *Curriculum Studies Handbook: The Next Moment, Critical Studies of Southern Place: A Reader*, and *Oxford Handbook of Hip Hop Music Studies*.

Bridget Turner Kelly is Associate Professor of Higher Education at Loyola University Chicago. She earned a Ph.D. in Social Foundations of Education at the University of Maryland with a concentration in higher education and student development. Dr. Kelly's scholarship is focused on the experiences of students of color on predominantly White campuses, women and faculty of color at research universities, and how all students can become socially just educators. More succinctly, her work highlights the mediating impacts of gender and race throughout women and people of color's experiences in higher education.

Norma A. Marrun is Assistant Professor in the Department of Teaching and Learning's Cultural Studies, International Education, and Multicultural Education (CSIEME) program at the University of Nevada, Las Vegas (UNLV). Her research interests include: schooling trajectories of Latina/o students, educational inequality and equity, and Chicana/Latina and women of color feminist epistemologies. She received her Ph.D. in Educational Policy Studies with a concentration in Latina/o Studies from the University of Illinois at Urbana-Champaign. Her current work explores students of color perceptions about the teaching workforce. As a co-founder and co-coordinator of the Multicultural Educational Services Alliance (MESA), she leads efforts to directly connect campus to community through family engagement.

OiYan Poon is an Assistant Professor of Higher Education Leadership at Colorado State University. Her research focuses on racial inequalities and injustices in higher education, Asian–American experiences with race and racism in education, affirmative action, and college admissions policies. Dr. Poon's scholarship has been recognized with awards from the American College Personnel Association and the Association for the Study of Higher Education. She earned her Ph.D. at UCLA in Race and Ethnic Studies in Education with a graduate certificate in Asian–American Studies, M.Ed. in College Student Affairs Administration at the University of Georgia, and B.S. at Boston College.

Ester Sihite is a Ph.D. candidate in Higher Education at Loyola University Chicago. Her research interests include community colleges, access for historically underrepresented populations, and educator cultural competency. Her dissertation explores how community college educators cultivate asset-based approaches to working with diverse students. She earned her M.A. in Student Development Administration from Seattle University and her B.A. in Psychology from the University of Washington.

Natasha Turman recently completed her Ph.D. in Higher Education at Loyola University Chicago. For the past four years, she has served as the Project Manager for the Multi-Institutional Study of Leadership (MSL), an international quantitative research study measuring socially responsible leadership. Dr. Turman's research interests cut across two distinct, yet complementary areas: gender and diversity in higher education and critical leadership education. These targeted foci allow her to examine who is excluded from the dominant narratives of leadership and post-secondary education, what systemic processes maintain this exclusion, and how institutions of higher education can be a catalyst for change.

Mirelsie Velazquez is Assistant Professor of Educational Studies and Women's and Gender Studies at the University of Oklahoma. As a historian of education, her work focuses on Latina/o urban and women's histories. Dr. Velazquez is completing a book manuscript on the history of Puerto Ricans in Chicago, centering on the community's activism around schooling concerns from the 1940s until the 1970s. Similarly, her work on Latina/Chicana feminism contextualizes the work of Latina mothers in demanding a sense of justice in the schooling lives of their communities. Dr. Velazquez' work has most recently appeared in the journals *Latino Studies, Centro*, and *Gender and Education*. She is a regularly invited speaker on issues of race and education, Latina/o communities, and Latina Feminism. Internationally, Dr. Velazquez works on centering conversations on Puerto Rican women's lives within a global understanding on colonialism.

Danielle Wallace is Associate Professor of Africana Studies and affiliated faculty in Women and Gender Studies at William Paterson University. She earned her Ph.D. in African–American Studies at Temple University. Her teaching and research interests include community-centered social justice education, the role of Black student organizations in historical and modern-day social movements, gender and sexual politics in the Black community, and the dating, marriage, and mate selection ideals of college educated Black men and women. In addition to her ongoing research on relationships and marriage, she is conducting research on the 1964 Paterson Uprising and its potential role in the establishment of a Black Students Union and Department of Black Studies at William Paterson University.

INDEX